Praise for Edward Lear's
The Complete Verse and Other Nonsense

"Strongly recommended . . . This is nonsense treated with the seriousness it deserves."
  —*New Statesman*

"Without doubt, Edward Lear's vision of nonsense has been incorporated deep in the fabric of our consciousness. . . . This new edition . . . shows the scale of Edward Lear's achievement, both as writer and illustrator. . . . Vivien Noakes, already a brilliant Lear biographer, proves herself also his perfect editor, her extensive scholarly notes not only hugely informative, but in a funny way complementing the nonsense, as though the daddy-longlegs has been togged up in a pea-green anorak."
  —*The Mail on Sunday*

"This definitive edition opens up to us the mind of the man who wrote that 'nonsense is the breath of my nostrils,' and reveals the unfolding of his particular, bizarre genius. . . . Anyone who has ever felt, for one reason or another, that their shoes were far too tight, and who has dreamt of fleeing humdrum reality, will find themselves consolingly at home in Lear's nonsense world."
  —Jackie Wullschlager, author of *Hans Christian Andersen* and *Inventing Wonderland*

PENGUIN BOOKS

THE COMPLETE VERSE AND OTHER NONSENSE

Edward Lear was born in Highgate in 1812. Sickly as a child, he had little formal education but was privately trained as an artist and earned a living as a landscape painter and ornithological illustrator. While employed as a draughtsman for Lord Stanley, heir to the Earl of Derby, who had a menagerie at his estate at Knowsley, Lear began to entertain the younger members of the family with his nonsense and drawings. He published his first book of nonsense, *A Book of Nonsense*, in 1846, under the pseudonym "old Derry Down Derry." That same year he gave a series of drawing lessons to Queen Victoria. At thirty-seven he enrolled at the Royal Academy Schools in London but stayed only a few months. A second edition of *A Book of Nonsense* appeared in 1855, and a third (under his own name) in 1861; the first American edition was published in 1863. In 1870 he published *Nonsense Songs, Stories, Botany, and Alphabets*, following it a year later with *More Nonsense, Pictures, Rhymes, Botany, Etc.* and in 1876 with *Laughable Lyrics; A Fourth Book of Nonsense Poems, Songs, Botany, Music, &c.* He traveled extensively throughout his life, continuing to write prolifically—poems, stories, songs, and whimsy-filled letters—and to draw and paint; several of his paintings were exhibited at the Royal Academy. In 1886, John Ruskin nominated *A Book of Nonsense* as the top of his list in his "Choice of Books" in the *Pall Mall Gazette*. Edward Lear died in January 1888.

Vivien Noakes is the author of the acclaimed biography *Edward Lear: The Life of a Wanderer* and *The Painter Edward Lear*. She edited *Edward Lear: Selected Letters* and was the Guest Curator of the major exhibition "Edward Lear 1812–1888" at the Royal Academy of Arts, London and the National Academy of Design, New York.

BY VIVIEN NOAKES

Edward Lear: The Life of a Wanderer (1968)

For Lovers of Edward Lear (ed. with Charles Lewsen) (1978)

Scenes from Victorian Life (ed.) (1979)

Edward Lear 1812–1888: the Catalogue of the
Royal Academy Exhibition (1985)

Edward Lear: Selected Letters (ed.) (1988)

The Painter Edward Lear (1991)

Catalogue of Isaac Rosenberg Material in the
Imperial War Museum (1998)

The Daily Life of the Queen: An Artist's Diary
(with Michael Noakes) (2000)

EDWARD LEAR

The Complete Verse and Other Nonsense

Compiled and edited with an Introduction and Notes by
VIVIEN NOAKES

PENGUIN BOOKS

PENGUIN BOOKS
Published by the Penguin Group
Penguin Group (USA) Inc., 375 Hudson Street, New York, New York 10014, U.S.A.
Penguin Group (Canada), 90 Eglinton Avenue East, Suite 700, Toronto, Ontario,
Canada M4P 2Y3 (a division of Pearson Penguin Canada Inc.)
Penguin Books Ltd, 80 Strand, London WC2R 0RL, England
Penguin Ireland, 25 St Stephen's Green, Dublin 2, Ireland (a division of Penguin Books Ltd)
Penguin Group (Australia), 250 Camberwell Road, Camberwell, Victoria 3124,
Australia (a division of Pearson Australia Group Pty Ltd)
Penguin Books India Pvt Ltd, 11 Community Centre, Panchsheel Park,
New Delhi – 110 017, India
Penguin Group (NZ), 67 Apollo Drive, Rosedale, North Shore 0632, New Zealand
(a division of Pearson New Zealand Ltd)
Penguin Books (South Africa) (Pty) Ltd, 24 Sturdee Avenue, Rosebank,
Johannesburg 2196, South Africa

Penguin Books Ltd, Registered Offices: 80 Strand, London WC2R 0RL, England

6 7 8 9 10

LIBRARY OF CONGRESS CATALOGING IN PUBLICATION DATA
Lear, Edward, 1812–1888.
[Nonsense verses]
The complete verse and other nonsense / Edward Lear ; compiled and
edited with an introduction and notes by Vivien Noakes.
p. cm.
Includes bibliographical references and index.
ISBN 978-0-14-200227-8 (pbk.)
1. Nonsense verses, English.   2. Nonsense literature, English.
I. Noakes, Vivien, 1937–
II. Title.
PR4879.L2 A6 2002
821'.8—dc21   2002028998

PRIVATE and KOMΦIDEMTIAL

Contents

The Complete Verse and Other Nonsense

Appendix

Acknowledgements

I owe a great debt to earlier editors of Lear's nonsense, who not only made his work available to readers in their own time, but have, in some cases, preserved in their editions nonsense that has subsequently disappeared. Of special importance is Lady Strachey, the niece of Frances, Lady Waldegrave who was married to one of Lear's closest friends, Chichester Fortescue. At a time when Lear's reputation was at its lowest, she edited two volumes of correspondence between Lear and her aunt and Fortescue, as well as *Queery Leary Nonsense* (1911) and *The Complete Nonsense Book* (1912). Where some other families disposed of Lear material, she preserved theirs so that it would be available to later scholars. Holbrook Jackson's *The Complete Nonsense of Edward Lear* (1947) has delighted generations of children. My most vivid memory of this book is seeing it tucked under the arm of our Latin mistress as she came in for the last Latin lesson of each term. My joy in what she read was as great as my dislike of the subject she normally taught, and, although I had known his nonsense from earliest childhood, this was my real introduction to the delights of Edward Lear.

Work on this edition has been under way, as a background to other research into Lear's life and work, since 1963. Those years have seen the death of a number of people without whom it could not have been achieved. Foremost among these is Philip Hofer, whose collection of Lear manuscripts – together with those of William B. Osgood Field – was deposited at the Houghton Rare Book and Manuscript Library, Harvard University, in 1942, making possible much of the Lear scholarship that has followed; my debt to him, as a scholar and a friend, is incalculable. I would also like to record my deep gratitude to George Buday, Herbert Cahoon, Arnold Clark, Donald Gallup, William

Hornby, Sheila Kerr, Herman Liebert, Mr and Mrs Robert Gillies Michell, Colonel William Prescott, Edward Selwyn and Susan, Lady Tweedsmuir. I am sad that they cannot see the ways in which their generous help contributed to the finished edition.

I would like to extend my warm thanks to W. H. Bond and Eleanor Garvey who, as successive Curators of Printing and Graphic Arts at the Houghton Library, offered me every facility for research in their incomparable collection of manuscripts. I have shared much hospitality and conversation with Justin Schiller in New York and London, and his willingness to make material available to me meant that I knew of manuscripts I might otherwise have missed. It is with gratitude that I dedicate this book to him. Frederick Koch graciously allowed me free access to his collection of Leariana, much of which is now on deposit in the Beinecke Library. Sir Thomas Barlow, Bt, the Hon. Mrs A. Buchan, Dr David Michell and James Farquharson were most generous in allowing me to use material which has come down through their families. To Charles Lewsen I am grateful for the hours and the ideas we shared. For help in many ways I would like to thank George Ainscow, Sir David Attenborough, Malcolm Brown, Maldwin Drummond, Stephen Guy, Maureen Lambourne, Iona Opie, Gordon Sauer and Derek Wise.

The staff of a number of libraries and museums have been both patient and helpful. For this, and for permission to reproduce material in their collections, I would like to thank the Beinecke Rare Book and Manuscript Library at Yale University, the Berg Collection in the New York Public Library, Brigham Young University, the British Library, the Butler Library at Columbia University, the Syndics of the Fitzwilliam Museum, Cambridge, the Houghton Rare Book and Manuscript Library at Harvard University, the Henry Huntington Library and Art Gallery, the National Library of Scotland, Penguin Books (the archives of Frederick Warne), the William R. Perkins Library at Duke University, the Pierpont Morgan Library, the Harry Ransom Humanities Research Center at the University of Texas at Austin, the Representative Church Body Library in Dublin, the University of Rochester Library, the Somerset Record Office, the Principal and Fellows of Somerville College, Oxford, the Robert Manning Strozier Library at Florida State University, Robert H. Taylor Collection, Department of Rare Books and Special Collections, Princeton University Library, the Tennyson Research Centre at Lincoln, the Trustees of the Victoria and

Albert Museum, and the Library of Westminster School. For permission to quote copyright material I would like to thank: the Trustees of Mrs C. H. A. Anstruther-Duncan for 'There was an old person whose legs', 'There was an old man whose delight', 'There was an old man who said,"See!"', 'There was an old man of Lodore', 'There was an old person so silly', 'There was an old man whose repose', 'There was an old man whose despair', 'There was an old person of Sidon', 'There was an old person whose mirth', 'There was an old lady of Leeds', 'There was an old man in a boat', 'There was an old man whose desire', 'There was an old person of Calais', 'There was an old man with a light', 'There was an old man who said "O! –' and 'There was an old man who made bold'; and Letters to Anna Duncan and Lady Duncan in *Bosh and Nonsense*; Faber and Faber Ltd for W. H. Auden's poem 'Edward Lear'; Fondation Martin Bodmer for 'Remminissenciz of Orgust 14 Aitnundrednaity' in *English and American Autographs in the Bodmeriana*; the Trustees of Lady Charnwood for 'Eggstrax from The Maloja Gazette' in *Call Back Yesterday*; James and Rosemary Farquharson for 'Eggstracts from the Roehampton Chronicle' in *Edward Lear: A New Nonsense Alphabet*; the late Denise Harvey for [Lear's adventures in Crete], plate 3, in *Edward Lear: The Cretan Journal*; H. P. Kraus, New York, for 'Oh! Pan!', second illustration to 'There was an Old Man of Nepaul', 'There was an old man who forgot', 'There was an old man of Orleans', 'There was an old man of the Dee' and 'There was an old person of Leith' in *Lear in the Original*; John Murray (Publishers) Ltd for drafts for a poem describing the later history of the Owl and the Pussy-cat in Angus Davidson, *Edward Lear: Landscape Painter and Nonsense Poet*, for 'Ribands and pigs', 'The Adventures of Mr Lear & the Polly [& the] Pusseybite on their way to the Ritertitle Mountains', 'Cold are the crabs that crawl on yonder hill' and [Nonsense Trees] in *Teapots and Quails*, and for [Lear's adventures on horseback], nos. 3, 4, 5, 10, 12, 14, 21, 25, 33, and 'The Hens of Oripò' in Susan Hyman *Edward Lear in the Levant*; *Poetry Review* for 'When the light dies away on a calm summer's eve' and 'From the pale and the deep'; the Royal Academy of Arts for 'I slept, and back to my early days', 'Portraites of the inditchenous beestes of New Olland', [Lear's adventures on horseback], nos. 2, 8, 26, 27, 'Object discovered in Beta' and 'O Digby my dear' in *Edward Lear 1812–1888: The Catalogue of the Royal Academy of Arts Exhibition*; the Trustees of Hugh Sharp for

'The Pobble and Princess Bink'; and *Sussex County Magazine* for 'Peppering Roads'; the Victoria and Albert Museum for six coloured birds. I have established copyright for previously unpublished material in *Selected Letters*, and for the illustrations, 'Scene in the Campagna of Rome', 'Ye poppular author & traveller in Albania & Calabrià, keepinge his feete warme', 'There was an old man with a Book', 'O dear! how disgusting is life!', Letter to Mrs Stuart Wortley [The Moon Journey] and illustration from a letter to Hallam Tennyson of 16 June 1884 in *Edward Lear: The Life of a Wanderer*; and 'Miss Fraser's Album' in *The Painter Edward Lear*.

I would like to thank Professor Christopher Ricks, whose enthusiasm for Lear led to the proposal for this edition. Copy-editing is always an exacting discipline, but with Lear the problems are exaggerated and I am grateful to Lindeth Vasey for her punctilious attention to detail. My thanks go also to my editor, Margaret Bartley, and to the designer, Peter Stratton.

Finally, I am grateful to the Society of Authors whose grant enabled me to open Windows on the world.

Every effort has been made to trace copyright owners, but if any have been inadvertently overlooked the publishers will be pleased to make the necessary arrangements at the first opportunity.

I would like to dedicate this edition to Justin Schiller

Abbreviations

NB Place of publication is London unless otherwise indicated.

AD	Angus Davidson, *Edward Lear: Landscape Painter and Nonsense Poet* (1938).
Beinecke	Beinecke Rare Book and Manuscript Library, Yale University.
BL	British Library.
B&N	Edward Lear, *Bosh and Nonsense* (1982).
BN (1846)	*A Book of Nonsense*, first edition.
BN (1861)	*A Book of Nonsense*, third, enlarged edition.
Bowen	Typescripts made from manuscripts formerly in the possession of Ann Lear, prepared in the 1930s by Eleanor Bowen. The manuscripts have since disappeared.
Brigham Young	Brigham Young University, Provo, Utah.
Byrom	T. Byrom, *Nonsense and Wonder: The Poems and Cartoons of Edward Lear* (New York, 1977).
CNB	*The Complete Nonsense Book*, ed. Lady Strachey (1912).
Columbia	Butler Library, Columbia University.
Diary	Edward Lear's diary, 1858–87, Houghton.
Drummond	Edgar Drummond.
Duke	William R. Perkins Library, Duke University, Durham, North Carolina.
Duncan	Manuscripts formerly in the possession of Lady Duncan, now on deposit in the Frederick R. Koch Collection, Beinecke.
Edin.	National Library of Scotland, Edinburgh.

ET	Emily Tennyson.
Farq.	Manuscripts formerly in the possession of William Prescott, now in the collection of J. J. Farquharson, Esq.
Florida	Robert Manning Strozier Library, Florida State University, Tallahassee, Florida.
Fort.	Chichester Fortescue, later Lord Carlingford.
G&F	*Edward Lear, 1968.* Catalogue of the exhibition held at Gooden & Fox, London.
HH	William Holman Hunt.
HJ	*The Complete Nonsense of Edward Lear*, ed. Holbrook Jackson (1947).
Houghton	Houghton Rare Book and Manuscript Library, Harvard University.
HT	Hallam Tennyson.
Huntington	Huntington Library and Art Gallery, San Marino, California.
IJ	Indian Journal. A manuscript account of Lear's travels in the sub-continent in the Houghton Rare Book and Manuscript Library, Harvard.
Koch	Frederick R. Koch Collection, Beinecke.
Kraus	*Lear in the Original: Drawings and Limericks by Edward Lear from his Book of Nonsense* (H. P. Kraus, New York, 1975).
LEL	*The Letters of Edward Lear*, ed. Lady Strachey (1907).
Lincoln	Tennyson Research Centre, Lincoln.
LL	Edward Lear, *Laughable Lyrics: A Fourth Book of Nonsense Poems, Songs, Botany, Music, &c.* (1877).
LLEL	*The Later Letters of Edward Lear*, ed. Lady Strachey (1911).
MN	Edward Lear, *More Nonsense, Pictures, Rhymes, Botany, Etc.* (1872).
NSS	Edward Lear, *Nonsense Songs and Stories* (1895).
NSSBA	Edward Lear, *Nonsense Songs, Stories, Botany, and Alphabets* (1871).
NYPL	Berg Collection, New York Public Library.

OED	*Oxford English Dictionary.*
OF	William B. Osgood Field, *Edward Lear on my Shelves* (New York, 1933).
Opie	*The Oxford Dictionary of Nursery Rhymes*, ed. Iona and Peter Opie (Oxford, 1951).
OYF	*Our Young Folks* (Boston, 1870).
PM	Pierpont Morgan Library, New York.
P of L	Sir Ian Malcolm, *The Pursuit of Leisure, & Other Essays* (1929).
Princeton	Robert H. Taylor Collection, Princeton University Library, New Jersey.
QLN	*Queery Leary Nonsense*, compiled by Lady Strachey (1911).
RA	Vivien Noakes, *Edward Lear 1812–1888: The Catalogue of the Royal Academy of Arts Exhibition* (1985).
Rochester	University of Rochester Library.
Schiller	Collection of Justin G. Schiller.
Selwyn	Revd E. Carus Selwyn.
SL	*Selected Letters*, ed. Vivien Noakes (Oxford, 1988).
T&Q	*Teapots and Quails*, ed. Angus Davidson and Philip Hofer (1953).
Taunton	Somerset Record Office, Taunton. This collection contains letters between Lear and Chichester Fortescue and Lady Waldegrave, pub. in *LEL* and *LLEL.*
Texas	Harry Ransom Humanities Research Center, University of Texas at Austin.
V&A	Victoria and Albert Museum, London.
VN	Vivien Noakes, *Edward Lear: The Life of a Wanderer* (first edition 1968).
Warne	Archives of the publisher, Frederick Warne (Penguin Books).
Westminster School	Library of Westminster School, London, containing a transcript by Charles Church of Lear's Greek journal.

Edward Lear

by W. H. AUDEN

Left by his friend to breakfast alone on the white
Italian shore, his Terrible Demon arose
Over his shoulder; he wept to himself in the night,
A dirty landscape-painter who hated his nose.

The legions of cruel inquisitive They
Were so many and big like dogs; he was upset
By Germans and boats; affection was miles away:
But guided by tears he successfully reached his Regret.

How prodigious the welcome was. Flowers took his hat
And bore him off to introduce him to the tongs;
The demon's false nose made the table laugh; a cat
Soon had him waltzing madly, let him squeeze her hand;
Words pushed him to the piano to sing comic songs;

And children swarmed to him like settlers. He became a
                                             land.

January 1939

Introduction

Edward Lear was born in Highgate,[1] then a pleasant rural village a few miles north of London, on 12 May 1812.[2] He was the twentieth of twenty-one children. His father, Jeremiah, was a successful London stockbroker, Past Master of the Fruiterers' Company and a Freeman of the City of London. At the time of Edward's birth, the family was living in quiet, middle-class comfort, but when he was about four his father's business collapsed. Lear later wrote that Jeremiah served a short prison sentence for fraud and debt,[3] but the evidence for this is conflicting. Certainly the family left Highgate, though they were to return, settling for a while in dingy lodgings in 'thrice odious New Street'[4] on the borders of the City.

Edward had little to do with his mother, and was brought up instead by his eldest sister, Ann. She was twenty-one years older than he, and after her death he wrote: 'Ever all she was to me was good, & what I should have been unless she had been my mother I dare not think.'[5] 'Do you remember dear Fred', she wrote to one of her brothers, 'what I used to call you many years ago? Your constant increase in *circumference* reminds me again of the *Norfolk Biffin* – what a fine specimen of this rounded fruit you must present!! I think I see you now how you used to run round the room after me when I compar'd you to the flat *spreading* Norfolk apple.'[6] This merriment, and her loving warmth and goodness, did much to balance the distress of Edward's childhood, and the importance of her influence on the future nonsense writer cannot be overemphasized. Already short-sighted and suffering from asthma and bronchitis, at the age of about five or six he developed epilepsy, an illness that affected his life profoundly. 'I suppose the ever=presence of the Demon since I was 7 years old would have prevented happiness under any sort of circumstance', he wrote in his seventieth year. 'It is a most merciful blessing that I have kept up as I have, & have not gone utterly to the bad mad sad.'[7] His use of the word Demon is significant, for at this time epilepsy was still associated with demoniac possession, making it a shameful, lonely disease. 'Alas! Alas! how fearful a birthright was mine!' he wrote less than a year before his death. 'I wonder if others suffer similarly? Yet I dare not ask or endeavour to know.'[8] In his adult life none of his many friends ever realized that he was epileptic, but privately he knew himself to be an oddity, a social outcast, even though the society that cast him out was not aware of it.

When he was about seven, the strange turbulence of his childhood began to show itself in swings of mood and bouts of acute depression which he called 'the Morbids'. Much later he recalled that 'the earliest of all the morbidnesses I can recollect must have been somewhere about 1819 – when my Father took me to a field near Highgate, where was a rural performance of gymnastic clowns &c., – & a band. The music was good, – at least it attracted me: – & the sunset & twilight I remember as if yesterday. And I can recollect crying half the night after all the small gaiety broke up – & also suffering for days at the memory of the past scene.'[9] His realization that happiness and beauty are transitory and that their going leaves an aching emptiness was a theme to which he returned in his nonsense.

Ann, and his second sister, Sarah, taught him to read and write, to play the piano and, most importantly of all, to draw and paint. He was briefly, and unhappily, at school, and had little to do with boys of his own age, but though he would always regret his lack of formal education, he felt that it left him poised 'on the threshold of knowledge',[10] eager to discover more.

In 1822 Sarah married and went to live in Arundel in Sussex, a small country town set between the rolling beauty of the South Downs and the bracing air of the English Channel. As a boy and young man Edward went frequently to stay with her, building a circle of young friends and discovering there the gentle beauty of downland countryside. From Bury Hill above Arundel the land falls away into the wide valley of the river Arun, spreading out towards the distant North Downs. '... [T]he vast – for it is really – vast – plain was wondrous to see', he wrote of another view in 1869. 'Doubtless there is something in SPACE by which the mind (leastways *my* mind,) can work & expand.'[11] All his life he sought wide horizons – both the real width of the landscape he explored in his travel and his drawings, and the symbolic width of tolerance expressed in the landscape of his nonsense, the great Gromboolian plain and the hills of the Chankly Bore.

It is from this time that his earliest writing has survived. Reading it we see in the youthful Lear a joyful ebullience and spontaneous sense of the ridiculous combined with quiet sensibility and a wistful sadness. One family – the Drewitts, for whom most of the surviving early work was written – was particularly important to him. 'I owe a great deal to you', he later told them, 'for had I not then known you – my school companions would have led me into a very different way of life.'[12] He had found an audience with whom he could share his sense of fun, and for them he played the role of clown. 'My Sussex friends always say that I can do nothing like other people',[13] he wrote, with a touch of pride, describing himself as '3 parts crazy – & wholly affectionate'.[14]

When Lear was about fifteen his family broke up. He would later speak melodramatically of being thrown out into the world without a penny, but Ann had a small inherited income and they set up house together in Gray's Inn Road. The childhood years were over, but their legacy remained. 'Considering all I remember to have passed through from 6 years old to 15 – is it not wonderful to be alive? – far more to be able to feel and write', he wrote forty years later.[15]

He at once began to earn his living by teaching drawing, by doing 'uncommon queer shop-sketches – selling them for prices varying from ninepence to four shillings', often to stagecoach passengers in inn yards, and by 'colouring prints, screens, fans; awhile making morbid disease drawings, for hospitals and certain doctors of physic'.[16] In about 1828 he was introduced to the ornithological illustrator Prideaux Selby, who was working on *Illustrations of British Ornithology*. The fashion for large, beautiful books of natural-history illustration reflected a growing interest in the newly discovered birds and animals brought back from scientific voyages around the world. Lear served an unofficial apprenticeship with Selby, and by 1830 he felt confident enough to begin a project of his own. The Gardens of the Zoological Society of London had opened in Regent's Park in 1829. In June 1830 he applied for permission to make drawings of the parrots there, and began work on *Illustrations of the Family of Psittacidæ, or Parrots*, one of the finest books of ornithological illustration ever published in England. It broke new ground, for it was the first book in imperial folio to be reproduced by lithography, the first devoted to a single family of birds and the first in which the artist worked almost entirely from nature, drawing living, moving birds rather than stuffed specimens. The work, which was issued to subscribers in folios, was an astonishing achievement for a boy still in his teens. Lear's drawings were compared to those of John James Audubon and he was elected an Associate of the Linnean Society. Two parrots would be named after him: *Anodorhynchus leari* (*Bonaparte*), the dark-blue hyacinthine or Lear's macaw from Brazil, which is now threatened with extinction, and *Lapochroa leari* (*Bonaparte*) or Lear's cockatoo.

The President of the Zoological Society at that time was Lord Stanley, heir to the Earl of Derby, who had built up an extensive menagerie at his family estate at Knowsley, near Liverpool. He was looking for a draughtsman who could make an accurate record of the birds and animals in his collection, and he asked Lear if he would undertake the work. It was an invitation that would have far-reaching consequences.

Between 1830 or 1831 and 1837 Lear travelled frequently to Knowsley, and more than a hundred of the beautiful, highly finished drawings of animals and birds he did at that time are preserved still in the library there. Lord Stanley's father, the twelfth earl, was then in his eighties. 'Dear old man! His joyous temperament, and his love of society and good cheer, made his guests as happy and merry as himself', one of his guests later recalled.[17] Shortly after Lear's arrival, Lord Derby noticed that his grandsons were disappearing from the dinner table as soon as they politely could. When he asked why this was, he was told that the young man in the Steward's room who had come to draw the animals and birds was such good company that they were going down to be with him. In that case, said the earl, he shall come up here and dine with us.[18]

Suddenly above stairs, Lear entertained the Knowsley guests, as he had his Sussex friends, with parodies of heart-rending songs to which he added ridiculous drawings. Not all of Lord Derby's visitors, however, appreciated his company. Lear found many of them 'hard & worldly critters' who 'hadn't a particle of taste, & young as I then was, I always felt that had it not been for the unvaried kindness of the Stanleys and Hornbys, they would hardly have been decently civil to the "dirty Artist" – ornithological & landscape painter'.[19] It was not only their lack of manners that maddened him; he disliked their affected ways, particularly the cultivated ennui and boredom which were considered indications of the wealth that raised them above the need for unseemly activity. For Lear, despite its difficulties, life was something to be experienced to the full, yet here were people who had the opportunity to do anything they chose, and who chose to do nothing. 'The uniform apathetic tone assumed by lofty society irks me dreadfully', he wrote; 'nothing I long for half so much as to giggle heartily and to hop on one leg down the great gallery – but I dare not.'[20]

But in the nursery it was another matter. Here he was in his element, entertaining the earl's great-grandchildren, grandnephews and grandnieces with his nonsense and drawings. When an unidentified friend introduced him to the limerick 'as a form of verse lending itself to limitless variety for Rhymes and Pictures', he set about composing verses and making drawings to which the children responded with 'uproarious delight and welcome at the appearance of every new absurdity'.[21]

Lear himself never used the word limerick, a name given to this kind of verse in the late nineteenth century after he had made it popular. Many ideas have been put forward as to its origin; the most convincing is that it was used extensively by the poetic school, Fili na Maighe, which flourished in County Limerick in the mid eighteenth century.[22] The origin of the verse form itself is lost in the obscurity of oral tradition, and it is here, rather than in earlier children's writing, that we find the fountain-head of Lear's writing.

'Nonsense is the breath of my nostrils', he wrote.[23] It is a philosophy as much as a genre. For him it was a response to 'this ludicrously whirligig life which one suffers from first & laughs at afterwards'.[24] Recorded nonsense goes back as far as classical Greek writing, but it was part of oral tradition long before that. It found its home among the less educated groups in society – including children. Its inversion of the natural order, joyful abandon and unaffected, robust humour demonstrated a spiritual freedom and independence which could temporarily ignore the oppression of sad inevitability.

In Old Comedy, Aristophanes' *The Birds* demonstrates its features most clearly. Here we find characters who step outside society into a created world where normal rules no longer apply; there are woods that open and skies with walls, humans who behave like birds and birds like humans, play on words, imitation and parody, meaningless musical refrains, nursery rhymes, singing, dancing, music played on crude rustic instruments and slapstick. Apart from sheer joy in its absurdity, a continuing characteristic of nonsense, Aristophanes used these elements to ridicule society and make political comment, aspects that would later move over into the new art of satire.

In the following centuries, and in different cultures, nonsense continued within the oral tradition and has come down to us in snatches of recorded testimony. We find it in the Roman feast of Saturnalia and in the Anglo-Saxon and medieval minstrels who sang their glees to the harp in great houses; we see it in the irreverent topsy-turvydom of the Feast of Fools, in Boy Bishops and Court jesters; it is preserved in the robust humour of some medieval poetry and in the mummers' plays. In the era of Renaissance Humanism, the wisdom of folly was proclaimed by Erasmus,[25] and a century later by Shakespeare's fools. It found its way into the music halls, and continues to this day in nursery rhymes and the antics of circus clowns.

By the mid nineteenth century, however, oral tradition was disappearing. Its principal enemies were the spread of education and the break-up of rural communities through widespread migration to the cities. In composing his limericks Lear was drawing, almost certainly unconsciously, on this age-old heritage. He was no antiquarian, but he found in the simplicity and energy of the oral tradition a perfect medium through which to express the enigma of the human situation, with its merriment and sad futility. He published his first book of limericks under the pseudonym of 'old Derry down Derry',[26] the fool of some mummers' plays. Traditionally the fool is an outsider, a man of lowly birth who can fling his hat in the air and speak the truth, and, like the Old Man of Port Grigor, in his limericks Lear upended the accepted view of the world as he celebrated his own personal Saturnalia.

The ennui that he found at Knowsley was not the only enemy of fullness of living in the early nineteenth century. Lower down the social scale the demands of gentility meant that spontaneity was curbed. The fiddle and the flute were giving way to the parlour piano, the traditional ballad to the sentimental song, and 'ladies were not encouraged to exercise their bodies except by dancing'.[27] Evangelical Christianity, meanwhile, taught that parents had a duty to curb their child's inherent sinfulness. The will, a demonstration of pride, must be broken. The body, the occasion of sin, must be denied all excess. The pleasures of song and dance, laughter and play, food and dress were worldly vanities that must be scorned. Where joy was synonymous with levity and merriment a step along the broad road to damnation, there was little place for Godwin's belief that the true object of education, like that of every other moral process, was the generation of happiness.[28]

The various forces that led to the curbing of man's true nature were reflected in much of the children's literature of the day. 'From the hour when children can speak, till they come to years of discretion or indiscretion, they are carefully prompted what to say, and what to think, and how to look, and how to feel', lamented Catherine Sinclair in her book *Holiday House*, published in 1839, in which she 'endeavoured to paint that species of noisy, frolicsome, mischievous children which is now almost extinct, wishing to preserve a sort of fabulous remembrance of days long past, when young people were like wild horses on the prairies, rather than like well broken hacks on the road; and when amidst many faults and many eccentricities, there was still some individuality of character and feeling allowed to remain'.[29]

Part of Lear's achievement was in broadening the scope of traditional nonsense and bringing it into the literary fold. Though now within the pages of a book, the element of performance is retained, created by the conjunction of words and picture. The two are inseparable. Together they set the scene and tell the story. The rhythm of the verse is a dance rhythm, but an awkward, big-footed dance, like a rustic jig. As with the clowns he saw on that memorable evening near Highgate, Lear's Old Persons leap and spin as they go with one prance from Turkey to France or twirl on their nose and their chin.

Like the author of the old tale in which Lazy Jack made the dumb girl laugh and speak again by the absurdity of his antics, Lear knew that laughter can open eyes and ears closed by fear. 'It is odd,' he said, 'how children like me',[30] but he was on their side as he shared with them the knowledge that, however absurd and distorted his Old Persons might appear, it was not in them, nor in the children themselves, but in the false standards all around that the real deception lay. 'There only remains a general, but very strong, pervading sense of wellbeing and innate rectitude from the standpoint of eight years old,' one child friend said of Lear, 'I knew he was "safe" and that I was safe and that we were all safe together, and that suspicion might at once be put aside.'[31] Despite their incongruity, there is in Lear's characters an honesty that is lacking in the improving literature of the time. Here are grown-ups doing things that grown-ups should never do. They rush and they fall, they eat and drink vastly, wear huge bonnets and wigs, play on crude instruments and dance hornpipes and jigs. They are immense and unmannerly, immoderate and strange, unabashed by their eccentricities and excess. Some even share their noses and beards with those free-flying creatures, the birds. They do not deceive, but share with the children both the folly of their actions and the reality of the human characteristics they display – carelessness, generosity, stupidity, greed. Above all, they are their own masters, ignoring the blandishments of 'They', that constrained, critical mass whom Walter de la Mare called 'perhaps [Lear's] greatest triumph' with 'their unanimity, their cogency, their scorn'.[32]

Lear was not, of course, the only children's writer of the time who offered his readers an escape from a world of anxiety into one of safety and imagination – nor were all children subjected to these fears – but he was the most influential. In an age when they were too often loaded with shame, he sought to free them. By facing both the good and the bad without criticism, he gave them an opportunity of coming affectionately to terms with themselves and other people, encouraging a good-natured acceptance of oddities and blindness to obvious faults which Erasmus describes as 'the sort of absurdity which is the binding force in society and brings happiness to life'.[33]

In the limericks these oddities and faults can be most clearly seen in the drawings, indeed Lear tells us that Madame de Bunsen 'would never allow her grandchildren to look at my books, inasmuch as their distorted figures would injure the children's sense of the beautiful'.[34] Where, in Aristophanes, actors wore masks to turn themselves into birds, Lear makes this transformation through his illustrations, whose control of form and strength of line came from his experience as a natural history draughtsman. Their uncluttered, deceptive simplicity was helped by his use of lithography – with which he was familiar through his ornithological work – rather than wood-engraving, the more usual method of reproduction in children's books of the time.

There is this same simplicity in Lear's use of words in the limericks – apart from the adjective in the last line. It is not usual for children's writers to share with their young readers words like ombliferous, borascible, propitious, umbrageous, incipient or oracular. He may use these words correctly or he may not. Often they are his own creation. Unlike Lewis Carroll, with the exception of 'Torrible' in 'The Jumblies', Lear did not favour portmanteau words with their layers of association. His nonsense words have no meaning, and he defied attempts by others to give them any. They were not, however, created in a vacuum. Where gibberish can be chaotic and threatening, his words follow accepted rules of word formation. His two most famous neologisms – 'runcible' and 'scroobious' – have adjectival suffixes, and his apparently capricious spelling has its own rationality, sometimes observing phonetic consistency, at others challenging this by imitating apparently illogical common usage. The Clangle-Wangle, he tells us, 'is more properly written, Clangel-Wangel',[35] because that is how it sounds, just as the tree of Lebanon is obviously a seeder tree or the year is Aitnundrednaity; on the other hand an apology is kneaded. Jean-Jacques Lecercle suggests that 'Nonsense breaks rules not by forgetting them, but by following them to the letter',[36] and for children there is a paradoxical reassurance, a feeling of shared conspiracy, when they come upon familiar forms in senseless words or crazy logic upending familiar ones. There is fun too in the euphony of incongruous usages and nonsensical phrases: '… on a signal being given all the Blue-Bottle-Flies began to buzz at once in a sumptuous and sonorous manner, the melodious and mucilaginous sounds echoing all over the waters, and resounding across the tumultuous tops of the transitory Titmice upon the intervening and verdant mountains, with a serene and sickly suavity only known to the truly virtuous'.[37]

In the 1830s, the close, detailed drawing and the time spent in the damp climate of north-east England were affecting Lear's eyesight and his chest. In 1835 he visited Ireland, and the following summer he was in the Lake District. As he made powerful and often dramatic drawings of the lakes and hills, he realized that he wanted to be a landscape painter. With encouragement from Lord Stanley – now the Earl of Derby – he left England for Rome, then the cosmopolitan art centre of the painting world.

Lear lived in Rome, with two extended visits to England, for the next eleven years. There are large gaps in our knowledge of what happened during this time, but from what has survived we can see that he continued to entertain his friends with absurd drawings and rhymes, and with illustrations of the adventures he had on his travels. His Knowsley connections gave him introductions into the English community there, with its patronage, and he began to establish a reputation as a painter. In 1846, during a visit to England, he was appointed drawing-master to Queen Victoria, who had admired his book recording his travels in the Abruzzi, and he published *A Book of Nonsense*, the limericks he had written and drawn for the children at Knowsley.

By 1848 revolution was spreading across Europe, and he realized that it was time to move on. He planned to return to England, but first he wanted to travel, to gather drawings from which he could later work in his studio. For the next fifteen months he moved from southern Italy to Sicily, then to Malta, Corfu, Greece, Turkey, Albania, Egypt and Palestine, making hundreds of drawings and recording his experiences in journals that he would later publish. Conditions were often primitive, but the sickly child had become an indomitable traveller. As he journeyed through scenery of dramatic sublimity and quiet beauty, he saw places and ways of life that few of his more cautious fellow countrymen could have imagined.

By the end of 1849 he was back in England. Before leaving Rome he had written to his close friend Chichester Fortescue:

What to do my dear Fortescue when I return to England!!??¿–¡¡! – (expressive of indelible doubt, wonder, & ignorance). *London* must be the place – & then comes the choice of 2 lines: – society – & half day's work – pretty pictures – petitmaître praise boundless – frequented studio – &c. &c. – wound up with vexation of spirit as age comes on that talents have been thrown away – or – *hard study* beginning at the root of the matter – the human figure – which to master alone would enable me to carry out the views & feelings of Landscape I know to exist within me.[38]

A bequest of £500 freed him for a time from the need to earn a living and, at the age of thirty-seven, he applied to become a student at the Royal Academy Schools in London. Little has survived from this period, but it seems that he stayed there for only a few months. The Academy course was spread over ten years, much of it spent making drawings from antique sculpture; for a man approaching his forties, who was happiest when exploring wild and beautiful countryside, it was an impossible constraint.

In 1852 he was introduced to the Pre-Raphaelite painter William Holman Hunt, and that summer they spent several weeks together. Hunt later recalled that Lear 'had the most unquenchable love of the humorous wherever it was found. Recognition of what was ridiculous made him a declared enemy to cant and pretension, and an entire disbeliever in posturers and apers of genius either in mien or in the cut of the coat and affectation of manners.'[39] Working with Hunt, he gained confidence in the use of oil paint. Things were going well, and during the fifties his reputation steadily increased so that by the end of the decade his work was beginning to command considerable sums. Then in 1861 came a turning point in Lear's career. Three things happened: Ann died; he published a new edition of *A Book of Nonsense* to such popular acclaim that he became a household name; and he devoted months to a large painting that was to be his most important work – a nine-foot-long oil painting of the Cedars of Lebanon. But the painting, though highly praised when it was first exhibited in Liverpool, was dismissed by critics in London. It did not sell, and by August 1867 Lear was writing: 'sometimes I consider as to the wit of taking my Cedars out of its frame & putting round it a border of rose-coloured velvet, – embellished with a fringe of yellow worsted with black spots, to protypify the possible proximate propinquity of predatorial panthers, – & then selling the whole for floorcloth by auction'.[40] The failure of this painting marked the beginning of the decline of his artistic career. Increasingly he had to rely on friends and earlier patrons to commission and buy his work.

From the mid-1850s he had begun to winter abroad, returning to London in the summer to exhibit his paintings. He continued to travel, revisiting Greece and Albania, Palestine and Egypt, and exploring Crete and Corsica. His favourite wintering place was the Ionian island of Corfu, then a British protectorate, but when the islands were returned to the Greeks in 1864 he had to leave with the rest of the expatriot community. He had hoped that he might stay on, instructing Fortescue, who was a Member of Parliament:

I want you to write to Lord Palmerston to ask him to ask the Queen to ask the King of Greece to give me a 'place' – As I have never asked anything of you before – I think I may rely on your doing this for me. I wish the place to be created a-purpos for me, & the title to be δ Αρχανοηδιφλναρίαποίοζ [First nonsense chatter maker], with permission to wear a fool's cap (or mitre) – 3 pounds of butter yearly & a little pig – and a small donkey to ride on. Please don't forget all this, as I have set my heart on it.[41]

He began to spend his winters on the Riviera, first in southern France, and then in Italy where, in 1870, he built himself a house in San Remo.

It was in these later years of disappointment and loneliness that Lear wrote his greatest nonsense, for it was now that he composed his stories and songs. I have written elsewhere[42] that travel was for Lear more than a search for paintable views, important though this was. The strange, more primitive ways of life he observed, and the magnificent grandeur of many remote places scarcely ever visited by foreigners, made him realize the rewards that might come from taking adventurous risks. Brought up as a sickly child, he faced hardships which drew forth unknown abilities and powers. In a process of self-discovery which greater caution would have made impossible, he demonstrated to himself that his life need not be ruled by his epilepsy; he discovered that, for all its suffering, the world was full of beauty and wonder. Above all, he found in these journeys a physical and spiritual freedom he had never imagined possible and which he sought to share in his nonsense songs. In the stories, which were written first, the excitement of visiting strange places and meeting curious creatures is marred by hazards and disagreeable happenings, but in the songs these threats have largely disappeared.

Two themes run through this later work: the rewards that may come if you have the courage to dare, and the need for tolerance and sympathetic understanding of oddities and social outcasts. Erasmus suggests that 'the two main obstacles to learning by experience are a sense of propriety which clouds the judgement and fear which advises against an undertaking once danger is apparent. Folly offers a splendid liberation from both of them. Few mortals realize how many other advantages follow from being free from scruples and ready to venture anything.'[43] Certainly Lear did not pretend that the great Gromboolian plain and the hills of the Chankly Bore can be reached easily; you have first to face a difficult voyage, as any voyage of real self-discovery must be. It takes courage to go to sea in a sieve, and it is no easy thing to sail away for a year and a day. As he launched his Jumblies, Lear knew that they were embarking on an adventure few had either the vision or the courage to share. Yet, suggest Iona and Peter Opie, 'Children seem to be instinctively aware that there is more to living than doing what is prudent and permitted.'[44] 'O Timballo! How happy we are,' exclaim the Jumblies, and 'How wise we are!' for however ridiculous they may appear with their green heads and their blue hands, and although theirs might seem to be a Ship of Fools, they know that it is the others, with their cautious warnings and anxious fears, who lack wisdom. Lear's nonsense songs are perhaps no more than a game, a jest, but it is a game with a purpose, for they demonstrate that only by taking risks and confronting dangers can you discover your real abilities and limitations. 'A true game is one that frees the spirit,' say the Opies. 'It allows of no cares but those fictitious ones engendered by the game itself. When the players commit themselves to the rhythm and incident ... they opt out of the ordinary world.'[45]

The first book of Lear's nonsense songs is filled with characters who opt out of the ordinary world. Most of them refuse to go back. Their readers, though, must return, but they may bring something with them. 'I am glad for a season to take an airing beyond the diocese of the strict conscience,' writes Charles Lamb, 'not to live always in the precincts of the law courts – but now and then, for a dream-while or so, to imagine a world with no meddling restrictions – to get into recesses whither the hunter cannot follow me ... I come back to my cage and my restraint the fresher and more healthy for it. I wear my shackles more contentedly for having respired the breath of imaginary freedom.'[46]

In his limericks Lear has taken us to the offshore islands of his nonsense world; with the songs he carries us to its mainland where the horizons are wide and clear. This world welcomes anyone, however different. It welcomes nature's oddest creatures – the Pelican, the Kangaroo, the Daddy Longlegs – thereby setting an immediate standard of perfectly proper strangeness. To children who knew that they could never attain the unreal perfection demanded of them, such a world – the creation of a man who saw himself as an oddity – must have represented a haven. I am what I am, proclaims the Scroobious Pip, and that is enough, for this is a place where they can be themselves, expressing their freedom in music and dance. No stranger group can ever have gathered than those who came together on the Quangle Wangle's Hat, and yet

> ...at night by the light of the Mulberry moon
> They danced to the Flute of the Blue Baboon,
> On the broad green leaves of the Crumpetty Tree,
> And all were as happy as happy could be,
> With the Quangle Wangle Quee.

Lear wrote that 'one finds that constant quiet sympathy is not only one of the most lovable qualities, but one of the very rarest',[47] but in his nonsense world it is a commonplace.

But it could not last. In his last nonsense song, 'The Dong with a Luminous Nose', we find a land where 'awful darkness and silence reign'. For all its merriment, one of the characteristics of pure nonsense is detachment. Here it has broken down. Real emotion has intruded, bringing with it the threat of vulnerability and loss, and, as the Jumblies sail away, the Dong is left for ever alone. It is an experience of rejection that Lear knew well, and from which he sought all his life to escape. For a while his created world had offered sanctuary, but in the end desolation and loneliness triumphed even there.

After 1876, although he occasionally tried to write new songs, and his letters to responsive correspondents were still filled with absurdity, only the autobiographical poems, 'How pleasant to know Mr Lear!', 'Some Incidents in the Life of my Uncle Arly', and the second part of 'Mr and Mrs Discobbolos', were successful. But his place as the Father of Nonsense was assured, and he was delighted when friends sent him cuttings from the February 1886 issue of the *Pall Mall Magazine*, in which John Ruskin, writing on his choice of books, said: 'Surely the most beneficent and innocent of all books yet produced for [families] is the Book of Nonsense, with its corollary carols? – inimitable and refreshing, and perfect in rhythm. I really don't know any author to whom I am half so grateful, for my idle self, as Edward Lear. I shall put him first of *my* hundred authors.'

The companion of Lear's old age, Foss the cat who 'has no end of a tail because it has been cut off',[48] died in September 1887. His master survived him by only a few months, dying in San Remo on 29 January 1888.

Writing to Lear in 1886, Emily Tennyson had said: 'However solitary your life has, for many years been, you must not forget that to you is given the precious gift of peopling the lives of many not only of this generation but of generations to come with good & beautiful things & thoughts, to say nothing of your own life of which so many think with a loving admiration very precious to them.'[49] These were sentiments endorsed by his closest friend, Franklin Lushington, who wrote after Lear's death: 'I have never known a man who deserved more love for his goodness of heart & his determination to do right; & I don't think any human being knew him better than I did. There never was a more generous or a more unselfish soul.'[50]

Notes

1. Lear's birthplace was actually in Holloway, close to the border with Highgate. Since he always refers to his home as being in Highgate, I have followed his practice here.

2. Lear's birth certificate gives his date of birth as 13 May, and he celebrated it on that day until at least 1848. Some time after this he began to keep it on 12 May. In a letter to Hubert Congreve of 12 May 1882 he writes: 'I ain't 70 till 11.30 tonight', and it seems likely that the late hour of his birth led to a misdating.

3. Diary, 27 April 1881.

4. 'Eclogue: *Vide* Collins "Hassan – or the Camel Driver"', l. 16 and see its headnote.

5. Diary, 17 January 1865.

6. Letter from Ann to Frederick Lear, 10 September 1847.

7. Diary, 31 July 1882.

8. Diary, 2 May 1887.

9. Diary, 24 March 1877.

10. Letter to Chichester Fortescue, 2 September 1859.

11. Diary, 26 September 1869.

12. Letter to Fanny Coombe, 27 November 1841.

13. Letter to C. Empson, 1 October 1831.

14. Letter to Fanny Coombe, 15 July 1832.

15. Diary, 29 March 1868.

16. 'By Way of Preface', *NSS*.

17. *The Diary of Frances, Lady Shelley, 1787–1817* (1912), p. 13.

18. Quoted in *AD*, p. 15. I have been unable to trace the source of this story.

19. Letter to Fortescue, 1 May 1884.

20. Letter to Miss Coobe, quoted in *AD*, p. 17.

21. Introduction to *MN*

22. Letter to the *Observer* from E. T. Hanrahan, M.E., Ph.D., 24 December 1967.

23. Letter to Norah Bruce, 24 December 1870.

24. Letter to William Holman Hunt, 7 July 1870.

25. D. Erasmus, *Praise of Folly* (1509), trans. Betty Radice (1971).

26. Title-page limerick of *BN* (1846).

27. G. M. Trevelyan, *English Social History* (1952), Vol. 4, p. 24.

28. William Godwin, *The Enquiry Concerning the Principles of Political Justice, and its Influences on General Virtue and Happiness* (1793).

29. Catherine Sinclair, *Holiday House: A Series of Tales &c.* (Edinburgh, 1839) p. 3.

30. Diary, 28 February 1862.

31. J. St Loe Strachey, Foreward to *The Lear Coloured Bird Book for Children* (1912).

32. Walter de la Mare, *Lewis Carroll* (1930), p. 17.

33. Erasmus, *Praise of Folly*, p. 92.

34. Quoted in Ian Malcolm, *The Pursuit of Leisure, & Other Essays* (1929), p. 118.

35. 'The History of the Seven Families of the Lake Pipple-Popple', chapter X.

36. Jean-Jacques Lecercle, *Philosophy of Nonsense: The Intuitions of Victorian Nonsense Literature* (1994), p. 48.

37. From 'The Story of the Four Little Children Who Went Round the World'.

38. Letter to Fortescue, 25 August 1848.

39. William Holman Hunt, *Pre-Raphaelitism and the Pre-Raphaelite Brotherhood* (1912), p. 332.

40. Letter to Fortescue, 9 August 1867.

41. Letter to Fortescue, 6 September 1863.

42. *RA*, p. 14.

43. Erasmus, *Praise of Folly*, p. 103.

44. Iona and Peter Opie, *Children's Games in Street and Playground* (1969), p. 263.

45. Ibid., p. 1

46. Charles Lamb, 'On the Artificial Comedy of the Last Century', in *Selected Prose*, ed. Adam Phillips (1985), p. 143.

47. Quoted in T. A. Nash, *The Life of Richard Lord Westbury* (1888), p. 51.

48. Letter to Fortescue, 28 February 1872. This description was given to Foss's predecessor, Potiphar, but it applied equally to the tailless Foss.

49. Letter from Emily Tennyson, 22 January 1886.

50. Letter from Franklin Lushington to Charles Street, 12 May 1888.

Table of Dates

Begins collaboration with John Gould on *The Birds of Europe* (1832–7), *A Monograph of the Ramphastidæ, or Family of Toucans* (1834) and *A Monograph of the Trogonidæ, or Family of Trogans* (1838).

From about 1830, employed by Sir William Jardine to do drawings for *Felinæ* (1834), *Pigeons* (1835) and *Parrots* (1836) in the series *The Naturalists' Library*, and by Thomas Bell, T. C.Eyton, George Gray and James Sowerby in ornithological and natural history works.

1832   Moves to 61 Albany Street, Regent's Park.
April Illustrations of the Family of Psittacidæ, or Parrots published in one volume.

1833   *July–August* Visits Amsterdam, Rotterdam, Berne and Berlin with John Gould.
Enrols at Sass's School of Art which prepares students for the entrance examination to the Royal Academy Schools (a fellow pupil is William Frith); it is not known how long he stayed.
September Father dies of a heart attack.

1834   Moves to 28 Southampton Row, Bloomsbury.

1835   *July–August* Visits Ireland with Arthur Penrhyn Stanley, later Dean of Westminster. His interest turns to landscape painting.

1836   *Dead Birds* exhibited at the Society of British Artists. His eyesight and general health deteriorate.
August–October Visits the Lake District. His interest in landscape grows.

1837   *The Screes, Wastwater, Cumberland* exhibited at the Society of British Artists, the first of his landscapes to be hung in a public exhibition.
Spring Second visit to the continent with Gould.
June–July Visits Devon and Cornwall.
July–December Travels through Belgium, Luxembourg, Germany and Switzerland to Florence.
3 December Arrives in Rome. Takes rooms at 39 Via del Balbuino.

1838   *May–August* Visits the Bay of Naples with James Uwins, and shares digs with Samuel and Hannah Palmer.

June Earliest known oil painting.

September Moves to 107 Via Felice.

1839   *May–October* Goes on a walking tour towards Florence, then stays at Civitella di Subiaco with a group of other artists.

1840   *Summer* At Civitella di Subiaco.

1841   *Spring* Returns to England. Publishes *Views in Rome and its Environs.*

September Visits Scotland with Phipps Hornby.

December Returns to Rome.

1842   *April–May* Visits Naples and Sicily.

1843   *July–October* Tours the Abruzzi with Charles Knight.

1844   *May* Mother dies of 'general decay'.

October Returns to the Abruzzi.

1845   *April* Meets Chichester Fortescue.

May Travels to England and takes rooms in Duke Street, St James's.

1846   *February* Publishes *A Book of Nonsense* under the pseudonym 'old Derry down Derry'. Composes his earliest known alphabet.

April Publishes *Illustrated Excursions in Italy,* Volume I.

July–August Gives a series of twelve drawing lessons to Queen Victoria, at Osborne and Buckingham Palace.

August Publishes *Illustrated Excursions in Italy,* Volume II.

Gleanings From The Menagerie And Aviary At Knowsley Hall is published.

December Returns to Rome.

1847   *May–October* Visits Sicily and southern Calabria with John Proby, and witnesses outbursts of revolution. Completes a large oil painting (50" x 76") of Civitella.

1848   *February* Meets Thomas Baring, later Lord Northbrook and Viceroy of India.

April–May As Italy becomes unsettled, Lear leaves Rome and travels via Malta to Corfu.

June–July Travels in Greece with Charles Church, and is taken ill with malaria.

August Arrives in Constantinople and convalesces.

September–December Travels across Greece into Albania.

December Returns to Malta and meets Franklin Lushington.

1849   *January–February* Visits Egypt and Sinai.

March Returns to Malta, then tours southern Greece with Lushington.

March–July Travels alone in the Morea and visits Janina, Vale of Tempe and Mount Olympus.

July Travels to England, where he takes rooms at Stratford Place, London w1.

September Inherits £500 from a family friend.

November–December Re-enrols at Sass's School of Art to prepare work for the entrance examination to the Royal Academy Schools.

1850   *January–before November* Student at the Royal Academy Schools.

Claude Lorraine's House on the Tiber exhibited at the Royal Academy, Lear's first work to hang there.

1851   *July–August* Visits Devon.

Publishes *Journals of a Landscape Painter in Albania, &c.* Meets Alfred and Emily Tennyson.

1852   *Summer* Meets William Holman Hunt, and spends the summer with him in Fairlight, Hastings. He stays on after Hunt leaves, until February 1853. Conceives a plan of illustrating Tennyson's poems.

The Acropolis of Athens, sunrise; Peasants assembling on the road to the Piræus exhibited at the British Institution, Lear's first work to hang there.

Autumn Publishes *Journals of a Landscape Painter in Southern Calabria, &c.*

1853   *February* Returns to London and takes rooms at 65 Oxford Terrace, Hyde Park.

Summer The City of Syracuse, one of two paintings exhibited in the Royal Academy, is chosen by Frederick Lygon as an Art Union Prize.

September–October In Leicestershire works on a painting *The Temple of Bassæ*.

November Publishes musical settings of four of Tennyson's poems. His health deteriorates.

December Travels to Egypt.

1854   *January–March* Goes up the Nile as far as the first cataract.

April Returns to England via Malta and southern France. At Oxford Terrace.

August–October Travels in Switzerland, then returns to London.

1855   Publishes a second edition of *A Book of Nonsense*.

A Calabrian Ravine and *A Devonshire Glen* exhibited at the Royal Society of British Artists, Lear's first work to hang there.

November Leaves England to winter in Corfu, travelling with Lushington who has been appointed to the Supreme Court of Justice there.

1856   *April* Employs Giorgio Kokali as his man-servant; he stays with Lear until his death.

August–October Travels via Albania and Greece to Mount Athos and Troy.

1857   *January* Returns briefly to Albania.

May Travels via Trieste and Venice to London, and takes rooms at 16 Upper Seymour Street, Portman Square.

August–October Visits Ardee, Ireland, with Fortescue.

November Returns to Corfu.

1858   *March–June* Travels to Petra, Palestine and Lebanon, then returns to Corfu.

August Travels to England, staying at Upper Seymour Street. Five more of his musical settings of Tennyson's poems are published.

November Leaves London to winter in Rome, taking rooms at Via Condotti.

1859   *March* The Prince of Wales visits his studio.

May Travels from Rome to London, staying at Upper Seymour Street.

July–November Takes rooms in St Leonard's, East Sussex, then returns to London to rooms at Stratford Place.

December Leaves London for Rome.

1860   *May* Tours the Bay of Spezzia, then returns to London, staying at Stratford Place. *The Temple of Bassæ* is bought by subscribers and given to the Fitzwilliam Museum, Cambridge.

   September Takes rooms at Oatlands Park Hotel, Weybridge to work on his paintings *The Cedars of Lebanon* and *Masada*.

   November Draws his first known nonsense botany. Publishes three more settings of Tennyson's poems.

1861   *January* Moves back to London, to Stratford Place.

   February Ann falls ill.

   11 March Ann dies.

   May–August Travels via Paris to Florence to do two paintings for Frances, Lady Waldegrave, returning home through Switzerland.

   September The Cedars of Lebanon is exhibited in Liverpool and receives favourable reviews.

   November Leaves London to winter in Corfu.

   December The third edition of *A Book of Nonsense* is published under his own name, and is a popular success.

1862   *March The Cedars of Lebanon* is exhibited in the Great International Exhibition in London, but it is hung high and is not well received.

   May Travels via Malta to London, staying at Stratford Place.

   November Returns to Corfu.

1863   *April–May* Tours the Ionian Islands.

   June Returns via Italy to England, staying at Stratford Place. The first American edition of *A Book of Nonsense* is published.

   December Publication of *Views in the Seven Ionian Islands*.

1864   *January* Returns to Corfu.

   April Gives up his home in Corfu, which is ceded to the Greeks, and travels via Athens to Crete.

   June Returns via Athens to England, staying at Stratford Place.

   November Leaves London to winter in Nice, at 61 Promenade des Anglais.

December Walks along the Corniche and visits San Remo for the first time.

1865   *February* Writes his first nonsense story, 'The History of the Seven Families of the Lake Pipple-Popple'.
April Returns to England, staying at Stratford Place.
June Possible date for the composition of his first nonsense song 'The Duck and the Kangaroo'. The Prince of Wales again visits his studio, and buys ten drawings.
July Publication of Lewis Carroll's *Alice's Adventures in Wonderland*.
November Travels to Venice to carry out two commissions for Lady Waldegrave.
December Travels to Malta.

1866   *April* Leaves Malta and returns to England, travelling via Corfu and the Dalmatian coast. At Stratford Place.
November Comes close to proposing marriage to Gussie Bethell.
December Leaves London for Egypt.
December–May 1867 Travels down the Nile as far as Wadi Halfa, then visits Gaza and Jerusalem.

1867   *June* Returns to England via Ravenna. At Stratford Place.
November Leaves London for the south of France, and takes rooms in Cannes.
December Writes 'The Owl and the Pussy-cat', the first nonsense song to be positively dated. Sells the *The Cedars of Lebanon* for less than a third of its original price.

1868   *April* Tours Corsica, then returns to England, staying at Stratford Place.
December Leaves London to winter in Cannes.

1869   *June* Travels to Paris to arrange for the reproduction of his pictures of Corsica.
July Arrives in London and takes rooms at 11 Duchess Street, Portland Place.
Considers buying land and building a house in England.
September Writes 'The Daddy Long-legs and the Fly'.
December Publication of *Journal of a Landscape Painter in Corsica*. Returns to Cannes.

1870   *February* Revisits San Remo to look at land which is
        for sale. 'The Owl and the Pussy-cat' is published in *Our
        Young Folks* (Boston), the first of his nonsense songs to be
        published.
        March Buys land in San Remo and begins to plan his
        new house.
        Summer Prepares nonsense for a new book.
        August Stays in Certosa del Pesio in the Italian Alps,
        and meets the Terry family for whom he draws and writes
        much nonsense, including nonsense cookery and botany,
        and the alphabet 'The Absolutely Abstemious Ass'.
        December Publication of *Nonsense Songs, Stories,
        Botany, and Alphabets.*

1871   *March* Moves into Villa Emily, San Remo.
        September Invited by Lord Northbrook to visit India.
        December Writes 'The Courtship of the Yonghy-Bonghy-
        Bò'. Publication of *More Nonsense, Pictures, Rhymes,
        Botany, Etc.*

1872   *May* Writes 'The Quangle Wangle's Hat'.
        June Visits England, and takes rooms at 6 Chandos
        Street, Cavendish Square.
        September Returns to San Remo.
        October Sets out for India, but turns back at Suez.
        November Foss the cat arrives.

1873   *May* Ill in bed, and makes the first drafts of 'Some
        Incidents in the Life of my Uncle Arly'. Writes 'The
        Pobble who has no Toes'.
        Summer Monastery of Megaspelion in the Morea
        exhibited at the Royal Academy, the last of his works
        to hang there in his lifetime.
        October Leaves a second time for India.
        November Arrives in Bombay.

1874   Travels in India and Ceylon.

1875   *January* Leaves India and returns to San Remo.
        June–September In England, taking rooms at 8 Duchess
        Street.
        September Returns to San Remo.

1876   *Summer* Prepares work for a new nonsense book.

bronchitis. Completes 'Some Incidents in the Life of my
Uncle Arly'.

February A Book of Nonsense is nominated by John
Ruskin as the top of his list in his 'Choice of Books' in the
Pall Mall Gazette. Makes final payment of the debt for
building Villa Tennyson.

July–September At Briánza.

1887   *July–September* At Adorno, Piedmonte.

26 September Death of Foss.

1888   *29 January* Lear dies. He is buried in San Remo.

March Franklin Lushington clears Lear's house, and
offers the return of letters to some correspondents, but
destroys most of his personal papers.

September Publication of the first collected edition of
Lear's four nonsense books in America and England.

Further Reading

The place of publication is London unless otherwise indicated.

Byrom, T., *Nonsense and Wonder: The Poems and Cartoons of Edward Lear* (New York, 1977). The fullest critical study to be devoted entirely to Lear's work.

Cammaerts, Emile, *The Poetry of Nonsense* (1925).

Chesterton, G. K., 'How Pleasant to know Mr Lear', in *A Handful of Authors: Essays on Books and Writers*, ed. Dorothy Collins (1953).

Colley, Ann C., 'Edward Lear's Limericks and the Reversals of Nonsense', *Victorian Poetry* 26: 3 (Autumn 1988), pp. 285–99.

—, *Edward Lear and the Critics* (Columbia, SC, 1993). This has the fullest bibliography relating to Lear criticism.

Copley, I. A., 'Edward Lear – Composer', *Musical Opinion*, 104: 1236 (October 1980), pp. 8–9, 12, 39.

Davidson, Angus, *Edward Lear: Landscape Painter and Nonsense Poet: 1812–1888* (1938).

Ede, Lisa, 'Edward Lear's Limericks and their Illustrations', in *Explorations in the Field of Nonsense*, ed. Wim Tigges (Amsterdam, 1987), pp. 103–16.

—, 'An Introduction to the Nonsense Literature of Edward Lear and Lewis Carroll', in *Explorations in the Field of Nonsense*, pp. 47–60.

Fowler, Rowena (ed.), *Edward Lear: The Cretan Journal* (Athens, 1984).

Hark, Ina Rae, 'Edward Lear: Eccentricity and Victorian *Angst*', *Victorian Poetry* 16 (1978), pp. 112–22.

—, *Edward Lear* (Boston, 1982).

Hofer, Philip, *Edward Lear as a Landscape Draughtsman* (Cambridge, MA, 1967).

Hofer, P. and R. Thompson, 'The Yonghy-Bonghy-Bò: i. The Poem. ii. The Music', *Harvard Library Bulletin* 15 (1967), pp. 229–37.

Huxley, Aldous, 'Edward Lear', in *On the Margin* (1923).

Hyman, Susan, *Edward Lear's Birds* (1980).

— (ed.), *Edward Lear in the Levant: Travels in Albania, Greece and Turkey in Europe 1848–1849* (1988).

Lear, Edward, *Bosh and Nonsense* (1982).

Lecercle, Jean-Jacques, *Philosophy of Nonsense: The Intuitions of Victorian Nonsense Literature* (1994).

Lehman, John, *Edward Lear and his World* (1977).

Levi, Peter, *Edward Lear* (1995).

Liebert, Herman, W. (ed.), *Lear in the Original: Drawings and Limericks by Edward Lear for his 'Book of Nonsense'* (New York, 1975).

Lord, John Vernon, *Illustrating Lear's Nonsense* (Brighton, 1991).

Lyons, A. K., T. R. Lyons and M. J. Preston, *A Concordance to the Complete Nonsense of Edward Lear* (Norwood, PA, 1980).

Malcolm, Ian, *The Pursuit of Leisure, & Other Essays* (1929).

Noakes, Vivien, *Edward Lear: The Life of a Wanderer* (1968), 4th revised edn (2003).

—, *Edward Lear 1812–1888: the Catalogue of the Royal Academy of Arts Exhibition* (1985). This has the fullest bibliography relating to all Lear's work, including his nonsense.

— (ed.), *Selected Letters* (Oxford, 1988).

—, *The Painter Edward Lear* (Newton Abbot, 1991).

Orwell, George, 'Nonsense Poetry', in *Shooting an Elephant and Other Essays* (1950).

Partridge, Eric, 'The Nonsense Words of Edward Lear and Lewis Carroll', in *Here, There and Everywhere. Essays Upon Language* (1950).

Pitman, Ruth, *Edward Lear's Tennyson* (Manchester, 1988).

Schiller, Justin G., *Nonsensus: Cross-referencing Edward Lear's original 116 limericks … together with a census of known copies of the genuine first edition* (Stroud, 1988).

Sewell, Elizabeth, *The Field of Nonsense* (1952). The classic study of nonsense.

Sherrard, Philip (ed.), *Edward Lear: The Corfu Years: a Chronicle Presented through his Letters and Journals* (Athens, 1988).

[Slade, B. C.] William B. Osgood Field, *Edward Lear on my Shelves* (New York, 1933).

Stewart, Susan A., *Nonsense: Aspects of Intertextuality in Folklore and Literature* (Baltimore, 1979).

Tigges, Wim, *An Anatomy of Literary Nonsense* (Amsterdam, 1988).

— (ed.), *Explorations in the Field of Nonsense* (Amsterdam, 1987).

A Note on the Texts

Lear published four volumes of nonsense, *A Book of Nonsense* (1846, 1855 and 1861), *Nonsense Songs, Stories, Botany, and Alphabets* (1871), *More Nonsense, Pictures, Rhymes, Botany, Etc.* (1872) and *Laughable Lyrics; A Fourth Book of Nonsense Poems, Songs, Botany, Music, &c.* (1877).

Frederick Warne bought the copyright of *A Book of Nonsense* in 1861, and in 1888 they acquired that of the rest of Lear's titles. After the 3rd edition, *A Book of Nonsense* remained unchanged until the 25th edition, the first to appear after Lear's death in January 1888. In this, three limericks were removed, the format was enlarged and it was retitled *The Book of Nonsense*. Also in 1888 *More Nonsense* was reissued, using the new format and containing only limericks, including the three taken from *A Book of Nonsense*.

In 1895 Warne separated the botany, alphabets and cookery from the songs and stories, and published them in two separate volumes as *Nonsense Botany and Nonsense Alphabets* and *Nonsense Songs and Stories* which included some new material – 'How pleasant to know Mr Lear!', 'Incidents in the Life of my Uncle Arly' [*sic*], 'Mr and Mrs Discobbolos: Second Part', 'The Heraldic Blazons of Foss the Cat' and a facsimile of 'The Duck and the Kangaroo'.

In 1911, Lady Strachey edited *Queery Leary Nonsense*, using entirely unpublished work, and, in 1912, *The Complete Nonsense Book* which incorporated the nonsense published by Lear plus some previously unpublished material. Subsequent years saw the publication in small, individual volumes of newly discovered manuscripts.

Work published by Lear himself went out of copyright in 1938, and new editions then began to appear. In 1947 came the publication of *The Complete Nonsense of Edward Lear* edited by Holbrook Jackson, the most enduring of these. It contained the material Lear had published arranged in four parts following the four volumes, and a fifth part comprising the material that first appeared in *Nonsense Songs and Stories*.

The purpose of this edition is to bring together Lear's nonsense, and the surviving poetry that is not nonsense, and to provide detailed notes. Much of the material has never before been published. As well as the poetry and prose there are also examples of nonsense drawings in the margins of his ornithological work, nonsense in landscape, illustrations to popular ballads, his travel adventures, diary entries, entire nonsense letters and nonsense extracts from otherwise straightforward letters (although few of Lear's letters can be called straightforward, since nonsense words and similes break into so many of them).

Most of the work has now been dated, which means that, for the first time, it can be arranged chronologically. This enables us not only to see the development of Lear's writing, but also to show how the life and nonsense interwove from boyhood to old age, creating a remarkable autobiographical compendium. Where dating has not been possible, for example with many of the limericks, the work is placed at the date of publication and arranged in the order in which it was published. Undated material that has not previously been published is placed where its style or content suggests a possible context.

Lear's own papers, including the manuscripts of nonsense he prepared for the printer and some proofs, are preserved at the Houghton Library, Harvard University, the result of the prescience of the American academic and collector, Philip Hofer, who bought many of the manuscripts when they came on to the market in the late 1920s and early 1930s, and encouraged his friend, William B. Osgood Field, to buy the rest. Both these collections were later deposited at Harvard, forming the single most important holding of Lear papers. Further material is held at the Somerset Record Office in Taunton, in the Warne archive and at the Tennyson Research Centre in Lincoln, although the latter has now been partly dispersed. Small collections still remain in the families for whom they were originally written and drawn, but other papers have passed through the sale rooms. Some of these now form significant groupings, in particular the Frederick R. Koch collection which is currently on deposit at the Beinecke Rare Book and Manuscript Library at Yale University and which contains, among others, nonsense prepared for the Duncan and Phipps Hornby families.

There are undoubtedly still papers in private collections that may yet come to light, but much has been destroyed. The letters and early poems which belonged to Lear's sister Ann were still in existence in South Africa in the late 1930s, but exhaustive searches have failed to find them. Fortunately, some at least were transcribed by Eleanor Bowen, the great-granddaughter of Lear's sister Sarah, and they now exist in a number of typescript copies. So too do some of the early poems that Lear wrote for his childhood friends, the Drewitts. Two important collections belonging to Lear's close friends, Franklin Lushington and Lord Northbrook, are known to have been destroyed. Reading the ebullient joyfulness of Lear's occasional nonsense, and observing how it burst forth at every opportunity, one realizes how fortunate we are that anything has survived from his early years in particular, and how sad it is that much more has not.

In selecting the text a number of guidelines have been followed. In the case of work published by Lear, priority has been given to the text he published, even where a number of manuscripts exist; significant variants are noted. Where work was published after his death, the published version has again been chosen, except where there are compelling reasons for replacing words or phrases with a manuscript variant, as, for example, the mistaken reading of the last line of 'Some Incidents in the Life of my Uncle Arly', or the typically phonetic 'dumms' for 'dumbs' in the same poem. Any such changes are given in the notes. Most previously unpublished material exists only in one copy, but where there is more than one manuscript, the one adjudged to be the final text is used. Where the poem survives in both manuscript and transcript, the manuscript is taken as the source. In the case of the Bowen papers, where only the typescript survives, there has been no opportunity to check their accuracy. However, in a handwritten note, Eleanor Bowen spoke of the care she had taken that the transcripts should be as accurate as possible.

As a general rule, the punctuation and capitals follow those given by Lear. However, in the published limericks and alphabets he was notoriously inconsistent in his use of these. In different editions the same limerick might have a comma, a full-point or nothing after a particular word, while surviving manuscripts offer a dash or a colon. Lear often capitalized nouns, but they sometimes have a capital letter in one line and a lower-case in the next. Such inconsistencies also occur in proper nouns, for example he gives us both 'Lake Pipple-Popple' and 'Lake Pipple-popple'. Where there is no apparent reason for these discrepancies the decision was made to establish consistency, but if there is any possibility that doing so might alter the sense or rhythm he intended they have been left as they are. Three of the four alphabets published here show a similar haphazard use of punctuation and capitals, and the same modifications, with the same caveats, have been applied. In previously unpublished limericks the punctuation and capitalization of the manuscript are followed. Full points after titles, for example Mr, have been omitted.

In the text of poems ampersands have been transcribed as 'and'; they have been retained in letters, in prose transcriptions, and in variants given in the notes. Numbers in the text of poems have been spelled out, for example 'twenty-two', but have been retained elsewhere, and in the notes to poems, for example '6'. Lear's spelling, apart from obvious spelling mistakes, has been scrupulously followed, and [sic] has been introduced only where there is a possibility that the given word might be thought to be a misprint. Illegible words have been rendered as '[ ]'. With a few exceptions, neologisms are not identified as such in the notes since it was felt that pedantry would destroy the spirit in which they were created. Lear's abbreviations, as, for example, 'thro'' for 'through' and 'e'en' for 'even', have been retained. Place names have been rendered in the text as he gave them, as in 'Sanremo', but have been given their modern spelling in any commentary.

Where Lear has not titled a poem, the first line is taken, with inverted commas, for example 'Gozo my child is the isle of Calypso'. Limericks have not been given titles, but groups of limericks have, in square brackets, for example [Limericks published in *More Nonsense*]. In prose and miscellaneous pieces, untitled work has been given a title which is placed in square brackets as, for example, [Lear's adventures on horseback]. Prose letters are headed with the name of the recipient, for example, Letter to Ruth Decie. Verse letters are headed either with the name of the recipient, or with the first line of the poem in inverted commas, depending on which is more appropriate.

Lear composed at least twenty-nine alphabets. Clearly these could not all be reproduced, and one example has been given of each of the formats he used. A note gives the dates of composition, the name of the recipient, a broad breakdown of contents and the publication details of the others.

The Complete Verse
and Other Nonsense

Eclogue

Vide Collins 'Hassan – or the Camel Driver'

In dreary silence down the bustling road
The Lears – with all their goods and chattels rode;
Ten carts of moveables went on before,
And in the rear came half-a-dozen more;
A Hackney-coach the Lears themselves enshrouds
To guard them from the gaze of vulgar crowds.
The vehicle has reached the turnpike gate, –
Where wond'ring toll-men, – throngs of people wait; –
The loaded carts their dusty way pursue, –
Shrill squeak the wheels, – dark London was in view.   10
With grief heart-rending then, those mournful folk
Thrice sighed – thrice wiped their eyes – as thus they
    spoke:
'Sad was the hour – and luckless was the day
When first from Bowman's Lodge we bent our way! –

'How little half the woes can we foresee,
Of that thrice odious New Street where we flee! –
Bethink thee Mother! – can we ever find
Half room enough for all these goods behind? –
Soon must those carts their precious loads resign, –
Then, what but noise and trouble shall be thine! –   20
Ye banished furnitures, that once did bear
In our last Halls a more than equal share,
Here, where no dark rooms shew their craving door,
Or mildewed lumberrooms make place for more,
In vain ye hope the comfort – space – to know,
Which dark rooms large or lumberrooms bestow, –
Here closets only – dwarfish rooms are found,
And scanty inconvenience rules around.
Sad was the hour and luckless was the day
When first from Bowman's Lodge we bent our way!   30

'What noisome thought could urge our parents so –
To leave the country and to London go!
The rural scene to change for houses, brown,
And barter health for the thick smoke of town!
What demon tempts him from our home to go
In horrid New Street to pour forth our woe? –
Oft – oft we've hoped this hour we ne'er might see,
Yet London – now at last we come to thee!
Oh! why was New Street so attractive made, –
Or why our Dad so easily betrayed?
Why heed we not as swift we ride along
The farewell peal of Highgate bells ding dong, –
Or wherefore think the flowery hedges hide, –
The grunting pigs, and fowls in speckled pride?
Why think we these less pleasing to behold
Than dirty streets which lead to houses old!
Sad was the hour and luckless was the day
When first from Bowman's Lodge we bent our way!

'Oh! cease our fears! all grumbling as we go,
While thought creates unnumbered scenes of woe, –
What if the mobs in all their ire we meet!
Oft in the dust we trace their crowded feet, –
And fearful – oft when day's November light
Yields up her yellow reign to gas-lit night,
By mischief roused they scour the streets, and fly,
While radical reform is all they cry:
Before them Death with fire directs their way,
Fills the loud yell and guides them to their prey.
Sad was the hour and luckless was the day
When first from Bowman's Lodge we bent our way.

'At that dread hour the noise of fire shall sweep –
If aught of rest we find, upon our sleep,
Or some rude thief bounce through the window – smash –
And wake our dozings with a hideous crash,
Thrice happy they – the Catharine Street poor –
From wish of town – from dread of fire secure!

40

50

60

They tempt no New Street, and no thieves they find! –
No carts of goods have they – before – behind! –
Sad was the hour and luckless was the day   70
When first from Bowman's Lodge we bent our way!

'Oh! Hapless Lears! – for that your care hath won, –
The large sidegarden will be most undone! –
Big swelled our hearts, on this same mournful day
When low the plants drooped down – as thus they seemed
    to say; –
"Farewell! ye Lears whom fruits could not detain! –
Whom flowrets drooping buds implored in vain! –
Yet as ye go may every blow fall down,
Weak as those buds on each receiving crown, –
So may ye see nor care – nor grievous fuss, –   80
Nor e're be cast to earth – to die like us! –"
Ah! might we safely to our home return –
Say to our garden – "Cease – no longer mourn! –"
Ah! might we teach our hearts to lose their fears,
And linger there our yet remaining years!'
They said – and ceased: lamenting o'er the day,
When first from Bowman's Lodge they bent their way.

To Miss Lear on her Birthday

Dear, and very dear relation,
Time, who flies without cessation, –
Who ne'er allows procrastination, –
Who never yields to recubation
Nor ever stops for respiration,
Has brought again in round rotation
The once a yearly celebration
Of the day of thy creation, –
When another augmentation
Of a whole year in numeration   10
Will be joined in annexation

To thy former glomeration
Of five seven-years' incalculation.
And in this very blest occasion
A thought has crossed my imagination,
That I 'neath an obligation
To make to thee a presentation,
(So 'tis the custom of our nation)
Of any trifling small donation,
Just to express my gratulation
Because of thy safe peragration
To one more long year's termination;
But having made an indagation
As to my moneyed situation,
(What must have been my indignation
Mortification, and vexation)
I tell you sans equivocation,
– I found – through dire depauperation,
A want of power – my sweet relation,
To practise my determination! –

So as the fates ordained frustration
I shortly ceased my lamentation
And, though it caused much improbation,
I set to work with resignation
To torture my imagination,
To spin some curious dication
To merit p'raps thine approbation, –
At least to meet thine acceptation,
And – after much deliberation
And 'mongst my thoughts much altercation,
I fixed that every termination
To every line should end in -ation! –
Now – since I've given this explanation,
Deign to receive my salutation
And let me breathe an aspiration
To thee – this day of thy creation.

First then, I wish thee, dear relation,
Many a sweet reduplication
Of this thy natal celebration:
And may'st thou from this first lunation   50
Unto thy vital termination
Be free from every derogation
By fell diseases' contamination,
Whose catalogic calculation
Completely thwarts enumeration, –
Emaciation, – fomentation,
With dementation – deplumation,
And many more in computation
For these are but an adumbration: –
– And may'st thou never have occasion   60
For any surgic operation
Or medical administration, –
Sanguification, – defalcation, –
Cauterization – amputation –
Rhabarbaration – scarification
And more of various designation: –
May'st thou be kept in preservation
From every sort of vitiation
By evil's dark depreciation: –
Intoxication – trucidation, –   70
From malversation – desecration –
From giving way to execration,
And every sinful machination: –
And in thy daily occupation –
Whether it be discalceation,
Or any other ministration
May'st thou not meet the least frustration;
May'st thou withstand all obtrectation
Thrown out to mar thy reputation; –
May'st thou be free from altercations   80
Or with thy word or thy relations; –
And (though it wants corroboration,
Yet not quite void of confirmation, –)
If as report gives intimation

You are about to change your station,
May every peaceful combination
Of bliss await your situation
In matrimonial elevation –
May'st thou be loved with veneration –
– By none be held in detestation, –
And towards thy life's advesperation,
When most are prone to [   ]
Their feeble limbs to desiccation, –
Their strength through years to deliquation, –
Their minds and brains to conquassation, –
Their failing speech to aberration, –
Their wearied taste to nauseation, –
                    then,
Then, may'st thou, – Oh dear relation,
Always receive refullerlation, –
Thy frame imbibe reanimation, –
Thy reason hold her wonted station
And keep her prudent scintillation,
Till thou descend'st by slow gradation
Unto thy final destination –
The long last home of all creation.
– This is my birthday aspiration; –
– Believe it, ever dear relation
Sincere without exaggeration –
In every individual ation! –
Sanguine – in each anticipation –
And kindly meant in perpetration.

Finis.

The Shady Side of Sunnyside

Woe worth the day when folly gave the signal
(Or rather Hymen) to old father Brignall,
To marry that same stupid 'Hurrum, – Scurrum',
Through whom we lost the sunny side of Durham!

That Sunnyside! how sweet it must have been!
My heart quite longs for such a lovely scene!
I think I see it now, – so wide and roomy, –
And then so brilliant always! – never gloomy! –

The sun that lighted up its eastern side,
Its beams upon the western multiplied, –   10
And gleamed at once o'er all its lakes and towers, –
Ah! at that rate, all Durham had been ours! –

– Had! – did I say? Alas – 'tis past recalling!
(Or else I'd spent a week or two in brawling)
No – no – don't fret – 'tis safe from every danger,
While in the awful clutches of the Grainger.

There's all their nasty children too, – before
We can get at it – each to have a paw
Upon that sweet – delightful sunny shore! –
– A breeding race – those Graingers! Known of yore!   20

Well, it's no use our thoughts to stew and ferret; –
'Figs on it' – I say – like Granny Skerritt; –
But when we *do* get into Durham's county, –
We'll pay those Grainger folks for all their bounty!

Yes – yes! so long o'er Sunnyside we've brooded, –
And our illustrious blood so long deluded, –
That when for that great rout we give the signals –
Oh! woe to Graingers [   ] and Brignalls! –

Journal
1829

November 2nd Monday evening – took my place –
Went to a dance at nine o'clock, –
Jigged all the colour out of my face
And reached my lodgings at crow of cock.

November 3rd Packed up my luggage till half past four,
Got up at six, and drank some tea,
And set off as cold as the frozen sea, –
Wished goodbye – took my hats and umbrella –
And shivered and shook to the White Horse cellar.
Sat on the top of the stage and four –
For Robinson half an hour or more, –
Rattled and rumbled down the Strand
Where the mudscrapers stood in a dingy band,
And rode away from London smoke,
Or ever the light of day had broke.
Chelsea and Fulham and Putney Bridge, –
And Kingston on Thames with its banks of sedge, –
Esher and Cobham, how cold they were! –
Oh! it was enough to make anyone swear!
– Thumped my feet till I made them ache, –
Took out provisions, a meal to make, –
Offered a sandwich, – (I had but three,) –
To my neighbour, who sat with a shaky knee,
'Sir' – said she with a glutinous grin,
'I'll thank you for *two*, as they seem but thin, –
And shall feel quite glad if you'll give one 'arter,
To this here young lady wot's my darter.' –
As good as her word was the brazen wretch,
Down went three sandwiches all at a stretch.
– Ripley – Guildford and Godalming too –
Whitley – Northchapel and Chittingfold gate –
Saw us looking as black and blue
As a spoonful of milk in an empty plate.

After the coach at Petworth ran –
(He and his wife,) a hugey man –
Quite as globose as a harvest moon,
Up he got, and 'twas B. Colhoun.
– Down Fittleworth Hill we made a dash,
And walked on foot up Bury Hill side, –
Half hot – half cold – like a luke-warm hash,   40
And as stiff as a lobster's claw – wot's tied.
Arundel town at length reached we,
As early as ten minutes after three.
Went to the Bank: found no one there –
Wanted a dinner – the cupboard was bare, –
Set off to Peppering – Cloky and I –
Over the hard chalk merrily –
Halfway there heard a horrible clack –
– Sister and nephews coming back –
Couldn't return with them – nonsense quite –   50
So posted away in the dusky light –
And five o'clock it might very well be,
Ere I caught a glimpse of the old elm tree,
And popped on my friends like a powder puff –
Ha – Ha – Ha – ! – it was merry enough!
Gobbled enough to choke Goliath –
Drank my tea – and sat by the fire;
Saw the baby – that unique child –
Who squeaked – and stared – and sniffed – and
      smiled; –
Then went to bed with a very good will   60
And fell asleep ere you'd swallow a pill.

November 4th   Wednesday, rose before the sun, –
And scrambled away o'er stile and gate, –
Left a note to say where I'd run, –
And got to Arundel – just at eight.
Breakfast over – up the hill,
With Sarah to Brookfield sallied forth,
White frost covering the country still, –
Just like a frozen syllabub froth:

70 Saw the children – ate some oys-
ters – and went out to see the boys: –
Found them performing sundry strides, –
Some by skates and some by slides, –
Went back, and fixed to come and stay
On Sunday next, then came away.
Found the wind blew vastly bitterly, –
Called at Lyminster – John at home, –
Looked at the plates of Roger's Italy, –
Talked of reform and Chancellor Brougham: –

80 Back to Arundel made a run, –
And finished a lunch at half past one:
Out again – and called at Tower
House, and staid for half an hour.
Walked again with Sister Sarah,
Through roads which surely never looked barer, –
Woods of gloomy and leafless trees,
All in a state of shiver and freeze:
Into the town again and dressed, –
Devoured a dinner with infinite zest: –

90 Went with the Streets to tea next door, –
Wardropers – Blanches and two or three more; –
Played at Backgammon and Chess with James,
– Got beaten, and gammoned at sundry games, –
Eat stewed oysters at supper time, – read
Original verses – and went to bed.

November 5th Thursday. Breakfasted. Cold again –
Dismal and half inclined to rain, –
Walked with Sarah to Hampton Beach, –
Saw the sea twirl like a vomiting leech, –

100 Walked up and down by the grumbling tide
Till our noses looked like Capsicums dried, –
Half-past eleven – left behind,
The soap-suddy waves, – and boisterous wind,
– After demolishing buns and bread –
And making our visages vulgarly red, –
Called at Brookfield for half a minute,

But didn't go in – for no one was in it, –
Went to Calceto and stayed some time
With Mrs George – till one o'clock chime, –
Then home again – And calls of course –   110
And dined upon mutton and capers sauce.
After dinner – popped next door –
And sat a dozen minutes or more, –
Went into Uncle Richard's – at first, –
Just in order to see Miss Hurst, –
But found a lot of people there –
So stayed – to drive away toothache and care.
– Back then we went then – one and all,
And here Miss Bischoff had a fall.
And then we reached, as we'd designed –   120
Miss Upperton's – And then we dined, –
And lastly, setting off again,
Just as the day was on the wane,
We got to Arundel at last,
At five o'clock – or rather past.

And thus Ma'am, in these dogg'rel verses
All the remarkable reverses
Of fortune, which we met, as how –
Through our strange wanderings, you know –
Conclusion now – by saying that I   130
Can never forget them certainly, –
And hoping that your wine may be
As good to all infinity
Of time, and that your pears mayn't spoil, –
But multiply – like Widow's oil –
I have the pleasure to sign here,
Myself – Yours most obliged –

                                        E. Lear.

Turkey Discipline
(adapted to the tune of 'Shades of Evening')

Horrid Turkeys! what a pother!
Leave my Mother's gulls alone!
We, alas! can get no other,
If those precious two are gone! –
Still you persevere! – You Monsters! –
Over you have come – pell-mell! –
Oh! my gulls! – if you come near them
I will utter such a yell!!!

'Bless my heart – nine monstrous turkeys! –
Gracious! – all the garden's full! –
And one great one with a jerk has
Pounced upon my favourite gull!'
– Through the noise of turkeys calling,
Now was heard, distinct and well,
From the Southern window squalling
Many a long and awful yell.

Down rushed Fanny and Eliza; –
– Screams and squeaks and yowlings shrill, –
– Gulls and turkeys with their cries a-
round them echoed o'er the hill: –
What would they not give to fetch them
Such a blow! – sad to tell –
As poor Fanny ran to catch them,
Evil turkeys – down she fell! –

'When the light dies away on a calm summer's eve'

When the light dies away on a calm summer's eve
And the sunbeams grow faint and more faint in the west,
How we love to look on, till the last trace they leave
Glows alone like a blush upon modesty's breast! –
Lonely streak! dearer far than the glories of day
Seems thy beauty – 'mid silence and shadow enshrined, –
More bright as its loneliness passes away –
And leaves twilight in desolate grandeur behind! –
So when grief has made lonely and blighted our lot,
And her icy cold chain o'er our spirits has cast,   10
Will not memory oft turn to some thrice hallowed spot,
That shines out like a star among years that are past?
Some dream that will wake in a desolate heart,
Every chord into music that long has been hushed,
Mournful echo! – soon still – for it tolls with a smart,
That the joys which first woke it, are long ago crushed!

'From the pale and the deep'

From the pale and the deep
    From the dark and bright –
From the violets that sleep –
    Away from light: –
From the lily that flashes
    At morn's glad call –
The bee gathers honey
    And sweets from all. –

There are hearts like bees
    In a world such as this,   10
That are given to please
    Through sorrow and bliss: –

Be the heaven of life
As dark as it will –
Amid pleasure and strife
They are smiling still.

They've a tear for the sad, –
But there's balm in their sigh, –
And they laugh with the glad
In sunshine and joy: –
They give hope to the gloom
Of the mourner's thrall –
Like the bee they find honey
And sweets in all.

Peppering Roads

If you wish to see roads in perfection –
A climax of cart-ruts and stones –
Or if you've the least predilection
For breaking your neck or your bones, –
If descents and ascents are inviting, –
If your ankles are strangers to sprains, –
If you'd ever a penchant for sliding, –
Then, to Peppering go by all means! –

Take a coach some dark night in November,
A party of four within side –
Ah! I once had that jaunt, I remember,
And really I pretty near died! –
First across to my neighbour I tumbled
Then into the next lady's lap,
For at ev'ry fresh rut we were jumbled
And jolted at ev'ry new gap! –

So that when we had finished our journey
   The coachman who opened the door
Found us tangled so very topturvy –
   We rolled out in one bundle, – all four.   20
And then we were so whisped together,
   Legs – dresses – caps – arms – blacks and whites,
That some minutes elapsed before ever
   They got us completely to rights! –

If you go in a gig, you are sure to
   Get lost in a mist on the hills, –
There's a gibbetted thief on a moor too,
   Your mem'ry with murder that fills. –
And besides, if you ride in what fashion
   You will – you are sure to get splashed,   30
Till you get quite incensed, in a passion,
   And peppery – like mutton that's hashed.

Or if, on some fine frosty morning,
   You make up your mind for a walk, –
Oh! ere such be your project – take warning,
   For sunbeams will liquify chalk! –
Step by step you get clogged so – for sartin,
   With chalk round your shoes like a rope, –
For to comfort – and eke Day and Martin! –
   You might as well walk upon soap! –   40

From one end of the walk to the other –
   It's one awful bootjack to feet –
One mighty pedestrial slither –
   For Christianlike progress unmeet! –
Oh! the Peppering roads! Sure 'tis fit there
   Should be some requital at last, –
So the inmates you find, when you get there,
   Amply pay you for all you have passed! –

Miss Fraser's Album

My Album's open; come and see; –
    What, won't you waste a thought on me?
Write but a word, a word or two,
    And make me love to think on you.

Give me of your esteem a sample;
    A line will be of price untold:
In gifts, the heart is all and ample,
    It makes them worth their weight in gold.

Here friends assemble, hand and heart,
    Whom life may sever, death may part,
Sweet be their deaths, their lives well spent,
    And this their friendship's merriment.

The lov'liest wreath that glows
    'Neath summer's hand entwining
A thousand flowerets shows
    In blinded beauty shining: –
The lowly bell – the blushing rose, –
    Their varied charms combining. –

And when the sunlight flies
    And day's hushed toils are ending –
The sounds of evening rise
    In mingled sweetness blending: –
And distant bells, and Zephyr's sighs
    To soothe, their joys are lending:

As round the flowing wreath
    Variety is smiling,
And o'er those sounds that breathe
    The silent air beguiling, –

Through ev'ry page of mine
  Th'unfading wreath we're twining,   30
Variety's sweet charms will shine,
  One blended whole combining. –

Ruins of the Temple of Jupiter Aegina, Greece

Many the feet that filled
  Thy halls and marble stairs
When the sun was used to gild
  Thy white-robed worshippers;
These were forms too bright and fair,
  Who were kneeling at thy shrine,
For their souls to feel the snare
  Of homage – false as thine: –
There were shouts of revelry
  From thy mount rose high and long,   10
And the dark and distant sea
  Used to echo back the song! –
And the far off glorious clashing
  Of thy cymbaled votary –
Came, through the soft air flashing,
  Like the sounds of years gone by.
Aegina! – they are fled –
  Thy fame hath perishèd! –

The moss is on thy walls –
  Silence and deep despair; –   20
And the ruin as it falls
  Gives the only echo there:
Thy music is not heard, –
  Thy high raised roof is gone, –
And the solitary bird
  Sits on the topmost stone: –
There are sunbeams ling'ring still,
  Through thy far white pillars seen

But they only seem to tell
   Of what thou once hast been! –
And oft in silence o'er thee,
   The dark cloud passes on –
And it sheds a deeper glory
   O'er thy wild oblivion! –
Aegina! – With the dead
   Thy fame hath perishèd! –

Type of thy parent clime! –
   In ages past away,
Greece was like thee sublime –
   Like thee was bright and gay! –
And on thy mount wert thou
   Shrined in thy orient sky,
A gem upon the brow
   Of her fair liberty! –
But Greece has fallen, like thee, –
   Desolate – wildly lone; –
Her sons – the brave and free,
   Forgotten and unknown: –
The echo of her fountains
   Seems her lost children's sigh, –
And on her lov'liest mountains
   Sits dark captivity! –
Aegina! – Greece! – the dead,
   And you have perishèd! –

The Bride's Farewell

Farewell Mother! tears are streaming
Down thy tender pallid cheek,
I, in gems and roses gleaming,
One eternal sunshine dreaming,
Scarce this sad farewell may speak.
Farewell Mother! now I leave thee,

And thy love unspeakable,
One to cherish – who may grieve me,
One to trust – who may deceive me,
Farewell Mother – fare thee well!   10

Farewell Father! thou art smiling,
Yet there's sadness on thy brow,
A mingled joy and languor wiling
All my heart from thee beguiling
Tenderness to which I go, –
Farewell Father thou didst bless me
Ere my lips thy name could tell,
He may wound – who should caress me
Who should solace – may distress me,
Father, guardian, – fare thee well!   20

Farewell Sister – thou are twining
Round me an affection deep,
Gazing on my garb so shining
Wishing joy, but ne'er divining
Why a blessèd bride should weep:
Farewell Sister – have we ever
Suffered wrath our breasts to swell,
Ere gave looks or words that sever?
Those who should be parted never,
Sister dearest – fare thee well.   30

Farewell Brother; thou art brushing
Gently off those tears of mine,
And the grief that fresh was gushing
Thy most holy kisses hushing,
Can I e'er meet love like thine?
Farewell, brave and gentle Brother
Those more dear than words can tell
Love me yet – although another
Claims Ianthe! Father, Mother,
All beloved ones, – Fare ye well!   40

Ruby –

Accidentally shot. November 23rd, 1829. –

Poor Ruby is dead! and before her no more
    From the hearth and the furze-bush the rabbit shall rise, –
For her barking is hushed and her bounding is o'er,
    And the birds will hop over the turf where she lies.

And the fire will shine down on the hearthrug at night,
    But poor Ruby will never repose there again, –
For her last sleep has closed up her eyelids, and light
    Will beam bright on her tomb to arouse her in vain.

To the churchyard no more when the service is done
    She will hasten to welcome her master and friends, –
Nor again chase her tail round and round in her fun, –
    For with life – Ruby's joy and her liberty ends. –

Poor dog! though the hand which so fondly she loved
    Was the same which in death made her dark eye grow dim, –
Yet, had language been hers – she would e'en have approved
    Of a deed e'er so fatal – if coming from him!

They'll miss thee – poor Animal! gentle and true,
    In the field and the parlour, [in both thou didst shine!]
For 'mongst dogs thou wast good ... and of mortals, how few,
    Can boast of a life half so faultless as thine! –

Thou wilt never come back! – Yet in some future day
    When the grass and the daisies have grown o'er thy head –
They will think of thee often at evening – and say
    When they look at thy hearthrug – 'Poor Ruby is dead!' –

Miss Maniac

Around my brain there is a chain, and o'er my fevered soul
A darkness like that solemn gloom which once through Egypt
  stole;

Sometimes I feel, but know not why, a fire within me burn,
And visions fierce and terrible, pursue where'er I turn;

Then I forget that earth is earth, and that myself am life,
And nature seems to die away in darkness, hell and strife.

But when my phrenzied fit is o'er, a dreary hour comes on, –

A consciousness of unknown things, – of reason overthrown.

Cold runs my blood from vein to vein – all vacant is mine eye,
And in my ears a sound of death, and dread eternity!

Then one by one my thoughts return, and from my grated cell
I gaze upon the mountain fir, the steep and woody dell;

And as I listen to the stream that dashes far below,
I pine for freedom as a joy I never more can know.

Beyond those far blue hills, I feel, was once my home of bliss,
And there my father's cottage stood, – a roof more blest than
  this.

Ah! now I think I see them come, the forms I used to love,
And hear the evening shepherd bell sound sweetly through our
  grove. –

But they are gone! – all past away – they only flash like rays
Of morning o'er my memory – my young – my happy days! –

They said that I was lovely then – and wreathed with flowers my
brow,

Oh! would my cheek had been as pale – my eye as dim as now! –

For love with all its pleasures came, but ah! its guilt came too,
And peace – fair twin to innocence, no more my bosom knew!

Oh – thou who falsely – darkly lured my frail fond heart astray,

Then left me like a broken flower, alone to waste away,

Where art thou now? doth ever thought, thy dark hour rush
across,

Of me, – forsaken – fallen me, – to goad thee with remorse? –

Or hast thou in the stream of life, 'mid scenes and forms more
sweet,

Forgot these tears that madd'ning mourn, my guilt and thy deceit? –

30

Go – lull more hearts with hopes of bliss, undreaming of a snare,

Till they awake to shame and feel – the pangs such bliss must bear.

Deceive! Deceive! – I loved thee once, therefore I will not
curse; –

But if my soul were bared to thee – Hell could not wish thee
worse! –

Yet, if a heart, e'en hard as thine, could feel but *half* the pain
Which woman's wounded bosom feels – 'twould ne'er deceive
again! –

Oh! when the bubble pleasure burst, how slowly time rolled by, –

My thoughts were grief – my looks were shame, – my every breath a sigh! –

Still – still I feel the scoffs of those who, with a cruel scorn,
Made doubly sad the memory of hours for ever gone, –   40

And still I hear my father's voice – as with a dreadful wrath

He cursed me with a bitter curse, and friendless drove me forth.

It was a cold and cheerless eve – and through the dark'ning sky
The wind swept past in hurried gusts, and shook the trees on
   high; –

My child was in my arms – my own – how quietly it slept!

I longed for morn yet feared it, and I wandered on and wept,

Till, worn with sorrow and fatigue, careless I sate me down,

And felt how doubly keen it is to mourn – and mourn alone!

Cold – cold we were – oh never since such chilling grief has
    press'd
Upon my heart whose strings seemed burst – and frozen in my
    breast;

And o'er my soul, like demon forms, dark recollections came,
My sorrows and my sins and all my pleasures bought with
    shame, –

Till through my brain they racked like fire, and every vein
    waxed hot,
And in confused despair, awhile e'en sorrow seemed forgot: –

Strange feelings, such as none but maniacs ever know or feel,
Rushed indistinctly on my mind, and reason seemed to reel,

Till, lost in unknown agony, I laughed as if in mirth,
Or shudd'ring – welcomed back the gloom of hell begun on
  earth:

Then madness first his scorching hand held o'er my withered
  brain, –

60 Ah – ha! – it was a deadly touch – but it never cooled again! –

'I slept, and back to my early days'

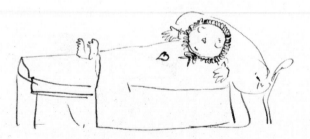

I slept, and back to my early days
Did wandering fancy roam –
When my heart vos light and my opes
   vos bright
And my own a appy ome.

When I dreamed I was young and hinnocent –
And my art vos free from care,
And my Parents smiled on their darling child,
And breathed for his [   ] a prayer.

Once again I was rising before the sun,
For in childhood I was told –
If its earliest ray on my head should play –
It would turn each tress to gold.

10

Once again I vos roaming through fields
    and flowers,
And I felt at each step new joys –
But I woke with a sigh that memory
Should revive what time destroys.

Resignation

'What must be must' or 'Baking Day'

I wish you would not mention it,
It gives me so much pain! –
Too soon by half I always know
'Tis baking day again! –
From pie to pie they hurry me, –
Loaves – tarts – preserves – and crusts –
And though I've not a moment's peace,
I cry – 'What must be, must!'

They bid me seek a change of fruit,
The charms which others see,   10
But – cherries – currants – plums – or pears –
They're all the same to me! –
'Tis true, I do not pluck the things,
Or clean 'em from the dust,
But though I don't – it's such a bore! –
Although 'What must be, must!'

They tell me pies are wanted now,
And eaten every day, –
They say they'll *always* have 'em too –
I only wish they may!   20
For my part, I'm so very sick
Of baking tarts and crust, –
I don't much think they'll catch me long,
To say – 'What must be, must!'

'I've just seen Mrs Hopkins – and read her the lines'

I've just seen Mrs Hopkins – and read her the lines,
(And they'll do for the mirror in print, she opines;) –
And so pray keep the book – till you've copied the rhyme,
For I shan't be in want of it now for some time.

I got home about five o'clock yesterday night –
As I fancy too you must have done – while 'twas light; –
For I saw you at Houghton – (I stood on the ridge
Upon Bury Hill side,) – and ride over the bridge.

I have sent you these numbers, by Robert – they'll be
An amusement perhaps to inspect after tea; –
They are beautiful things – and I think they're not dear
For both reading – and pictures. Good Bye. Edward Lear.

Ode to the little China Man

Who art thou – sweet little China Man? –
   Your name I want to know
With your lovely face so pale and wan –
   With a high diddle diddledy do. –

Your high cheek bones: – your screwed up mouth,
   How beautiful they be! –
And your eyes that ogle from north to south,
   With a high diddle diddledy dee! –

And your cultivated eyebrows too! –
   That depend from either eye! –   10
(I'm sure it's a fashion entirely new!) –
   With a high diddle diddledy di! –

But ev'ry one – (as the Frenchman said) –
   Ev'ry one to his way, –
(When he boiled in a pipkin his grandmother's head,) –
   With a high diddle diddledy da! –

Int'resting Mortal! – Whence art thou? –
   In figure surpassed by few! –
Tell us thy name – is it 'Chum-chu-wow'? –
   With a high diddle diddledy du? –   20

The little man fetched a sort of a sneer –
   As he made his sage reply –
While he twisted his eyebrow round his ear,
   With a high diddle diddledy dy. –

'Good folks' – (and he shook his noddle-ding-dong)
   'It's enough for you to know –
That in spite of my eyebrows – two feet long –
   I'm Miss Eliza's beau!!' –

Peppering Bell
On the marriage of Miss D—

At Burpham Church, the only bell
   The crazy tower can boast of
Is fractured like a walnut-shell
   Whose kernel's made the most of;
They thump its back, with many a whack,
   To set sweet tones a'flowing,
And each seventh day, the people say,
   'Hark! Hark! – the bell is going!'

But tired of such a horrid gong
    The Burphamites oft grumble,
10   'Why can't we have a good ding-dong, –
    And not that wretched dumb bell?'
Oh – be content with what heaven's sent,
    Nor be so very knowing –
For – Ah! – I fear, too soon you'll hear
    A better belle is going!

Letter to Harry Hinde

Dear Harry Hinde,
If you've a mind, –
This evening at eight,
Or hardly so late,
Being at leisure,
With very great pleasure,
I find I can come
To go with you home; –
(And drink of thy tea,
As I promised to thee:)
10 Yet – prithee don't, Harry,
By any means tarry
If this evening you should be
Engaged – for that would be
To me – the huge source
Of a deal of remorse;
For you know, if it won't suit,
I can bring up my flute
To skiggle and squeak
Any night of the week.
20 – Dask, now, I go to my dinner,
For all day I've been a-
way at the West End,
Painting the best end

Of some vast Parrots
As red as new carrots, –
(They are at the museum, –
– When you come you shall see 'em, –)
I do the head and neck first; –
– And ever since breakfast 30
I've had one bun merely!
So – yours quite sincerely
                                   E.L.

Scrawl

Dear Ann –

I conjecture you'll like it no worse
If I write you this evening a letter in verse, –
But such an epistle as this, Ma'am, I tell ye – can't
Anyhow prove either pleasant or elegant, –
For writing by night – I am quite in a flurry
And nervously warm – like a dish of stewed curry.

I left Mrs Street upon yesterday morning,
(If my hand shakes – you'll know it's occasioned by
       yawning)
And really they used me the whole of the time
With such kindness – it can't be explained in a rhyme!
They stuffed me with puddings – chops – cutlets – and pies,
Wine and cakes (I was going to say up to my eyes
But I thought 'twas so vulgar it lacked this addition:
They crammed and they stuffed me, yea, unto repletion.)
Exceedingly careful were they of my health,
And I scarcely left home at all – saving by stealth;
– They never allowed me to walk by the river
For said they – 'Lest the fogs disagree with your liver! –'
And as for a stroll through a valley – ''twere odds
If I went – that I didn't fall over the clods! – '
– 'Might I go and look over the Castle?' – 'Oh! Sidi
Mahommed!! – Suppose you should hap to grow giddy!
And pitch from the top over turrets and all –
Such a wap! breaking most of your bones in the fall! –'
So I stayed still at home and worked hard at my drawings,
And looked at the rooks – and sat hearing their cawings,
And walked out a little – a small pit-a-pat –
And endeavoured with heart and with soul to grow fat;
And indeed – just excepting – I sometimes am lame –
I don't seem in health or complexion the same; –
For my face has grown lately considerably fatter –

And has less the appearance of clarified batter
Than when, so malad, I left London turmoiled,
As pale as a sucking pig recently boiled.

Little Charles – I must say, seems improved on the whole –
But at books he's extremely dull – poor little soul! –
But the other child – Freddie – is noon night and morn
The most horrid young monkey that ever was born –
Such violent passions and tears in an ocean,
He kept the whole house in a constant commotion.   40

I now am ensconced in my favourite abode –
Which is Peppering, you know – with its sprain-ancle road;
They are all just as kind as they ever have been –
And the fields are beginning to look very green.
I have never procured yet a teal or a widgeon
But am drawing a very magnificent pigeon.
And as for my visits I'm going for to eat o-
f a dinner today with my friends at Calceto;
I leave this here place upon Saturday next,
Or on Sunday (I'll try to remember the text! –)   50
And stay ...

Letter to Fanny Jane Dolly Coombe

My dear Niece – par adoption –
   I shall not apologize for my departure from established rules so far
as to write to one so very juvenile as yourself, – as, – from the unusual
precocity of talent which you exhibited when but 6 months old I have
every reason to conclude you are by this time able to read writing; –
neither shall I excuse myself for quoting a foreign tongue – since I have
little doubt but that if you can master English – you are equally au fait
at French; – nor shall I offer any extenuation for the bad formation of
my letters – for I write by Candlelight – & in a hurry. – My letter indeed
is addressed to you – solely from a staunch belief that your whole kin-   10
dred – friends – connexions – & acquaintances are dead & departed –

& that you, – being the youngest – are the most likely to have survived so general a wreck – thus my epistle will prove a species of dead letter – & should by rights have been preluded by a *dead*ication. Faint hopes – however sometimes reanimate my mentals, & should the sundry folks below mentioned be still on the earth – I should thank you to convey their several messages to each, – which indeed is my principal reason for troubling you with so many skewers & pothooks. If you cannot yet speak your ideas – my love – you can squeak them you know.

Tell your Aunt Eliza – that on the evening before she left London – I was taken ill – with my old complaint in the head – so much so as to be unable to walk home – which consequently prevented me from meeting her at the Coach on the following morning. By a singular fatality – also – her tortoise died the next day. Thank my friend – your uncle Robert – for his recent letter – dated March 27th! – Tell him also – that when I ask for beasts or birds – it is only because I feel more pleasure in drawing from those given me by my intimate friends – than I could do from those otherwise come by – not from my being unable to get at specimens. – Having a rather Zoological connexion – & being about to publish British Quadrupeds – I have now living – 2 Hedgehogs, all the sorts of mice – weasels – Bats &c – & every beast requisite except a Pine Marten, – all of which, my dear child – I should be glad to present you with – did I suppose you could make the slightest use of them whatever.

Present my profound respects – to Mr W. Wardroper Esquire – with my best thanks for his friendly communications. I am glad that his Pamphlet – 'on curing Dropsy in Gallinaceous animals,' – has so extensive a sale. Pray – my dear – tell the 2 above mentioned friends never to incommode themselves in the least about writing to me, as they are aware how obtuse my feelings are, & that I bear being forgotten with much nonchalance.

Congratulate with Mrs Street from me, – on her recovery from her fall into the mill-pond – & from the 18 Paralytic strokes with which she was subsequently attacked: – my sister Ann is much gratified with her frequent correspondence in spite of her infirmities. – Should you see John Sayres – beg as a favour that he will not so continually torment me with graphic attentions.

Tell your papa – that I have been to the Opera & have heard Paganini – both of which pleasures have greatly contributed to widen the crack which nature had originally made in my brain.

Give my kindest regards & best respects to your Grandpapa and Grandmama – Father & Mother – Uncle George – and Aunt Eliza – who are not correspondents of mine – ask any body to kiss you from me – & believe me – My dear Dolly –

> Your 3 parts crazy – & wholly affectionate
> Uncle Edward.

'Oh! Pan!'

Oh! Pan!
You dear old man! –
Pray let us into your grotto, –
It is so extremely hot oh!
We've been at the *Pan*theon
A'seeing all as to be seen –
And now we're all tired and pale
And afraid of a *coup de soleil*.
So open your grotto –
It is so dreadfully hottoh!
Pan – Pan – darling old man!

10

Letter to George Coombe

My dear George – I'm convinced I am thoroughly cracked; –
I've waited a week e're your parcel I packed
In order to send it down free of post, yester=
=day, – by the hands of my Argyllshire sister, –
To save you an eightpence, – & all this is one of my
Violent fits of unusual economy: –
Mr Curtis's note you must know after all
Was the primary cause of my sending at all. –
So what was my horror in reaching today
In my bookcase – to find an aperient pill –
Which there has been thrust for these three weeks away –
To find the said note lying staring there still!
I declare I'd as soon have mounted a dragon! I
Felt quite dismayed with an impromptu agony. –
So now, – after thinking and reasoning and posing
I've made up my mind to the act of enclosing –
The entomological gentleman's letter, –
With a hope that my memory may shortly grow better.

Please the pigs! – Well, to call a new topic; – today,
I've seen *Miss* and Miss *Margaret Wat*kins; they stay
Number 9 – Woburn Place – but that's nothing to you –
Though it fills very nicely a distich or two: –
Miss Margaret Watkins was dressed in pea-green –
As fine a young lady as never was seen; –
And I never remember – (except a great Dutchman
Who at Rotterdam sat at [the] end of a barge –
You might travel through Europe, yet scarcely see such man,)
– To have seen any creature one quarter so large. –

James Winkworth – Esq. – of the Royal Berks Corps –
Rides often by here – on a long-tailed grey horse –
And for fun – I should make such another bad rhyme, –
I'll conclude – and I dare say you'll think it's high time. –

10

20

30

Remember me pray to all yours – and the dear
Little dotties, – write soon – ever yours,

    Edward Lear

The Nervous Family

We're all nervous, very very nervous,
And we're all nervous at our house in town,
There's myself, and my Aunt, and my Sister, and my Mother, –
And if left in the dark we're all quite frightened at each other!
Our Dog runs away if there's a stranger in the house,
And our great Tabby Cat is quite frightened at a mouse, –
    For she's *so* nervous, very very nervous,
    And we're *all* nervous at our house in Town.

My poor shaking Aunt can't work at her needle,
And my shaking hand spills half my cup of tea –   10
When wine at her dinner my timid Sister's taking –
She drops it on the table, so much her hand is shaking –
And my poor old shaky Mother, when to take her snuff she tries
To pop it in her nose, – o! she pops it in her eyes.
    For she's so nervous, very very nervous,
    And we're *all* nervous at our house in Town.

We all at dinner, shake – shake at carving,
And as for snuffing candles, we all put out the light;
T'other evening after dinner we all to snuff did try,
But my Aunt couldn't do it, nor my Sister, nor could I;   20
'Child! Give *me* the snuffers!' – said my mother in a flout –
'*I'll* show you how to do it!' – so she did, and snuffed it *out*,
    For she's so nervous, very very nervous, –
    And we're all of us nervous at our house in Town.

Thus far is part of an old published song. – the rest is mine. EL.

We're getting much too nervous to go out to dinner
For we all sit a'shaking, just like puppets upon wires.
I'm too nervous to speak loud, so I'm scarcely ever able
To ask for what I want, or to talk across the table; –
And my poor shaking Aunt where'er she sits, is sure to see,
30   Some sympathising Jelly always shaking vis à vis, –
Which makes her *more* nervous, very very nervous, –
And we're all of us nervous at our house in Town.

We're too nervous to get ready in time to go to church,
So we never go at all, since we once went late one day;
For the Clergyman looked *at* us, with a dreadful sort of frown,
And my poor shaky Mother caught his eye and tumbled down;–
And my Aunt and Sister fainted, – and tho' with care and pain
We dragged them slowly out, – yet we've never been again –
And we're all nervous, very very nervous,
40   And we're all of us nervous at our house in Town.

Our nerves in stormy weather are particularly *bad*,
And a single peal of thunder is enough to drive us *mad*.
So, when a storm comes on, we in a fright begin
To lock ourselves in closets where the lightning can't come in.
And for fear a little thunder to our nervous ears should come,
We each turn a barrel organ, and my Mother beats a drum,
For we're all nervous, very very nervous,
And we're all nervous at our house in Town.

The Nervous Family
Alternative version

My Aunt said I must marry, since there was none but I,
And the family would all be lost, if I should chance to die,
And we're all &c.

So we talked it o'er and o'er, but what with cons and pros,
It was long before we settled to whom I should propose.
    For we're all &c.

At last it was decided, and trembling off I set,
And I learnt my speech by heart, for fear I should forget,
    For we're all &c.

10

I found she was alone, but when we were together,
I considered what to talk about, and hit upon the weather,
    For we're all &c.

I thought of my proposal, but that I'd quite forgot;
And could only mumble out, 'Don't you think it very hot?'
    For we're all &c.

I twiddled with my thumbs, and I look'd upon the floor;
And the Lady look'd at me, which made me *shakier* than
      before,
    For we're all &c.

So I fairly ran away, for I could not stammer out,
And she never could discover what the deuce I came about,
    For we're all &c.

20

And having failed the first time, for fear of being derided,
I shall never try again – or at least I'm not decided,
    For we're all &c.

'The gloom that winter casts'

The gloom that winter casts
　　How soon the heart forgets –
When summer brings at last –
　　The sun that never sets.
So love – when hope first gleams
　　Forgets its former pain –
Amidst those sunny beams
　　Which ne'er shall set again.

'My dear Mrs Gale – from my leaving the cradle'

My dear Mrs Gale – from my leaving the cradle
　　Till now I have never such agony known,
What use *is* a Punch bowl without any ladle, –
　　Be it Ivory – Silver – Wood – China – or bone? –

My Landlady rushes and foams in a flurry –
　　Her Ladles for Punch and her Ladles for Soup,
Besides all her Ladles for Butter and Curry,
　　She vows are all – 'smished' in one family Group!

Then dear Mrs Gale – have a little compassion
　　If it's only a Ladle full – send me in one! –
And I'll ever proclaim you in my estimation –
　　The most '*Ladle-like*' personage under the sun! –

Portraites of the inditchenous beestes of New Olland

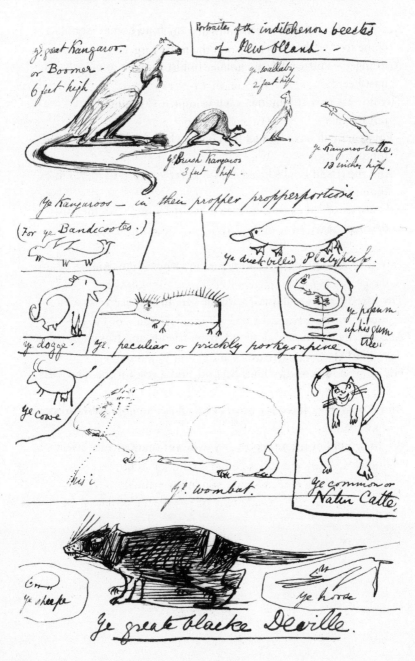

'My Sweet Home is no longer mine'

And Ah! when life's summer is flown – my fond home – should I
   come to thee then –
A stranger – unfriended and lone – couldst thou be to me what thou
   hast been!
Thy flowers may still bloom – but in vain; – thy tall elms may wave,
   not for me; –
– For years will have broken the chain, which hath bound me so
   fondly to thee,
– And the friend I once loved so will never – return to thee, fair as
   thou art,
And not as of old canst thou ever – Sweet Home! – soothe this
   desolate heart! –

Fare thee well! I will never forget – the scenes of my youth's happy
   day: –
Thy loved haunts will dwell with me yet, and cheer me thro' life's
   lonely way.
And ah! 'tis not ours to despond, from friends and from home though
   we part –
10 For Hope points to dwellings beyond, and a rest for the lone weary
   heart. –
And though, e'er life's day-dream shall close, amid far distant scenes I
   may roam, –
Bright symbol of future repose, – I will ever think of thee sweet
   home! –

[Illustrations for 'Kathleen O'More']

My Love still I think that I see her once more – But alas! She has left me below to deplore – My own little Kathleen – My poor little Kathleen – my Kathleen O'More

Her hair glossy black her eyes were of blue – Her color still changing – her smile ever new – so pretty was Kathleen, &c &c &c &c –

She milked the dun cow – which ne'er offered to stir, Tho wicked it was it was gentle to her – so kind was my Kathleen – &c &c &c &c &c

She sat by the Door one cold afternoon – To hear the wind blow, & to look at the Moon – so pensive was Kathleen &c &c &c

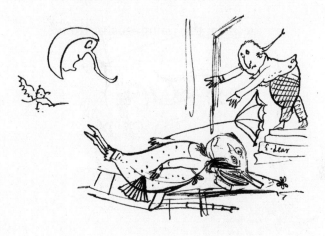

Cold was the night breeze as blow'd round her door. It *killed* my poor
Kathleen she drooped from that hour – & I lost my poor Kathleen
– &c &c &c

The bird of all birds as I loves the best Is the robin as builds in the
Churchyard her nest, for he seems to watch Kathleen – *hop* lightly
on Kathleen &c &c &c

Scene in the Campagna of Rome

[Lear's adventures on horseback]

1. L[ear] & K[night] leave Frascati – July 28th 1842. – Villa Taverna.

L. contemplates a ferocious horse with feelings of distrust.

2. Frascati. V. Taverna.

L. declares that he considers his horse far from tame.

3. Frascati. V. Taverna.

L. casually seats himself on the wrong side of his saddle.

4. V. Taverna. Frascati.

L. changes his position for the sake of variety.

5. V. Mondragone. Frascati.

L. perceives he has not seated himself properly.

6. K. & [L.] commence their journey.

L. is advised by K. to hold his reins short.

7. Frascati. Villa Mondragone.

L. is politely requested by K. to stop his horse.

8. M[onte] Porzio.

K. enquires amiably of L. if his stirrups are sufficiently short.

9. M. Porzio.

K. & L. are pursued by an irascible ox.

10. K. & L. pass M. Porzio & M. Compatri.

L. is requested by K. not to rise so exceedingly high from his saddle.

11. Monte Compatri.

L. descends an unsatisfactory hill in a pensive manner.

12. K. & L. pass Colonna.

L. is besought by K. to sit back on his saddle.

13. near Gallicano.

L. is immersed in an indefinite quagmire.

14. K. & L. arrive at Gallicano.

L. is informed by K. that he had better put his feet nearer to his horse's sides.

15. Ponte Lupo: – near Gallicano.

K. entreats L. to observe a large bridge called Ponte Loophole.

21. K. & L. proceed to Tivoli.

L. becomes suddenly and imperceptibly entangled in an obstructive Olive=tree.

23. K. & L. visit the temple by moonlight.

K. & L. discern a predominant Ghost.

25. Tivoli – K. & L. commence their journey back to Frascati.

L. is confidentially assured by the groom that he has mounted his horse incorrectly.

26. K. & L. pass through San Gregorio.

K. affectionately induces L. to perceive that a thornbush has attached itself to his repugnant horse.

27. K. & L. pass Casape & Poli, returning by Gallicano to Zagarolo.

L. is much disturbed by several large flies.

33. K. & L. proceed from Zagarolo to Frascati.

K. & L. are attacked by several very venomous Dogs in the vicinity of Colonna.

[Limericks for the 1846 and 1855 editions
of *A Book of Nonsense*]

There was an old Derry down Derry,
Who loved to see little folks merry;
    So he made them a Book,
    And with laughter they shook,
At the fun of that Derry down Derry!

There was an Old Man of Coblenz,
The length of whose legs was immense;
He went with one prance, from Turkey to France,
That surprising Old Man of Coblenz.

There was an Old Man of Peru,
Who watched his wife making a stew;
But once by mistake, in a stove she did bake,
That unfortunate Man of Peru.

There was an Old Man of the Hague,
Whose ideas were excessively vague;
He built a balloon, to examine the moon,
That deluded Old Man of the Hague.

There was an Old Man of Leghorn,
The smallest as ever was born;
But quickly snapped up he, was once by a puppy,
Who devoured that Old Man of Leghorn.

There was a Young Lady of Bute,
Who played on a silver-gilt flute;
She played several jigs, to her uncle's white pigs,
That amusing Young Lady of Bute.

There was an Old Man of Calcutta,
Who perpetually ate bread and butter;
Till a great bit of muffin, on which he was stuffing,
Choked that horrid Old Man of Calcutta.

There was an Old Person of Chester,
Whom several small children did pester;
They threw some large stones, which broke most of his bones,
And displeased that Old Person of Chester.

There was a Young Lady whose eyes,
Were unique as to colour and size;
When she opened them wide, people all turned aside,
And started away in surprise.

There was an Old Man of Kilkenny,
Who never had more than a penny;
He spent all that money, in onions and honey,
That wayward Old Man of Kilkenny.

There was an Old Man of Kamschatka,
Who possessed a remarkably fat cur;
His gait and his waddle, were held as a model,
To all the fat dogs in Kamschatka.

There was an Old Man of Columbia,
Who was thirsty, and called out for some beer;
But they brought it quite hot, in a small copper pot,
Which disgusted that Man of Columbia.

There was an Old Man of Berlin,
Whose form was uncommonly thin;
Till he once, by mistake, was mixed up in a cake,
So they baked that Old Man of Berlin.

There was an Old Person of Tartary,
Who divided his jugular artery;
But he screeched to his wife, and she said, 'Oh, my life!
Your death will be felt by all Tartary!'

There was an Old Man of the Cape,
Who possessed a large Barbary Ape;
Till the Ape one dark night, set the house on a light,
Which burned that Old Man of the Cape.

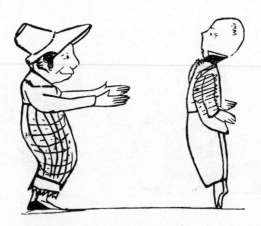

There was an Old Person of Burton,
Whose answers were rather uncertain;
When they said, 'How d'ye do?' he replied, 'Who are you?'
That distressing Old Person of Burton.

There was an Old Man of Vienna,
Who lived upon Tincture of Senna;
When that did not agree, he took Camomile Tea,
That nasty Old Man of Vienna.

There was an Old Man of th' Abruzzi,
So blind that he couldn't his foot see;
When they said, 'That's your toe,' he replied, 'Is it so?'
That doubtful Old Man of th' Abruzzi.

There was an Old Man of Corfu,
Who never knew what he should do;
So he rushed up and down, till the sun made him brown,
That bewildered Old Man of Corfu.

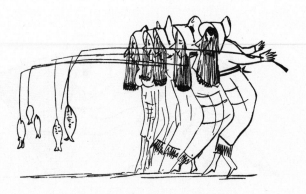

There was an Old Man of Marseilles,
Whose daughters wore bottle-green veils;
They caught several fish, which they put in a dish,
And sent to their Pa' at Marseilles.

There was an Old Man of Nepaul,
From his horse had a terrible fall;
But, though split quite in two, by some very strong glue,
They mended that Man of Nepaul.

There was an Old Man of the Isles,
Whose face was pervaded with smiles;
He sung high dum diddle, and played on the fiddle,
That amiable Man of the Isles.

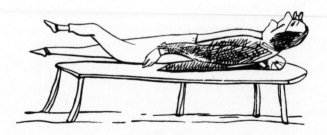

There was an Old Man of Moldavia,
Who had the most curious behaviour;
For while he was able, he slept on a table,
That funny Old Man of Moldavia.

There was an Old Man of Vesuvius,
Who studied the works of Vitruvius;
When the flames burnt his book, to drinking he took,
That morbid Old Man of Vesuvius.

There was a Young Lady of Tyre,
Who swept the loud chords of a lyre;
At the sound of each sweep, she enraptured the deep,
And enchanted the city of Tyre.

There was an Old Person of Rheims,
Who was troubled with horrible dreams;
So, to keep him awake, they fed him with cake,
Which amused that Old Person of Rheims.

There was a Young Lady of Hull,
Who was chased by a virulent Bull;
But she seized on a spade, and called out – 'Who's afraid!'
Which distracted that virulent Bull.

There was an Old Man of Quebec,
A beetle ran over his neck;
But he cried, 'With a needle, I'll slay you, O beadle!'
That angry Old Man of Quebec.

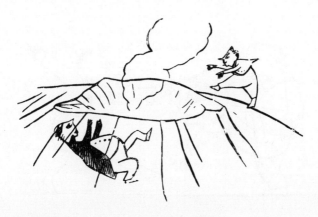

There was an Old Person of Gretna,
Who rushed down the crater of Etna;
When they said, 'Is it hot?' He replied, 'No, it's not!'
That mendacious Old Person of Gretna.

There was an Old Person of Prague,
Who was suddenly seized with the plague;
But they gave him some butter, which caused him to mutter,
And cured that Old Person of Prague.

There was an Old Man of the Dee,
Who was sadly annoyed by a flea;
When he said, 'I will scratch it' – they gave him a hatchet,
Which grieved that Old Man of the Dee.

There was an Old Man of the West,
Who wore a pale plum-coloured vest;
When they said, 'Does it fit?' he replied, 'Not a bit!'
That uneasy Old Man of the West.

There was an Old Man of Peru,
Who never knew what he should do;
So he tore off his hair, and behaved like a bear,
That intrinsic Old Man of Peru.

There was a Young Lady of Troy,
Whom several large flies did annoy;
Some she killed with a thump, some she drowned at the pump,
And some she took with her to Troy.

There was a Young Lady of Clare,
Who was sadly pursued by a bear;
When she found she was tired, she abruptly expired,
That unfortunate Lady of Clare.

There was a Young Lady of Norway,
Who casually sat in a doorway;
When the door squeezed her flat, she exclaimed, 'What of that?'
This courageous Young Lady of Norway.

There was a Young Lady of Sweden,
Who went by the slow train to Weedon;
When they cried, 'Weedon Station!' she made no observation,
But thought she should go back to Sweden.

There was an Old Man of the South,
Who had an immoderate mouth;
But in swallowing a dish, that was quite full of fish,
He was choked, that Old Man of the South.

There was an Old Person of Ischia,
Whose conduct grew friskier and friskier;
He danced hornpipes and jigs, and ate thousands of figs,
That lively Old Person of Ischia.

There was a Young Lady whose nose,
Was so long that it reached to her toes;
So she hired an Old Lady, whose conduct was steady,
To carry that wonderful nose.

There was an Old Man of Madras,
Who rode on a cream-coloured ass;
But the length of its ears, so promoted his fears,
That it killed that Old Man of Madras.

There was an Old Lady whose folly,
Induced her to sit in a holly;
Whereon by a thorn, her dress being torn,
She quickly became melancholy.

There was an Old Man of the Coast,
Who placidly sat on a post;
But when it was cold, he relinquished his hold,
And called for some hot buttered toast.

There was an Old Person of Troy,
Whose drink was warm brandy and soy;
Which he took with a spoon, by the light of the moon,
In sight of the city of Troy.

There was an Old Person of Buda,
Whose conduct grew ruder and ruder;
Till at last, with a hammer, they silenced his clamour,
By smashing that Person of Buda.

There was an Old Person of Sparta,
Who had twenty-five sons and one daughter;
He fed them on snails, and weighed them in scales,
That wonderful Person of Sparta.

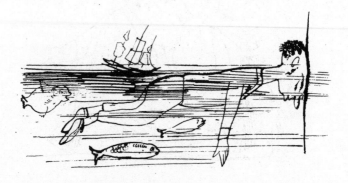

There was an Old Sailor of Compton,
Whose vessel a rock it once bump'd on;
The shock was so great, that it damaged the pate
Of that singular Sailor of Compton.

There was an Old Man of Apulia,
Whose conduct was very peculiar;
He fed twenty sons, upon nothing but buns,
That whimsical Man of Apulia.

There was an Old Person of Hurst,
Who drank when he was not athirst;
When they said, 'You'll grow fatter,' he answered, 'What matter?'
That globular Person of Hurst.

There was a Young Lady of Turkey,
Who wept when the weather was murky;
When the day turned out fine, she ceased to repine,
That capricious Young Lady of Turkey.

There was a Young Lady of Dorking,
Who bought a large bonnet for walking;
But its colour and size, so bedazzled her eyes,
That she very soon went back to Dorking.

There was an Old Person of Rhodes,
Who strongly objected to toads;
He paid several cousins, to catch them by dozens,
That futile Old Person of Rhodes.

There was an Old Man of Cape Horn,
Who wished he had never been born;
So he sat on a chair, till he died of despair,
That dolorous Man of Cape Horn.

There was an Old Man of Jamaica,
Who suddenly married a Quaker!
But she cried out – 'O lack! I have married a black!'
Which distressed that Old Man of Jamaica.

There was an Old Man of the West,
Who never could get any rest;
So they set him to spin, on his nose and his chin,
Which cured that Old Man of the West.

There was an Old Man of the East,
Who gave all his children a feast;
But they all ate so much, and their conduct was such,
That it killed that Old Man of the East.

There was a Young Lady of Poole,
Whose soup was excessively cool;
So she put it to boil, by the aid of some oil,
That ingenious Young Lady of Poole.

There was an Old Man of Dundee,
Who frequented the top of a tree;
When disturbed by the crows, he abruptly arose,
And exclaimed, 'I'll return to Dundee.'

There was an Old Man of New York,
Who murdered himself with a fork;
But nobody cried though he very soon died, –
For that silly Old Man of New York.

There was an Old Man of the North,
Who fell into a basin of broth;
But a laudable cook, fished him out with a hook,
Which saved that Old Man of the North.

There was a Young Lady of Wales,
Who caught a large fish without scales;
When she lifted her hook, she exclaimed, 'Only look!'
That extatic Young Lady of Wales.

There was an Old Man of the Nile,
Who sharpened his nails with a file;
Till he cut off his thumbs, and said calmly, 'This comes –
Of sharpening one's nails with a file!'

There was an Old Man of Bohemia,
Whose daughter was christened Euphemia;
Till one day, to his grief, she married a thief,
Which grieved that Old Man of Bohemia.

There was an Old Man of the Wrekin,
Whose shoes made a horrible creaking;
But they said 'Tell us whether, your shoes are of leather,
Or of what, you Old Man of the Wrekin?'

There was an Old Person of Cheadle,
Was put in the stocks by the beadle;
For stealing some pigs, some coats, and some wigs,
That horrible Person of Cheadle.

There was an Old Person of Ems,
Who casually fell in the Thames;
And when he was found, they said he was drowned,
That unlucky Old Person of Ems.

There was a Young Lady of Welling,
Whose praise all the world was a telling;
She played on the harp, and caught several carp,
That accomplished Young Lady of Welling.

There was an Old Lady of Prague,
Whose language was horribly vague;
When they said, 'Are these caps?' she answered, 'Perhaps!'
That oracular Lady of Prague.

There was an Old Person of Cadiz,
Who was always polite to all ladies;
But in handing his daughter, he fell into the water,
Which drowned that Old Person of Cadiz.

There was a Young Lady of Russia,
Who screamed so that no one could hush her;
Her screams were extreme, no one heard such a scream,
As was screamed by that Lady of Russia.

There was a Young Lady of Parma,
Whose conduct grew calmer and calmer;
When they said, 'Are you dumb?' she merely said, 'Hum!'
That provoking Young Lady of Parma.

There was a Young Girl of Majorca,
Whose aunt was a very fast walker;
She walked seventy miles, and leaped fifteen stiles,
Which astonished that Girl of Majorca.

There was an Old Man of Kildare,
Who climbed into a very high chair;
When he said, – 'Here I stays, – till the end of my days,'
That immovable Man of Kildare.

[Other early limericks]

There was an old man who forgot,
That his tea was excessively hot;
When they said 'Let it cool' – He answered 'You fool!
I shall pour it back into the pot.' –

There was an old man of Orleans,
Who was given to eating of beans;
Till once out of sport, he swallowed a quart,
That dyspeptic old man of Orleans.

There was an old man of the Dee,
Who always was partial to tea;
Buttered toast he abhorred, and by muffins was bored,
That uncommon old man of the Dee.

There was an old person of Leith,
Who had the most dolorous teeth;
So she had a new set. 'I'll eat quantities yet,'
Said that fortunate woman of Leith.

There was an old person whose legs,
Bore a striking resemblance to pegs;
When they said, 'Can you toddle?' he answered – 'I waddle,
What else *should* I do with my legs?'

There was an old man whose delight,
Was to play on the trumpet all night;
When they said, 'You're a bore!' he answered, 'What for?
Mayn't I play on the trumpet all night?'

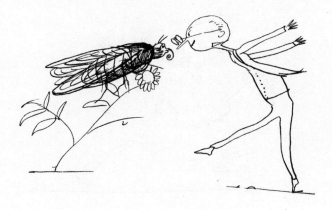

There was an old man who said, 'See!
I have found a most beautiful bee!'
When they said, 'Does it buzz?' he answered, 'It *does*,
I never beheld such a bee!'

There was an old man of Lodore,
Who heard the loud waterfall roar;
But in going to look, he fell into a brook,
And he never was heard of no more.

There was an old person so silly,
He poked his head into a lily;
But six bees who lived there, filled him full of despair,
For they stung that old person so silly.

There was an old man whose repose,
Consisted in warming his toes;
When they said, 'Are they done?' he answered, 'What fun!
Do you think I'm a'cooking my toes?'

There was an old man whose despair,
Induced him to purchase a bear;
He played on some trumpets, and fed upon crumpets,
Which rather assuaged his despair.

There was an old person of Sidon,
Who bought a small pony to ride on;
But he found him too small to leap over a wall,
So he walked, that old person of Sidon.

There was an old person whose mirth,
Induced him to leap from the earth;
But in leaping too quick, he exclaimed, 'I'm too sick
To leap any more from the earth.'

There was an old lady of Leeds,
Who was always a'doing good deeds;
She sate on some rocks with her feet in a box,
And her neck was surrounded by beads.

There was an old man in a boat,
Who complained of a pain in his throat;
When they said, 'Can you screech?' he replied, 'I beseech
You won't make any noise in my boat!'

There was an old man whose desire,
Was to sit with his feet in the fire;
When they said, 'Are they 'ot?', he replied, 'No, they're not!
You must put some more coals on the fire.'

There was an old person of Calais,
Who lived in a blue marble palace;
But on coming downstairs, he encountered some bears,
Who swallowed that person of Calais.

There was an old man with a light,
Who was dressed in a garment of white;
He held a small candle, with never a handle,
And danced all the merry long night.

There was an old man who said 'O! –
Let us come where the humble bees grow!
There are no less than five sitting still on a hive,
Singing songs to their children below.'

There was an old man who made bold,
To affirm that the weather was cold;
So he ran up and down, in his grandmother's gown,
Which was woollen, and not very old.

There was an old man whose Giardino
Produced only one little bean o!
When he said – 'That's enough!' – They answered,
  'What stuff!
You never can live on *one* bean o!'

There was an old man whose Giardino
Was always so cheerful and green O –
Every hour he could spare, – He sate in a chair
In the midst of his summer Giardino.

There was an old person of Sheen,
Whose carriage was painted pea=green;
But once in the snow the horse would not go,
Which disgusted that person of Sheen.

There was a young lady of Harwich,
Who built a remarkable carriage;
It held just one hundred – so everyone wondered –
And cried – 'Gracious me! what a carriage!'

There was an old person of Shields,
Who rambled about in the fields;
But, being infirm, he fell over a worm
And sighed that he'd ever left Shields.

There was an old person whose tears
Fell fast for a series of years;
He sat on a rug, and wept into a jug
Which he very soon filled full of tears.

The Hens of Oripò

The agèd hens of Oripò,
   They tempt the stormy sea;
Black, white and brown, they spread their wings,
   And o'er the waters flee;
And when a little fish they clutch
   Athwart the wave so blue,
They utter forth a joyful note, –
   A cock-a-doodle-doo!
O! Oo! Oripò – Oo! the hens of Oripò!

The crafty hens of Oripò,
   They wander on the shore,
Where shrimps and winkles pick they up,
   And carry home a store;

For barley, oats, or golden corn,
  To eat they never wish,
All vegetably food they scorn,
  And only seek for fish.
O! Oo! Oripò – Oo! the hens of Oripò!

The wily hens of Oripò,
  Black, white and brown and gray,   20
They don't behave like other hens;
  In any decent way.
They lay their eggs among the rocks,
  Instead of in the straw,
. . . . ,
. . . .
O! Oo! Oripò – Oo! the hens of Oripò!

The nasty hens of Oripò,
  With ill-conditioned zeal,
All fish defunct they gobble up,   30
  At morn or evening meal.
Whereby their eggs, as now we find,
. . . .
A fishlike ancient smell and taste
  Unpleasant doth pervade.
O! Oo! Oripò – Oo! the hens of Oripò!

'A was an Ant'

A

A was an Ant
Who seldom stood still,
And he made a small house
On the side of a hill.
a!
Little brown ant!

B

B was a Butterfly
Purple and green,
A more beautiful butterfly
Never was seen.
b!
Butterfly bright!

C

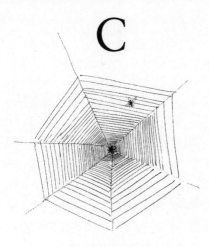

C was a Cobweb
Which caught a small fly,
Who tried to escape
From the spider so sly.
c!
Cobweb and Fly!

D

D was a Duck
With spots on his back,
Who lived in the water
And sometimes said Quack!
d!
Dear little duck!

E

E was an Elephant
Vast as to size,
With tusks and a trunk
And two small squinny eyes!
  e!
 Elephant's eyes!

F

F was a Fan
Which was purple and green,
The most beautiful fan
That had ever been seen.
  f!
 Fine little fan!

G

G was a Goat
With a beautiful coat,
But his horns were too curly
Which made him quite surly.
g!
Cross little goat!

H

H was a Hat,
But the brim was too wide,
And the crown was too flat
And all of one side.
h!
What a bad hat!

I

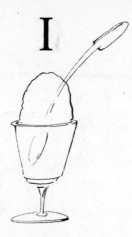

I was some Ice
Which was awfully nice,
But which nobody tasted
And so it was wasted.
        i!
    Very cold ice!

J

J was some Jujubes
Exceedingly sweet,
And they were (by some persons)
Esteemed quite a treat.
        j!
    Sweet little jujubes!

K

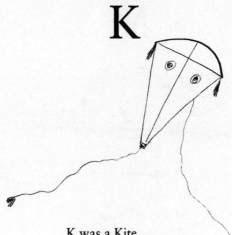

K was a Kite
Which flew up on high,
All over the houses
And into the sky.
            k!
    Fly away kite!

L

L was a Lamp
So beauteous and bright,
Which illumined a room
On a very dark night.
            l!
    Luminous lamp!

M

M was a Mouse
With a very long tail,
But he never went out
In the rain or the hail.
m!
Poor little mouse!

N

N were some Nuts
Which were perfectly brown,
And being quite ripe
They all tumbled down.
n!
Tumble down nuts!

O

O was an Owl
Who objected to light
When he made a great noise
Every hour in the night.
o!
Noisy old owl!

P

P was a Pudding
As round as the moon,
And when it was cut
It was helped with a spoon.
p!
Elegant pudding!

Q

Q was a Quail
With a very short tail,
Having fed upon corn
Ever since he was born.
q!
Queer little quail!

R

R was a Rabbit
Who had a bad habit
Of nibbling the flowers
In the gardens and bowers.
r!
Naughty old rabbit!

S

S was a spoon
Which I certainly think
Was placed in some tea
To assist you to drink.
　　s!
　Silvery spoon!

T

T was a Top
Which turned round and round,
And fell to the ground
With a musical sound.
　　t!
　Turn about top!

U

U was an Urn
With hot water in it,
To bubble and burn
And make tea in a minute.
u!
Useful old urn!

V

V was a Veil
With pink spots upon it,
Tied round with a string
Round a bottle green bonnet.
v!
Very fine veil!

W

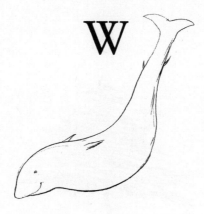

W was a Whale
With a dreadful long tail,
Who rushed all so frantic
Across the Atlantic.
w!
Roll about whale!

X

X was King Xerxes
Who more than all Turks is
Renowned for his fashion
Of screaming with passion.
x!
Shocking old Xerxes!

Y

Y was a Yew
Which flourished and grew
By a lovely abode
Quite close to the road.
y!
Dark little yew!

Z

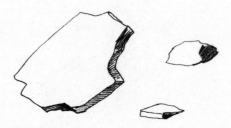

Z was some Zinc
Which caused you to wink
When you saw it so bright
In the summer sunlight.
z!
Pretty bright zinc!

'Ribands and pigs'

Ribands & pigs,
Helmets & Figs,
Set him a jigging & see how he jigs.

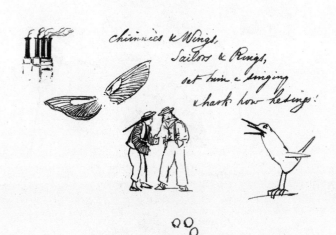

Chimnies & Wings,
Sailors & Rings,
Set him a singing & hark how he sings!

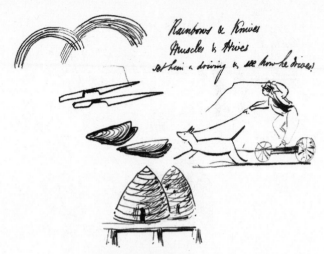

Rainbows & Knives
Muscles & Hives
Set him a driving & see how he drives!

Houses & Kings
Whiskers & Swings
Set him a stinging & see how he stings –

Herons & Sweeps
Turbans & Sheeps,
Set him a weeping & see how he weeps

Eagles & pears,
Slippers & Bears,
Set him a staring & see how he stares!

Tadpoles & Tops,
Teacups & Mops,
Set him a hopping & see how he hops!

20

Teapots, & Quails,
Snuffers & snails,
Set him asailing & see how he sails!

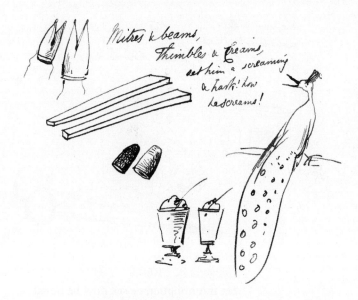

Mitres & beams,
Thimbles & Creams,
Set him a screaming & hark! how he screams!

Lobsters & owls,
Scissors and fowls,
Set him a howling & hark how he howls! –

30

Saucers & tops,
Lobsters & Mops,
Set it a hopping, & see how he hops!

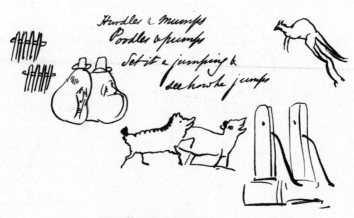

Hurdles & Mumps
Poodles & pumps
Set it a jumping & see how he jumps

Trumpets & Guns
beetles & buns –
Set him a running & see how he runs

Puddings & beams
Cobwebs & creams
Set him a screaming & hear how he screams!

40

Cutlets & eyes –
Swallows & pies
Set it a flying & see how it flies

Watches & Oaks,
Custards & Cloaks
Set him a poking & see how he pokes

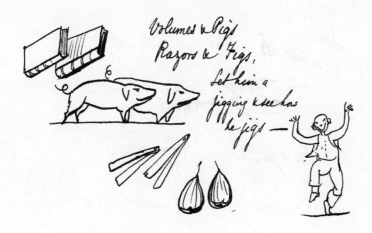

Volumes & Pigs
Razors & Figs,
Set him a jigging & see how he jigs –

50

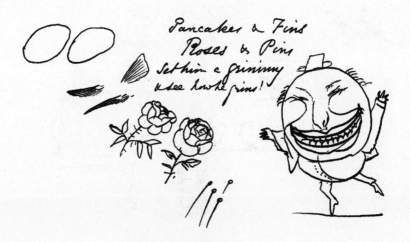

Pancakes & Fins
Roses & Pins
Set him a grinning & see how he grins!

Scissors & Fowls,
Filberts & Owls
Set him a howling & see how he howls –

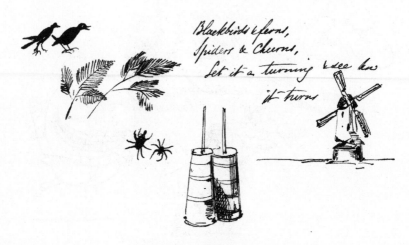

Blackbirds & ferns,
Spiders & Churns,
Set it a turning & see how it turns

Wafers & Bears,
Ladders & Squares,
Set him a staring & see how he stares!

Tea Urns & Pews,
Muscles & Jews,
Set him a mewing and hear how he mews –

Sofas & bees,
Camels & Keys
Set him a sneezing & see how he'll sneeze!

70

Bonnets, & Legs,
Steamboats & Eggs,
Set him a begging & see how he begs.

Houses & Kings,
Oysters & Rings
Set him a singing & see how he sings!

Rainbows & Wives
Puppies & Hives,
Set him a driving & see how he drives!

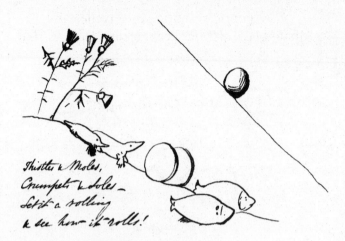

80

Thistles & Moles,
Crumpets & Soles –
Set it a rolling & see how it rolls!

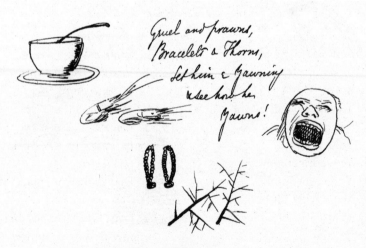

Gruel and prawns,
Bracelets & Thorns,
Set him a yawning & see how he yawns!

Ye poppular author & traveller in
Albania & Calabrià, keepinge his feete warme

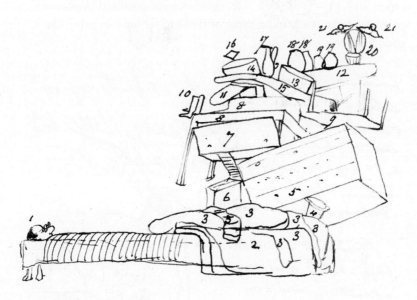

1. Ye traveller.
2. Ye Railwaie rugge.
3. Ye author his vestmentes.
4. his hatteboxe.
5. Ye Cheste of draweres
6. Ye chaire
7. Ye large cheste.
8. Ye washingtable
9. Ye dressing table.
10. Ye traveller his bootes.
11. Ye sparkling looking glasse.
12. Ye table.

13. Ye tinne tubbe
14. Ye china tub.
15. Ye matting rolled uppe.
16. Ye quadrangular
    pincushione.
17. Ye jugge.
18. Ye flaskes of gunnepowder.
19. Ye picklejarres.
20. Ye beautiful chaire made of
    wickerworke
21. Ye peaceful cherubbes that
    appeared to ye author
    when he fell asleepe.–

[Lear at the Royal Academy Schools]

I tried with 51 – little boys: – & 19 of us were admitted. And now I go with a large book and a piece of chalk to school every day like a good little boy. –

There was an old person of Ramleh,
Who purchased a little green Gamleh
As well as three pigs, some mice, and some figs,
All of which he took with him to Ramleh.

'O! Mimber for the County Louth'

O! Mimber for the County Louth
   Residing at Ardee!
Whom I, before I wander South,
   Partik'lar wish to see; –

I send you this – that you may know
   I've left the Sussex shore,
And coming here two days ago
   Do cough for evermore.

Or gasping hard for breath do sit
   Upon a brutal chair,
For to lie down in Asthma fit
   Is what I cannot bear.

10

Or sometimes sneeze: and always blow
   My well-developed nose,

And altogether never know
   No comfort nor repose.

All through next week I shall be here,
   To work as best I may
On my last picture, which is near-
   er finished every day.

But after the thirteenth, – (that's Sunday)
   I must – if able – start
(Or on the Tuesday if not Monday)
   For England's Northern part.

And thence I only come again
   Just to pack up and run,
Somewhere where life may less be pain,
   And somewhere where there's sun.

So then I hope to hear your ways
   Are bent on English moves,
For that I trust once more to gaze
   Upon the friend I loves.

(Alas! Blue Posts I shall not dare
   To visit e're I go –
Being compulsed to take such care
   Of all the winds as blow.)

But if you are not coming now
   Just write a line to say so –
And I shall still consider how
   Ajoskyboskybayso.

No more my pen: no more my ink:
   No more my rhyme is clear.
So I shall leave off here I think. –
      Yours ever,
         Edward Lear.

'Washing my rose-coloured flesh and brushing my beard with a hairbrush'

Dear F,

Washing my rose-coloured flesh and brushing my beard with a
   hairbrush, –
– Breakfast of tea, bread and butter, at nine o'clock in the morning,
Sending my carpetbag onward I reached the Twickenham station,
(Thanks to the civil domestics of good Lady Wald'grave's
   establishment,)
Just as the big buzzing brown booming bottlegreen bumblebizz boiler
Stood on the point of departing for Richmond and England's
   metropolis.

I say – (and if I ever said anything to the contrary I hereby retract it) –
I say – I took away altogether unconsciously your borrowed white
   filigree handkerchief;

After the lapse of a week I will surely return it,
And then you may either devour it, or keep it, or burn it, –   10
Just as you please. But remember I have not forgotten,
After the 26th day of the month of the present July,
That is the time I am booked for a visit to Nuneham.

Certain ideas have arisen and flourished within me,
As to a possible visit to Ireland, – but nobody
Comes to a positive certainty all in a hurry;
If you are free and in London, next week shall we dine at the *Blue*
   Posts?

Both Mrs Clive and her husband have written most kindly
Saying the picture delights them (the Dead Sea) extremely. –

20 Bother all painting! I wish I'd 200 per annum!
– Wouldn't I sell all my colours and brushes and damnable messes!
Over the world I would rove, North South East and *West* I would –
Marrying a black girl at last, and slowly preparing to walk into
    Paradise!

A week or a month hence, I will find time to make a queer Alphabet,
All with the letters beversed and beaided with pictures,
Which I shall give, (but don't tell him just yet,) to Charles Braham's
    little one.

Just only look in the Times of today for accounts of the Lebanon!

Now I must stop this jaw and write myself quite simultaneous,
Yours with a l[ ] affection – the globular foolish Topographer.

E.L.

From a letter to George Grove

I hasten to inform you that in a wood very near here, there are Toad-stools of the loveliest and most surprising colour and form: – orbicular, cubicular and squambingular, and I even thought I perceived the very rare Pongchámbinnibóphilos Kakokreasópheros among others a few days back. You have therefore nothing better to do than to come with Penrose and hunt up and down St George's Hill for the better carrying out of the useful and beastly branch of science you have felt it your duty to follow. Provided also that you bring your own cooking utensils you may dine off your gatherings though I won't partake of the feast, my stomach being delicate.

'But ah! (the Landscape painter said,)'

But ah! (the Landscape painter said,)
A brutal fly walks on my head
And my bald skin doth tickle;
And so I stop distracted quite,
(With itching skin for who can write?)
In most disgusting pickle –
   & merely sign myself
                   Yours affectionately
                   Edward Lear

[Additional limericks for the 1861 edition
of *A Book of Nonsense*]

There was an Old Man with a beard,
Who said, 'It is just as I feared! –
Two Owls and a Hen, four Larks and a Wren,
Have all built their nests in my beard!'

There was a Young Lady of Ryde,
Whose shoe-strings were seldom untied;
She purchased some clogs, and some small spotty dogs,
And frequently walked about Ryde.

There was an Old Man with a nose,
Who said, 'If you choose to suppose
That my nose is too long, you are certainly wrong!'
That remarkable Man with a nose.

There was an Old Man on a hill,
Who seldom, if ever, stood still;
He ran up and down, in his Grandmother's gown,
Which adorned that Old Man on a hill.

There was a Young Lady whose bonnet,
Came untied when the birds sate upon it;
But she said, 'I don't care! all the birds in the air
Are welcome to sit on my bonnet!

There was a Young Person of Smyrna,
Whose Grandmother threatened to burn her;
But she seized on the Cat, and said, 'Granny, burn that!
You incongruous Old Woman of Smyrna!'

There was an Old Person of Chili,
Whose conduct was painful and silly;
He sate on the stairs, eating apples and pears,
That imprudent Old Person of Chili.

There was an Old Man with a gong,
Who bumped at it all the day long;
But they called out, 'O law! you're a horrid old bore!'
So they smashed that Old Man with a gong.

There was an Old Lady of Chertsey,
Who made a remarkable curtsey;
She twirled round and round, till she sunk underground,
Which distressed all the people of Chertsey.

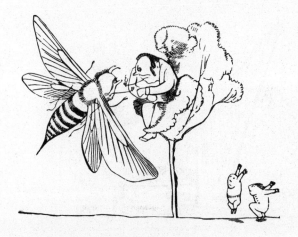

There was an Old Man in a tree,
Who was horribly bored by a Bee;
When they said, 'Does it buzz?' he replied, 'Yes it does!
It's a regular brute of a Bee!'

There was an Old Man with a flute,
A sarpint ran into his boot;
But he played day and night, till the sarpint took fright,
And avoided that man with a flute.

There was a Young Lady whose chin,
Resembled the point of a pin;
So she had it made sharp, and purchased a harp,
And played several tunes with her chin.

There was an Old Man in a boat,
Who said, 'I'm afloat! I'm afloat!'
When they said, 'No! you ain't!' he was ready to faint,
That unhappy Old Man in a boat.

There was a Young Lady of Portugal,
Whose ideas were excessively nautical;
She climbed up a tree, to examine the sea,
But declared she would never leave Portugal.

There was an Old Person of Leeds,
Whose head was infested with beads;
She sat on a stool, and ate gooseberry fool,
Which agreed with that person of Leeds.

There was a Young Person of Crete,
Whose toilette was far from complete;
She dressed in a sack, spickle-speckled with black,
That ombliferous person of Crete.

There was an Old Man who supposed,
That the street door was partially closed;
But some very large rats, ate his coats and his hats,
While that futile old gentleman dozed.

There was an Old Person whose habits,
Induced him to feed upon Rabbits;
When he'd eaten eighteen, he turned perfectly green,
Upon which he relinquished those habits.

There was an Old Person of Dover,
Who rushed through a field of blue Clover;
But some very large bees, stung his nose and his knees,
So he very soon went back to Dover.

There was an Old Person of Basing,
Whose presence of mind was amazing;
He purchased a steed, which he rode at full speed,
And escaped from the people of Basing.

There was an Old Person of Philæ,
Whose conduct was scroobious and wily;
He rushed up a Palm, when the weather was calm,
And observed all the ruins of Philæ.

There was an Old Man with a poker,
Who painted his face with red okre;
When they said, 'You're a Guy!' he made no reply,
But knocked them all down with his poker.

There was an Old Person of Mold,
Who shrank from sensations of cold;
So he purchased some muffs, some furs and some fluffs,
And wrapped himself from the cold.

There was an Old Man of Melrose,
Who walked on the tips of his toes;
But they said, 'It ain't pleasant, to see you at present,
You stupid Old Man of Melrose.'

There was a Young Lady of Lucca,
Whose lovers completely forsook her;
She ran up a tree, and said, 'Fiddle-de-dee!'
Which embarrassed the people of Lucca.

There was an Old Person of Cromer,
Who stood on one leg to read Homer;
When he found he grew stiff, he jumped over the cliff,
Which concluded that Person of Cromer.

There was an Old Person of Tring,
Who embellished his nose with a ring;
He gazed at the moon, every evening in June,
That ecstatic Old Person of Tring.

There was an Old Man on some rocks,
Who shut his wife up in a box;
When she said, 'Let me out,' he exclaimed, 'Without doubt,
You will pass all your life in that box.'

There was an Old Man in a pew,
Whose waistcoat was spotted with blue;
But he tore it in pieces, to give to his nieces, –
That cheerful Old Man in a pew.

There was an Old Man who said, 'How, –
Shall I flee from this horrible Cow?
I will sit on this stile, and continue to smile,
Which may soften the heart of that Cow.'

There was an Old Man of Whitehaven,
Who danced a quadrille with a Raven;
But they said – 'It's absurd, to encourage this bird!'
So they smashed that Old Man of Whitehaven.

There was an Old Person of Dutton,
Whose head was so small as a button;
So to make it look big, he purchased a wig,
And rapidly rushed about Dutton.

There was an Old Man who said, 'Hush!
I perceive a young bird in this bush!'
When they said – 'Is it small?' He replied – 'Not at all!
It is four times as big as the bush!'

There was an Old Person of Bangor,
Whose face was distorted with anger;
He tore off his boots, and subsisted on roots,
That borascible Person of Bangor.

There was an Old Man with a beard,
Who sat on a horse when he reared;
But they said, 'Never mind! you will fall off behind,
You propitious Old Man with a beard!'

There was an Old Person of Anerly,
Whose conduct was strange and unmannerly;
He rushed down the Strand, with a Pig in each hand,
But returned in the evening to Anerly.

There was an Old Person of Spain,
Who hated all trouble and pain;
So he sate on a chair, with his feet in the air,
That umbrageous Old Person of Spain.

There was an Old Man who said, 'Well!
Will *nobody* answer this bell?
I have pulled day and night, till my hair has grown white,
But nobody answers this bell!'

There was an Old Man with an owl,
Who continued to bother and howl;
He sate on a rail, and imbibed bitter ale,
Which refreshed that Old Man and his owl.

There was an Old Man at a casement,
Who held up his hands in amazement;
When they said, 'Sir! you'll fall!' he replied, 'Not at all!'
That incipient Old Man at a casement.

There was an Old Person of Ewell,
Who chiefly subsisted on gruel;
But to make it more nice, he inserted some mice,
Which refreshed that Old Person of Ewell.

There was an Old Man of Aôsta,
Who possessed a large Cow, but he lost her;
But they said, 'Don't you see, she has rushed up a tree?
You invidious Old Man of Aôsta!'

There was an Old Man, on whose nose,
Most birds of the air could repose;
But they all flew away, at the closing of day,
Which relieved that Old Man and his nose.

General appearance of a distinguished Landscapepainter – at Malta –
his hair having taken to a violent excess of growth of late.

Eggstracts from the Roehampton Chronicle

Object discovered in Lambda
16 August 1862

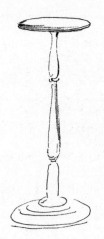

This remarkable instance of Snumphus, or Peppi-grottified Fungus, (growing on a lofty stalk or stem & resembling a Mushroom on Stilts,) has just been discovered in Lambda: – but at the time of our Reporter's departure, nothing was deter-mined as to its previous=present, or past=future condition, nature, or circumstances. Our reeders shall however be jooly informed of any further inwestigations on the topic.

Object discovered in Lambda
September 28 1862

We are glad to present our readers with a concise and convalescent illustration of the most remarkable Object discovered in our age – & which is at present causing immense sensation & suffusion in the whole of the civilised world. – This, which is as interesting in its associations as it is singular & beautiful in form, is formed of a jetlike material with devellopements of gold borders all round it & the name 'Lambda' in distinct letters on its fuliginous face.

The use of the object is at present undetermined; – but it is obvious

that it was once, (at an unbeknownly antique period,) the actual prop-
erty of the illustrious & unfortunate Lambda.

That Lambda is not recorded by any authentic author to have been
at Roehampton is advanced by some antiquarians who are desirous of
diminishing the value of this priceless object as an objection to this
theory: – but it does not follow that Lambda did not send or give the
article in question to other persons. – And to all well conditioned indi-
viduals the simple fact of Lambda's name being written on the object
itself is a full & painful guarantee of its indescribable interest.

Whether the Object in question be Lambda's Snuffbox, or Helmet,   10
or Culinary=pipkin, – or dispatch box, time alone, that unveiler of
obscure antidotes can eventually devellope: – but on those ignorant &
disgusting creatures, who have ventured to suggest that this object is a
Coalscuttle no further observation is necessary than that they cannot
lay claim to the title of rational human beings, & that they ought to be
altogether abolished & pisoned at the earliest aggravating & aggressive
opportunity following this notice.

Object discovered in Thêta
November 1 1862

It is seldom that we have to call the attention of   20
our readers to so many objects of antiquarian
interest, discovered in one spot as the present lat-
est & obviously melancholy article the portrait of
which we subjoin, & which has been quite recent-
ly discovered in Thêta. Which its origin and use
and effect are wholly, (if not almost,) unbeknown
to the enlightened & choragic population of the
surrounding hemisphere.

On the upper part of the perpendicular &
columnar structure of the object is a cross bar –   30
painfully suggestive of the manner in which the
amiable Thêta met with her afflicting & philhar-
monic fate, – (such is the tradition of the country,)
– by accidentally mistaking herself for a cloak &
hanging herself on the obtrusive Cloak=peg till her

futile & invaluable life was extinct. But there are others (it is due to the interests of science to state,) who contend that the singular object in question is the gigantic & fossil remnant of an extinct brute partaking of the nature of the ostrich & the domestic caterpillar, habitually walking on 3 feet, its neck, head, & expansive antennæ fixed on to the summit of its elongated body, & its general appearance at once surprising & objectionable. –

Of these conjectures, who shall say, which is the true, which the false, – or which the neither either one or t'other?

10   These doubts cannot be now obspiculated, nor indeed can they entirely be ever expressed. To give our readers an accurate portrait of the Object is our own sole & soporific duty.

Object discovered in Beta

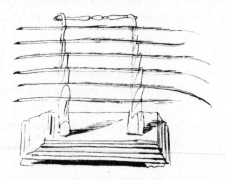

July 11 1863

We are delighted to acquaint our Readers, (& more especially Harkee! o logical Readers,) that fresh discoveries are on the point of being about to be expected to be supposed to be made at Clarence House Roehampton, – of which the accompanying drawing represents one of the most interesting hitherto offered to the pusillanimous public. The
20   object in question was found in Beta & is of an indescribable form & indefinable color: and although some idiotic contemporaries have argued that it is intended to hold pens, there cannot be the smallest doubt that it is the Stand on which the spears of the remarkable & distinguished Beta were kept when she was not using them. For it is well

known that Beta never grew to more than 3 feet 1 inch high – & consequently the penlike but warlike instruments above delineated are quite adapted to her size. Moreover their having been discovered in the apartment which for countless ages has been named after that small but indomitable person, is a parapumphilious proof that requires no other illustration except to the perception of owls, apes, geese, pigs, beetles, or donkies.

Q.E.D.

Letter to Ruth Decie

My dear little tiny child,

You will excuse my familiar mode of addressing you, because, you know, – you have as yet got no Christian name – ; – & to say – 'my dear Miss Decie' would be as much too formal, as 'my dear Decie' would be too rude. But as your Grandmama has written to me that you are just born I will write to congratulate you, & possibly this is one of the first letters you have as yet received. One of the old Greek Tragedians says – and I am sure you will not think me impertinent in translating what he says – μὴ φῦναι &c because there has not been time hitherto to buy you a Greek Dictionary, (& I feel sure you cannot read Sophocles with-   10
out, – besides, the Dictionaries are so fat & heavy I am certain you could not use them comfortably to yourself & your nurse,) – μὴ φῦναι &c – which means 'it is better never to have [been] born at all, or if born, – to die as soon as possible.' But this I wholly dissent from: & on the contrary I congratulate you heartily on coming into a world where if we look for it there is far more good & pleasure than we can use up – even in the longest life. And you in particular will find that you have – all quite without any of your own exertions – a mother & a father, – a grandmother & a grandfather, – some uncles, – an extremely merry brother (who propels himself along the floor like a compasses,) a con-   20
servatory & a croquet ground, & a respectable old cove who is very fond of small children & will give you an Alphabet bye & bye. – I therefore advise you to live & laugh as long as you can for your own pleasure, & that of all your belongings.

Please tell your Grandmama that I also wished to stop when the

carriage passed but couldn't – & say also, that I will write to her again
shortly. And now my dear you have read enough for the present. Good
night, & believe me,
     Your affte. old friend
       Edward Lear.
Give my love to your Papa & Mama.

There was an old person of Páxo,
Which complained when the fleas bit his back so;
    But they gave him a chair
    And impelled him to swear,
Which relieved that old person of Páxo.

'She sits upon her Bulbul'

She sits upon her Bulbul
    Through the long long hours of night –
And o'er the dark horizon gleams
    The Yashmack's fitful light.
The lone Yaourt sails slowly down
    The deep and craggy dell –
And from his lofty nest, loud screams
    The white-plumed Asphodel.

'O Digby my dear'

O Digby my dear
It is perfectly clear
   That my mind will be horridly vext,
If you happen to write,
By ill luck, to invite
   Me to dinner on Saturday next.

For this I should sigh at
That Mrs T Wyatt
   Already has booked me, o dear!
So I could not send answer   10
To you – 'I'm your man, Sir!' –
     Your loving fat friend,
      Edward Lear.

There was an old man with a Book –
Who said, 'Only look! Only look! –
   Obsquation, – obsgration, –
   At Waterloo station –
Enquire if there ain't such a Book!'

Letters to Evelyn Baring

Toosdy

Dear Baring, –

Disgustical to say, I must beg you to thank His Excellency from me, & to relate that I cannot come. I was engaged to dine with the De Vere's, but am too unwell with awful cold in the head & eyes to go out at all.

I have sent for 2 large tablecloths to blow my nose on, having already used up all my handkerchiefs. And altogether I am so unfit for company that I propose getting into a bag and being hung up to a bough of a tree till this tyranny is overpast. Please give the serming I send to His Excellency.

Yours sincerely,
Edward Lear

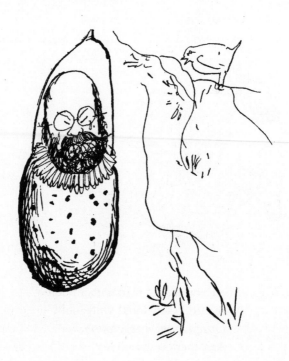

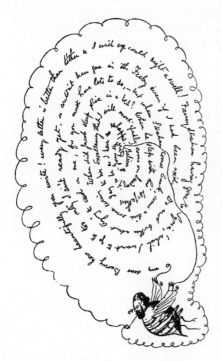

[my dear Baring how beautifully you write! every letter is better than t'other & I wish eye could right as well! Fancy Strahan having gone to Syria! which I want to go to too only I ain't ready yet, so couldn't have gone in the Feeby even if I had been ax'd. Do not bother about trying to cawl on me, for you must have lots to do, – but when Strahan comes back, come & dine some evening. When did Jacob sleep five in a bed? When he slep with his 4=fathers. Say to his Excellency that I will most gladly come on Sunday if so be as I have no relapps. Believe me, Yours sincerely]

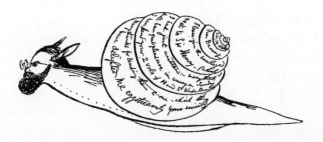

[Feb. 19. 1864 Dear Baring Please give the encloged noat to Sir Henry – (which I had just written: – & say that I shall have great pleasure in coming on Sunday. I have sent your 2 vols of Hood to Wade Brown. Many thanks for lending them to me – which they have delighted me eggstreamly Yours sincerely]

[deerbaringiphowndacuppelloffotografsthismawningwitchisendjoo
thereiswunofeechsortsoyookankeepbothifyooliketodoosoanwenyoo=
=haveabetterwunofyourselfletmehavit.

    Yossin seerly,
     DwdL[ear]]

Letter to Nora Decie

My dear Nora,

    As it is most probable that you are less occupied than your mama or grandmama, I have written to you to beg you to tell them I am on the point of leaving Corfu, & that I am going to Athens & Candia, & may probably be in England by the end of June.

    Will you say also that I am very sorry not to have been able to write all the winter, but I have done the same to everybody, & I don't think I shall ever write much more. I passed through Nice on my way hither but only arrived late at night & set off early next morning, but I wish you could thank Mrs Riley for her letter – which was very useful. (*Nice* my dear does not mean *nice* (like sugarplums & pudding, –) but it is a town chockfull of houses, & it is called *Nice* as if it was written *niece*, which means Frank's daughter's relationship to you, only he has not got any daughters yet.)

    Everybody here is packed up & going away, & we are all & every one of us cross & disagreeable & sorry & in a fuss & bothered. I should not however advise you to use the words 'bother' or 'chockfull' – for they are not strictly lady like expressions.

I hope Frank & Ruth are well, & your mother & father: give my love to them, & to your grandmama & grandpapa. Good bye my dear; I am going to start tomorrow, having sent my luggage away, & intending myself to go by sea, as it is cheaper than going by the steamer. I therefore join Captn. Deverill's 3 geese, & we are going to swim all the

way round Cape Matapan & so to the Piræus as fast as we can.

[Lear's adventures in Crete]

Plate 1

The Landscape painter perceives the Moufflons on the tops of the Mountains of Crete.

Plate 2

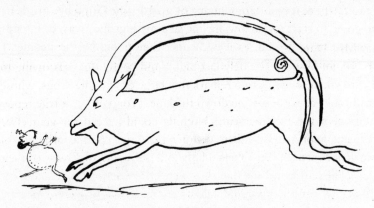

The Landscape painter escapes (with difficulty –) from an enraged Moufflon.

Plate 3

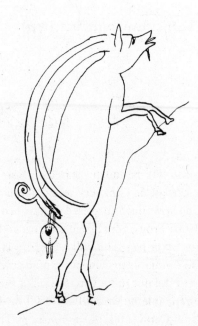

The landscape painter is enabled to ascend some of the highest tops of the Mountains of Crete by sticking on to a Moufflon's Horns.

Letters to Anna Duncan and Lady Duncan

Dear Miss Duncan,

[...] I got home very safely last night, and partly this was owing to the care taken of me by two remarkably large & amiable Frogs, whose arms I took, & who saw me down the lane. (You will see a true representation of the fact overleaf.) Nothing could exceed the genteel & intelligent expression of their countenances, except the urbanity of their deportment and the melancholy and oblivious sweetness of their voices. They informed me that they were the parents of nine and forty tadpoles of various ages and talents some of whom were expecting shortly to emigrate to Malvern and Mesopotamia.

Believe me,

    Yours sincerely,

      Edward Lear

My Dear Lady Duncan,

You & Miss Duncan will be much pleased to hear what occurred just after you left yesterday, & I am very sorry you had not happened to stay longer. Imagine how much surprised & gratified I was by a visit from the two considerate Frogs, who brought their two Eldest Tadpoles also to see me. On the other page you will see a correct drawing of the interview. Both of these amiable persons were much pleased with my 2 Lamps, which I regret I did not show you, & one of them was so good as to say that if he were able he would have tried to carry one of the Lamps as far as Maison Carab[ucel] to let you see it. They did not stay above 20 minutes, as they had a good way to go home, & I was vexed that there was nothing but a piece of cold lamb in the house & some

Marsala, both of which they declined, saying that either Watercresses or small beetles would have been pleasant, but that they were not hungry. I did not quite know at first how to be civil to the Tadpoles, as I found that owing to their long tails they could not sit on chairs as their parents did: I therefore put them into a wash-hand basin, & they seemed happy enough.

Such kind attentions from foreign persons quite of a different race, & I may say nature from our own, are certainly most delightful: and none the less so for being so unexpected. The Frogs were as good as to add that had I had any oil paintings they would have been glad to purchase one – but that the damp of their abode would quite efface water-color art.

Believe me,

   Yours sincerely,

    Edward Lear

The History of the Seven Families of the Lake Pipple-Popple

CHAPTER I
INTRODUCTORY

In former days – that is to say, once upon a time, there lived in the Land of Grambleamble, Seven Families. They lived by the side of the great lake Pipple-Popple (one of the Seven Families, indeed, lived *in* the Lake), and on the outskirts of the City of Tosh, which, excepting when it was quite dark, they could see plainly. The names of all these places you have probably heard of, and you have only not to look in your Geography books to find out all about them.

Now the Seven Families who lived on the borders of the great lake Pipple-Popple, were as follows in the next Chapter.

CHAPTER II
THE SEVEN FAMILIES

There was a Family of Two old Parrots and Seven young Parrots.

There was a Family of Two old Storks and Seven young Storks.

There was a Family of Two old Geese and Seven young Geese.

There was a Family of Two old Owls and Seven young Owls.

There was a Family of Two old Guinea Pigs and Seven young Guinea Pigs.

There was a Family of Two old Cats and Seven young Cats.

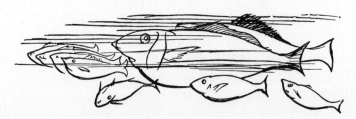

And there was a Family of Two old Fishes and Seven young Fishes.

CHAPTER III
THE HABITS OF THE
SEVEN FAMILIES

The Parrots lived upon the Soffsky-Poffsky trees, – which were beautiful to behold, and covered with blue leaves, – and they fed upon fruit, artichokes, and striped beetles.

The Storks walked in and out of the Lake Pipple-Popple, and ate frogs for breakfast and buttered toast for tea, but on account of the extreme length of their legs, they could not sit down, and so they walked about continually.

The Geese, having webs to their feet, caught quantities of flies, which they ate for dinner.

The Owls anxiously looked after mice, which they caught and made into sago puddings.

The Guinea Pigs toddled about the gardens, and ate lettuces and Cheshire cheese.

The Cats sate still in the sunshine, and fed upon sponge biscuits.

The Fishes lived in the Lake, and fed chiefly on boiled periwinkles.

And all these Seven Families lived together in the utmost fun and felicity.

CHAPTER IV
THE CHILDREN OF THE
SEVEN FAMILIES ARE SENT AWAY

One day all the Seven Fathers and the Seven Mothers of the Seven Families agreed that they would send their children out to see the world.

So they called them all together, and gave them each eight shillings and some good advice, some chocolate drops, and a small green morocco pocket-book to set down their expenses in.

They then particularly entreated them not to quarrel, and all the parents sent off their children with a parting injunction.

'If,' said the old Parrots, 'you find a Cherry, do not fight about who should have it.'

'And,' said the old Storks, 'if you find a Frog, divide it carefully into seven bits, but on no account quarrel about it.'

And the old Geese said to the Seven young Geese, 'Whatever you do, be sure you do not touch a Plum-pudding Flea.'

And the old Owls said, 'If you find a Mouse, tear him up into seven slices, and eat him cheerfully, but without quarrelling.'

And the old Guinea Pigs said, 'Have care that you eat your Lettuces, should you find any, not greedily but calmly.'

And the old Cats said, 'Be particularly careful not to meddle with a Clangle-Wangle, if you should see one.'

And the old Fishes said, 'Above all things avoid eating a blue Bosswoss, for they do not agree with Fishes, and give them a pain in their toes.'

So all the Children of each Family thanked their parents, and making in all forty-nine polite bows, they went into the wide world.

CHAPTER V

THE HISTORY OF THE

SEVEN YOUNG PARROTS

The Seven young Parrots had not gone far, when they saw a tree with a single Cherry on it, which the oldest Parrot picked instantly, but the other six, being extremely hungry, tried to get it also. On which all the Seven began to fight, and they scuffled,

and huffled,

and ruffled,

and shuffled,

and puffled,

and muffled,

and buffled,

and duffled,

and fluffled,

and guffled,

and bruffled, and

screamed, and shrieked, and squealed, and squeaked, and clawed, and snapped, and bit, and bumped, and thumped, and dumped, and flumped each other, till they were all torn into little bits, and at last

there was nothing left to record this painful incident, except the Cherry and seven small green feathers.

And that was the vicious and voluble end of the Seven young Parrots.

CHAPTER VI
THE HISTORY OF THE
SEVEN YOUNG STORKS

When the Seven young Storks set out, they walked or flew for fourteen weeks in a straight line, and for six weeks more in a crooked one; and after that they ran as hard as they could for one hundred and eight
10   miles: and after that they stood still and made a himmeltanious chatter-clatter-blattery noise with their bills.

About the same time they perceived a large Frog, spotted with green, and with a sky-blue stripe under each ear.

So, being hungry, they immediately flew at him, and were going to divide him into seven pieces, when they began to quarrel as to which of his legs should be taken off first. One said this, and another said that, and while they were all quarrelling the Frog hopped away. And when they saw that he was gone, they began to chatter-clatter,

blatter-platter,

20   patter-blatter,

matter-clatter,

flatter-quatter,

more violently than ever. And after they had fought for a week they pecked each other all to little pieces, so that at last nothing was left of any of them except their bills.

And that was the end of the Seven young Storks.

CHAPTER VII
THE HISTORY OF THE
SEVEN YOUNG GEESE

When the Seven young Geese began to travel, they went over a large plain, on which there was but one tree, and that was a very bad one.

So four of them went up to the top of it, and looked about them, while the other three waddled up and down, and repeated poetry, and their last six lessons in Arithmetic, Geography, and Cookery.

Presently they perceived, a long way off, an object of the most interesting and obese appearance, having a perfectly round body, exactly resembling a boiled plum-pudding, with two little wings, and a beak, and three feathers growing out of his head, and only one leg.

So after a time all the Seven young Geese said to each other, 'Beyond all doubt this beast must be a Plum-pudding Flea!'

On which they incautiously began to sing aloud,

> 'Plum-pudding Flea,
> Plum-pudding Flea,
> Wherever you be,

O come to our tree,
And listen, O listen, O listen to me!'

And no sooner had they sung this verse than the Plum-pudding Flea began to hop and skip on his one leg with the most dreadful velocity, and came straight to the tree, where he stopped and looked about him in a vacant and voluminous manner.

On which the Seven young Geese were greatly alarmed, and all of a tremble-bemble; so one of them put out his long neck, and just touched him with the tip of his bill, – but no sooner had he done this than the Plum-pudding Flea skipped and hopped about more and more and higher and higher, after which he opened his mouth, and, to the great surprise and indignation of the Seven Geese, began to bark so loudly and furiously and terribly that they were totally unable to bear the noise, and by degrees every one of them suddenly tumbled down quite dead.

So that was the end of the Seven young Geese.

CHAPTER VIII
THE HISTORY OF THE
SEVEN YOUNG OWLS

When the Seven young Owls set out, they sate every now and then on the branches of the old trees, and never went far at one time.

And one night when it was quite dark, they thought they heard a Mouse, but as the gas lamps were not lighted, they could not see him.

So they called out, 'Is that a Mouse?'
On which a Mouse answered, 'Squeaky-peeky-weeky, yes it is.'
And immediately all the young Owls threw themselves off the tree,

meaning to alight on the ground; but they did not perceive that there
was a large well below them, into which they all fell superficially, and
were every one of them drowned in less than half a minute.

So that was the end of the Seven young Owls.

CHAPTER IX
THE HISTORY OF THE
SEVEN YOUNG GUINEA PIGS

10

The Seven young Guinea Pigs went into a garden full of Gooseberry-
bushes and Tiggory-trees, under one of which they fell asleep. When
they awoke, they saw a large Lettuce which had grown out of the
ground while they had been sleeping, and which had an immense num-
ber of green leaves. At which they all exclaimed,

> 'Lettuce! O Lettuce!
> Let us, O let us,
> O Lettuce leaves,
> O let us leave this tree and eat
> Lettuce, O let us, Lettuce leaves!'

20

And instantly the Seven young Guinea Pigs rushed with such
extreme force against the Lettuce-plant, and hit their heads so vividly

against its stalk, that the concussion brought on directly an incipient transitional inflammation of their noses, which grew worse and worse and worse and worse till it incidentally killed them all Seven.

And that was the end of the Seven young Guinea Pigs.

CHAPTER X
THE HISTORY OF THE
SEVEN YOUNG CATS

The Seven young Cats set off on their travels with great delight and rapacity. But, on coming to the top of a high hill, they perceived at a long distance off a Clangle-Wangle (or, as it is more properly written, Clangel-Wangel), and in spite of the warning they had had, they ran straight up to it.

(Now the Clangle-Wangle is a most dangerous and delusive beast, and by no means commonly to be met with. They live in the water as well as on land, using their long tail as a sail when in the former element. Their speed is extreme, but their habits of life are domestic and superfluous, and their general demeanour pensive and pellucid. On summer evenings they may sometimes be observed near the Lake Pipple-Popple, standing on their heads and humming their national melodies: they subsist entirely on vegetables, excepting when they eat veal, or mutton, or pork, or beef, or fish, or saltpetre.)

The moment the Clangle-Wangle saw the Seven young Cats approach, he ran away; and as he ran straight on for four months, and the Cats, though they continued to run, could never overtake him, – they all gradually *died* of fatigue and exhaustion, and never afterwards recovered.

And this was the end of the Seven young Cats.

CHAPTER XI
THE HISTORY OF THE
SEVEN YOUNG FISHES

The Seven young Fishes swam across the Lake Pipple-Popple, and into the river, and into the Ocean, where most unhappily for them, they saw on the 15th day of their travels, a bright blue Boss-Woss, and instantly swam after him. But the Boss-Woss plunged into a perpendicular,

     spicular,

      orbicular,

       quadrangular,

        circular depth of soft mud,

where in fact his house was.

And the Seven young Fishes, swimming with great and uncomfortable velocity, plunged also into the mud quite against their will, and not being accustomed to it, were all suffocated in a very short period.

And that was the end of the Seven young Fishes.

CHAPTER XII
OF WHAT OCCURRED SUBSEQUENTLY

After it was known that the Seven young Parrots,
and the Seven young Storks,
and the Seven young Geese,
and the Seven young Owls,
and the Seven young Guinea Pigs,
and the Seven young Cats,
and the Seven young Fishes,
10 were all dead, then the Frog, and the Plum-pudding Flea, and the
Mouse, and the Clangel-Wangel, and the Blue Boss-Woss,
all met together to rejoice over their good fortune.

And they collected the Seven Feathers of the Seven young Parrots,
and the Seven Bills of the Seven young Storks, and the Lettuce, and the
Cherry, and having placed the latter on the Lettuce, and the other
objects in a circular arrangement at their base, they danced a hornpipe
round all these memorials until they were quite tired; after which they
gave a tea-party, and a garden-party, and a ball, and a concert, and then
returned to their respective homes full of joy and respect, sympathy,
20 satisfaction, and disgust.

CHAPTER XIII
OF WHAT BECAME OF THE PARENTS
OF THE FORTY-NINE CHILDREN

But when the two old Parrots,
 and the two old Storks,
 and the two old Geese,
 and the two old Owls,
 and the two old Guinea Pigs,
 and the two old Cats,
 and the two old Fishes,
became aware by reading in the newspapers, of the calamitous extinction of the whole of their families, they refused all further sustenance; and sending out to various shops, they purchased great quantities of Cayenne Pepper, and Brandy, and Vinegar, and blue Sealing-wax, besides Seven immense glass Bottles with air-tight stoppers. And having done this, they ate a light supper of brown bread and Jerusalem Artichokes, and took an affecting and formal leave of the whole of their acquaintance, which was very numerous and distinguished, and select, and responsible, and ridiculous.

CHAPTER XIV
CONCLUSION

And after this, they filled the bottles with the ingredients for pickling, and each couple jumped into a separate bottle, by which effort of course they all died immediately, and became thoroughly pickled in a few minutes; having previously made their wills (by the assistance of the most eminent Lawyers of the District), in which they left strict orders that the Stoppers of the Seven Bottles should be carefully sealed up with the blue Sealing-wax they had purchased; and that they themselves in the Bottles should be presented to the principal museum of the city of Tosh, to be labelled with Parchment or any other anti-congenial succedaneum, and to be placed on a marble table with silver-gilt legs, for the daily inspection and contemplation, and for the perpetual benefit of the pusillanimous public.

And if ever you happen to go to Gramble-Blamble, and visit that museum in the city of Tosh, look for them on the Ninety-eighth table in the Four hundred and twenty-seventh room of the right-hand corridor of the left wing of the Central Quadrangle of that magnificent building; for if you do not, you certainly will not see them.

The Duck and the Kangaroo

Said the Duck to the Kangaroo,
  'Good gracious! how you hop!
Over the fields and the water too,
  As if you never would stop!
My life is a bore in this nasty pond,
And I long to go out in the world beyond!
  I wish I could hop like you!'
  Said the Duck to the Kangaroo.

'Please give me a ride on your back!'
  Said the Duck to the Kangaroo.   10
'I would sit quite still, and say nothing but "Quack,"
  The whole of the long day through!
And we'd go to the Dee, and the Jelly Bo Lee,
Over the land, and over the sea; –
  Please take me a ride! O do!'
  Said the Duck to the Kangaroo.

Said the Kangaroo to the Duck,
   'This requires some little reflection;
Perhaps on the whole it might bring me luck,
   And there seems but one objection,
Which is, if you'll let me speak so bold,
Your feet are unpleasantly wet and cold,
   And would probably give me the roo-
   matiz!' said the Kangaroo.

Said the Duck, 'As I sate on the rocks,
   I have thought over that completely,
And I bought four pairs of worsted socks
   Which fit my web-feet neatly.
And to keep out the cold I've bought a cloak,
And every day a cigar I'll smoke,
   All to follow my own dear true
   Love of a Kangaroo!'

Said the Kangaroo, 'I'm ready!
    All in the moonlight pale;
But to balance me well, dear Duck, sit steady!
    And quite at the end of my tail!'
So away they went with a hop and a bound,
And they hopped the whole world three times round;
    And who so happy, – O who,
    As the Duck and the Kangaroo?   40

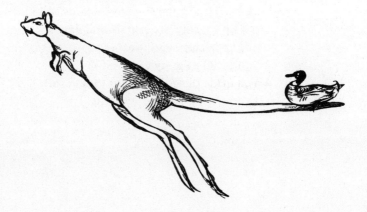

'Gozo my child is the isle of Calypso'

Gozo my child is the isle of Calypso
That naughty young woman who made egg flip so
And all day long with a spoon did sip so,
And every morn in the sea did dip so
Whereon Ulysses seeing her strip so
And all her beautiful ringlets drip so
From her beautiful head to her beautiful hipso
Because her curls she never would clip so,
– Took to staying away from his ship so,
And she his mariners all did tip so
And fed them with chickens that had the pip so
For fear he should ever give her the slip so
And over the ocean start for a trip so
    Singing – (with peculiar sweetness–) '*This* is
I who have wheedled the wily Ulysses,
With kurls and kobwebs and kustards and kisses
        Gip so, whip so, crip so, and quip so
        Flip so, bip so, rip so and zip so –
            O naughty Calypso!
Which made the little hills for to skip so!'

Stratford Place Gazette

7th August 1866
(9534th Edition)

ALARMING AND HORRIBLE EVENT

We regret to state that at 4 P.M. this day the well known Author &
Landscape painter Edward Lear committed sukycide by throwing
hisself out of a 5 pair of stairs winder. The cause of this amazing &
obsequious conclusion to a well spent & voracious life, we understand
to be as follies: – Mr L, having returned from a visit to some friends at
Hastings, wrote to them on his return to London begging them immee-   10
jiately to forward a book called 'The Gothe & the Un' which he
supposed he had left at their house. On this day however, the said book
tumbled spongetaneously out of a coat which had not been opened or
shaken or examined or craxpaxified in any way whatsoever; on seeing
which the unfortunate Gentleman tore his hair promiscuous, & bitter-
ly reproached his self with the trouble he had given to Mrs and Mr G.

Scrivens, likewise Mr Bennell: & finally giving way to dishpear, opened the window & leaped 4th into the street – to the extreme surprise & delight of some little children playing on the pavement, – the alarm of the thinking part of the neighbourhood, & the eminent annoyance to his own ribs and existence. Our readers will doubtless drop a tear over this brutal & harmonious occurrence, a view of which, (sketched by our special artist who happened to be passing,) we present them with our liveliest regards & compliments.

[Three miscellaneous limericks]

There was an old person who said –
'Do you think I've a very large head?'

There was an old man who felt pert
When he wore a pale rosecoloured shirt.
   When they said – 'Is it pleasant?'
   He cried – 'Not at present –
It's a *leetle* too short – is my shirt!'

There was an old person who sung,
'Bloo – Sausages! Kidnies! and Tongue!
   Bloo! Bloo! my dear Madam,
   My name is Old Adam.
Bloo! Sausages – Kidnies, and Tongue!'

The Adventures of Mr Lear & the Polly [& the] Pusseybite on their way to the Ritertitle Mountains

Mr Lear goes out a walking with a Polly & the Pusseybite.

Mr Lear, feeling tired, & also the Polly & the Pusseybite, sit down on a wall to rest.

Mr Lear, the Polly & the Pusseybite go into a shop to buy a Numbrella, because it began to rain.

Mr L., the P. & the P.B. having purchased umbrellas, proceed on their walk.

Mr L. & the P. & the P.B. arrive at a bridge, which being broken they do not know what to do.

Mr L., the P. & the P.B. all tumble promiscuous into the raging river & become quite wet.

[lacuna]

Mr Lear & the P. & the P.B. pursue their journey in a benevolent boat.

Mr L. & the P. & the P.B. incidentally fall over an unexpected Cataract, & are all dashed [to] atoms.

[lacuna]

The 2 venerable Jebusites fasten the remains of Mr L., the P. & the P.B. together, but fail to reconstruct them perfectly as 3 individuals.

Mr Lear & the Pusseybite & the Polly cat & the 2 Jebusites & the Jerusalem Artichokes and the Octagonal Oysterclippers all tumble into a deep hole & are never seen or distinguished or heard of never more afterwards.

'O Thuthan Thmith! Thweet Thuthan Thmith!'

My dear Mitheth Digby,
Thankth for your note: I will come on Thunday. But whatth been a matter with Digby? I hope he ith better than he wath. I am compothing a thong to thing now that my teeth have thuffered tho mutth, & it theemth to me that it will produthe a thenthation in the muthical thphereth.

O Thuthan Thmith! Thweet Thuthan Thmith!
I thit in thilenth clothe to thee
And lithtning to thy thongthtreth lipth
I watth the tholemn thtately thipth
Acroth the thounding thilver thea!
 And thith – o! thith!
 I thay ith blith –
 Thweet Thuthan Thmith!
 Thweet Thuthan Thmith!

The thlender Thrimp itth gambolth playth, 10
The thiny thprightly fitheth thwim, –
The thandy thore, the dithtant hillth, –
All thethe I watth; – but nothing thillth
The thindy that my bothom fillth
In gathing on thy thape tho thlim!
 With burthting thobth
 My thoft thoul throbth –
 Thweet Thuthan Thmith!
 Thweet Thuthan Thmith!

I hope, if I publith thith that you will thubthcribe for thikthty or theventy copieth.
 My love to Digby.
  Yourth thintherely,
   Edw Lear.

The Story of the Four Little Children
Who Went Round the World

Once upon a time, a long while ago, there were four little people whose names were

VIOLET,   SLINGSBY,   GUY, and LIONEL;

and they all thought they should like to see the world. So they bought a large boat to sail quite round the world by sea, and then they were to come back on the other side by land. The boat was painted blue with green spots, and the sail was yellow with red stripes; and when they set off, they only took a small Cat to steer and look after the boat, besides an elderly Quangle-Wangle, who had to cook the dinner and make the tea; for which purposes they took a large kettle.

For the first ten days they sailed on beautifully, and found plenty to eat, as there were lots of fish, and they had only to take them out of the sea with a long spoon, when the Quangle-Wangle instantly cooked them, and the Pussy-cat was fed with the bones, with which she expressed herself pleased on the whole, so that all the party were very happy.

During the day-time, Violet chiefly occupied herself in putting salt-water into a churn, while her three brothers churned it violently, in the hope that it would turn into butter, which it seldom, if ever did; and in the evening they all retired into the Tea-kettle, where they all managed to sleep very comfortably, while Pussy and the Quangle-Wangle managed the boat.

After a time they saw some land at a distance; and when they came to it, they found it was an island made of water quite surrounded by earth. Besides that, it was bordered by evanescent isthmusses with a great Gulf-stream running about all over it, so that it was perfectly beautiful, and contained only a single tree, 503 feet high. 10

When they had landed, they walked about, but found to their great surprise, that the island was quite full of veal-cutlets and chocolate-drops, and nothing else. So they all climbed up the single high tree to discover, if possible, if there were any people; but having remained on the top of the tree for a week, and not seeing anybody, they naturally concluded that there were no inhabitants, and accordingly when they came down, they loaded the boat with two thousand veal-cutlets and a million of chocolate drops, and these afforded them sustenance for more than a month, during which time they pursued their voyage with the utmost delight and apathy.

After this they came to a shore where there were no less than sixty-five great red parrots with blue tails, sitting on a rail all of a row, and all fast asleep. And I am sorry to say that the Pussy-cat and the Quangle-Wangle crept softly and bit off the tail-feathers of all the sixty-five parrots, for which Violet reproved them both severely.

Notwithstanding which, she proceeded to insert all the feathers, two hundred and sixty in number, in her bonnet, thereby causing it to have a lovely and glittering appearance, highly prepossessing and efficacious.

The next thing that happened to them was in a narrow part of the sea, which was so entirely full of fishes that the boat could go on no further; so they remained there about six weeks, till they had eaten nearly all the fishes, which were Soles, and all ready-cooked and covered with shrimp sauce, so that there was no trouble whatever. And as the few fishes who remained uneaten complained of the cold, as well as of the difficulty they had in getting any sleep on account

of the extreme noise made by the Arctic Bears and the Tropical Turn-spits which frequented the neighbourhood in great numbers, Violet most amiably knitted a small woollen frock for several of the fishes, and Slingsby administered some opium drops to them, through which kindness they became quite warm and slept soundly.

Then they came to a country which was wholly covered with immense Orange-trees of a vast size, and quite full of fruit. So they all landed, taking with them the Tea-kettle, intending to gather some of the Oranges and place them in it. But while they were busy about this, a most dreadfully high wind rose, and blew out most of the Parrot-tail feathers from Violet's bonnet. That, however, was nothing compared with the calamity of the Oranges falling down on their heads by millions and millions, which thumped and bumped and bumped and thumped them all so seriously that they were obliged to run as hard as they could for their lives, besides that the sound of the Oranges rattling on the Tea-kettle was of the most fearful and amazing nature.

Nevertheless they got safely to the boat, although considerably vexed and hurt; and the Quangle-Wangle's right foot was so knocked about, that he had to sit with his head in his slipper for at least a week.

10

This event made them all for a time rather melancholy, and perhaps they might never have become less so, had not Lionel with a most praiseworthy devotion and perseverance, continued to stand on one leg and whistle to them in a loud and lively manner, which diverted the whole party so extremely, that they gradually recovered their spirits, and agreed that whenever they should reach home they would subscribe towards a testimonial to Lionel, entirely made of Gingerbread and Raspberries, as an earnest token of their sincere and grateful infection.

After sailing on calmly for several more days, they came to another country, where they were much pleased and surprised to see a countless

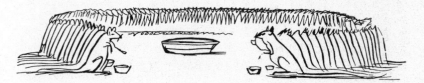

multitude of white Mice with red eyes, all sitting in a great circle, slowly eating Custard Pudding with the most satisfactory and polite demeanour.

And as the Four Travellers were rather hungry, being tired of eating nothing but Soles and Oranges for so long a period, they held a council as to the propriety of asking the Mice for some of their Pudding in a humble and affecting manner, by which they could hardly be otherwise than gratified. It was agreed therefore that Guy should go and ask the Mice, which he immediately did; and the result was that they gave [him] a Walnut-shell only half full of Custard diluted with water. Now, this displeased Guy, who said, 'Out of such a lot of Pudding as you have got, I must say you might have spared a somewhat larger quantity!' But no sooner had he finished speaking than all the Mice turned round at once, and sneezed at him in an appalling and vindictive manner, (and it

is impossible to imagine a more scroobious and unpleasant sound than that caused by the simultaneous sneezing of many millions of angry Mice,) so that Guy rushed back to the boat, having first shied his cap into the middle of the Custard Pudding, by which means he completely spoiled the Mice's dinner.

By-and-by the Four Children came to a country where there were no houses, but only an incredibly innumerable number of large bottles without corks, and of a dazzling and sweetly susceptible blue colour. Each of these blue bottles contained a Blue-Bottle-Fly, and all these interesting animals live continually together in the most copious and rural harmony, nor perhaps in many parts of the world is such perfect and abject happiness to be found. Violet, and Slingsby, and Guy, and Lionel, were greatly struck with this singular and instructive settle-ment, and having previously asked permission of the Blue-Bottle-Flies (which was most courteously granted), the Boat was drawn up to the shore and they proceeded to make tea in front of the Bottles; but as they

had no tea-leaves, they merely placed some pebbles in the hot water, and the Quangle-Wangle played some tunes over it on an Accordion, by which of course tea was made directly, and of the very best quality.

The Four Children then entered into conversation with the Blue-Bot-tle-Flies, who discoursed in a placid and genteel manner, though with a slightly buzzing accent, chiefly owing to the fact that they each held a small clothes-brush between their teeth which naturally occasioned a fizzy extraneous utterance.

'Why,' said Violet, 'would you kindly inform us, do you reside in bottles? and if in bottles at all, why not rather in green or purple, or indeed in yellow bottles?'

To which questions a very aged Blue-Bottle-Fly answered, 'We found the bottles here all ready to live in, that is to say, our great-great-great-great-great-grandfathers did, so we occupied them at once. And when the winter comes on, we turn the bottles upside-down, and conse-quently rarely feel the cold at all, and you know very well that this could not be the case with bottles of any other colour than blue.'

'Of course it could not,' said Slingsby, 'but if we may take the liber-ty of inquiring, on what do you chiefly subsist?'

'Mainly on Oyster-patties,' said the Blue-Bottle-Fly, 'and, when these are scarce, on Raspberry Vinegar and Russian leather boiled down to a jelly.'

'How delicious!' said Guy.

To which Lionel added, 'Huzz!' and all the Blue-Bottle-Flies said 'Buzz!'

At this time, an elderly Fly said it was the hour for the Evening-song to be sung; and on a signal being given all the Blue-Bottle-Flies began to buzz at once in a sumptuous and sonorous manner, the melodious and mucilaginous sounds echoing all over the waters, and resounding across the tumultuous tops of the transitory Titmice upon the intervening and verdant mountains, with a serene and sickly suavity only known to the truly virtuous. The Moon was shining slobaciously from the star-bespringled sky, while her light irrigated the smooth and shiny sides and wings and backs of the Blue-Bottle-Flies with a peculiar and trivial splendour, while all nature cheerfully responded to the cerulæan and conspicuous circumstances.

In many long-after years, the Four little Travellers looked back to that evening as one of the happiest in all their lives, and it was already past midnight, when – the Sail of the Boat having been set up by the Quangle-Wangle, the Tea-kettle and Churn placed in their respective positions, and the Pussy-cat stationed at the Helm – the Children each took a last and affectionate farewell of the Blue-Bottle-Flies, who walked down in a body to the water's edge to see the Travellers embark.

As a token of parting respect and esteem, Violet made a curtsey quite down to the ground, and stuck one of her few remaining Parrot-tail

feathers into the back hair of the most pleasing of the Blue-Bottle-Flies, while Slingsby, Guy, and Lionel offered them three small boxes, containing respectively, Black Pins, Dried Figs, and Epsom Salts: and thus they left that happy shore for ever.

Overcome by their feelings, the Four little Travellers instantly jumped into the Tea-kettle, and fell fast asleep. But all along the shore for many hours there was distinctly heard a sound of severely suppressed sobs, and of a vague multitude of living creatures using their pocket-handkerchiefs in a subdued simultaneous snuffle – lingering sadly along the wallopping waves as the boat sailed farther and farther away from the Land of the Happy Blue-Bottle-Flies.

10 Nothing particular occurred for some days after these events, except that as the Travellers were passing a low tract of sand, they perceived an unusual and gratifying spectacle, namely, a large number of Crabs and Crawfish – perhaps six or seven hundred – sitting by the water-side, and endeavouring to disentangle a vast heap of pale pink worsted, which they moistened at intervals with a fluid composed of Lavender-water and White-wine Negus.

'Can we be of any service to you, O crusty Crabbies?' said the Four Children.

'Thank you kindly,' said the Crabs, consecutively. 'We are trying to 20 make some worsted Mittens, but do not know how.'

On which Violet, who was perfectly acquainted with the art of mitten-making, said to the Crabs, 'Do your claws unscrew, or are they fixtures?'

'They are all made to unscrew,' said the Crabs, and forthwith they deposited a great pile of claws close to the boat, with which Violet uncombed all the pale pink worsted, and then made the loveliest Mittens with it you can imagine. These the Crabs, having resumed and screwed on their claws, placed cheerfully upon their wrists, and walked away rapidly on their hind-legs, warbling songs with a silvery voice and 30 in a minor key.

After this the Four little People sailed on again till they came to a vast and wide plain of astonishing dimensions, on which nothing whatever could be discovered at first; but as the Travellers walked onward, there appeared in the extreme and dim distance a single object, which on a nearer approach and on an accurately cutaneous inspection, seemed to be somebody in a large white wig sitting on an arm-chair made of Sponge Cakes and Oyster-shells. 'It does not quite look like a human being,' said Violet, doubtfully; nor could they make out what it really was, till the Quangle-Wangle (who had previously been round the world), exclaimed softly in a loud voice, 'It is the Co-operative Cauliflower!'

And so in truth it was, and they soon found that what they had taken for an immense wig was in reality the top of the cauliflower, and that he had no feet at all, being able to walk tolerably well with a fluctuating and graceful movement on a single cabbage stalk, an accomplishment which naturally saved him the expense of stockings and shoes.

Presently, while the whole party from the boat was gazing at him with mingled affection and disgust, he suddenly arose, and in a somewhat plumdomphious manner hurried off towards the setting sun, – his legs supported by two superincumbent confidential cucumbers, and a large number of Waterwagtails proceeding in advance of him by three-   10

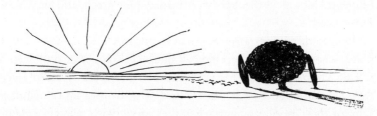

and-three in a row – till he finally disappeared on the brink of the western sky in a crystal cloud of sudorific sand.

So remarkable a sight of course impressed the Four Children very deeply; and they returned immediately to their boat with a strong sense of undeveloped asthma and a great appetite.

Shortly after this the Travellers were obliged to sail directly below some high overhanging rocks, from the top of one of which, a particularly odious little boy, dressed in rose-coloured knickerbockers, and with a pewter plate upon his head, threw an enormous Pumpkin at the boat, by which it was instantly upset.   20

But this upsetting was of no consequence, because all the party knew how to swim very well, and in fact they preferred swimming about till after the moon rose, when the water growing chilly, they sponge-taneously entered the boat. Meanwhile the Quangle-Wangle threw back the Pumpkin with immense force, so that it hit the rocks where the malicious little boy in rose-coloured knickerbockers was sitting, when, being quite full of Lucifer-matches, the Pumpkin exploded sur-reptitiously into a thousand bits, whereon the rocks instantly took fire, and the odious little boy became unpleasantly hotter and hotter and
10   hotter, till his knickerbockers were turned quite green, and his nose was burned off.

Two or three days after this had happened, they came to another place, where they found nothing at all except some wide and deep pits full of Mulberry Jam. This is the property of the tiny Yellow-nosed Apes who abound in these districts, and who store up the Mulberry Jam for their food in winter, when they mix it with pellucid pale peri-winkle soup, and serve it out in Wedgwood China bowls, which grow freely all over that part of the country. Only one of the Yellow-nosed Apes was on the spot, and he was fast asleep: yet the Four Travellers
20   and the Quangle-Wangle and Pussy were so terrified by the violence and sanguinary sound of his snoring, that they merely took a small cup-ful of the Jam, and returned to re-embark in their Boat without delay.

What was their horror on seeing the boat (including the Churn and the Tea-kettle), in the mouth of an enormous Seeze Pyder, an aquatic and ferocious creature truly dreadful to behold, and happily only met with in these excessive longitudes. In a moment the beautiful boat was bitten into fifty-five-thousand-million-hundred-billion bits; and it instantly became quite clear that Violet, Slingsby, Guy, and Lionel could no longer preliminate their voyage by sea.

The Four Travellers were therefore obliged to resolve on pursuing their wanderings by land, and very fortunately there happened to pass by at that moment, an elderly Rhinoceros, on which they seized; and all four mounting on his back, the Quangle-Wangle sitting on his horn

and holding on by his ears, the Pussy-cat swinging at the end of his tail, they set off, having only four small beans and three pounds of mashed potatoes to last through their whole journey.

They were, however, able to catch numbers of the chickens and turkeys, and other birds who incessantly alighted on the head of the Rhinoceros for the purpose of gathering the seeds of the rhododendron plants which grew there, and these creatures they cooked in the most translucent and satisfactory manner, by means of a fire lighted on the end of the Rhinoceros' back. A crowd of Kangaroos and Gigantic Cranes accompanied them, from feelings of curiosity and complacency, so that they were never at a loss for company, and went onward as it were in a sort of profuse and triumphant procession.

Thus, in less than eighteen weeks, they all arrived safely at home, where they were received by their admiring relatives with joy tempered with contempt; and where they finally resolved to carry out the rest of their travelling plans at some more favourable opportunity.

As for the Rhinoceros, in token of their grateful adherence, they had him killed and stuffed directly, and then set him up outside the door of their father's house as a Diaphanous Doorscraper.

Growling Eclogue
Composed at Cannes, December 9th, 1867

(Interlocutors – Mr Lear and Mr and Mrs Symonds)

Edwardus. – What makes you look so black, so glum, so cross?
Is it neuralgia, headache, or remorse?

Johannes. – What makes you look as cross, or even more so?
Less like a man than is a broken Torso?

E. – What if my life is odious, should I grin?
If you are savage, need I care a pin?

J. – And if I suffer, am I then an owl?
May I not frown and grind my teeth and growl?

E. – Of course you may; but may not I growl too?
May I not frown and grind my teeth like you?   10

J. – See Catherine comes! To her, to her,
Let each his several miseries refer;
She shall decide whose woes are least or worst,
And which, as growler, shall rank last or first.

Catherine. – Proceed to growl, in silence I'll attend,
And hear your foolish growlings to the end;
And when they're done, I shall correctly judge
Which of your griefs are real or only fudge.
Begin, let each his mournful voice prepare,
(And, pray, however angry, do not swear!)   20

J. – We came abroad for warmth, and find sharp cold!
Cannes is an imposition, and we're sold.

E. – Why did I leave my native land, to find
Sharp hailstones, snow, and most disgusting wind?

J. – What boots it that we orange trees or lemons see,
If we must suffer from *such* vile inclemency?

E. – Why did I take the lodgings I have got,
Where all I don't want is: – all I want not?

J. – Last week I called aloud, O! O! O! O!
30   The ground is wholly overspread with snow!
Is that at any rate a theme for mirth
Which makes a sugar-cake of all the earth?

E. – Why must I sneeze and snuffle, groan and cough,
If my hat's on my head, or if it's off?
Why must I sink all poetry in this prose,
The everlasting blowing of my nose?

J. – When I walk out the mud my footsteps clogs,
Besides, I suffer from attacks of dogs.

E. – Me a vast awful bulldog, black and brown,
40   Completely terrified when near the town;
As calves, perceiving butchers, trembling reel,
So did *my* calves the approaching monster feel.

J. – Already from two rooms we're driven away,
Because the beastly chimneys smoke all day:
Is this a trifle, say? Is this a joke?
That we, like hams, should be becooked in smoke?

E. – Say! what avails it that my servant speaks
Italian, English, Arabic, and Greek,
Besides Albanian: if he don't speak French,
50   How can he ask for salt, or shrimps, or tench?

J. – When on the foolish hearth fresh wood I place,
It whistles, sings, and squeaks, before my face:
And if it does unless the fire burns bright,
And if it does, yet squeaks, how can I write?

E. – Alas! I needs must go and call on swells,
That they may say, 'Pray draw me the Estrelles.'
On one I went last week to leave a card,
The swell was out – the servant eyed me hard:
'This chap's a thief disguised,' his face expressed:
If I go there again, may I be blest!   60

J. – Why must I suffer in this wind and gloom?
Roomattics in a vile cold attic room?

E. – Swells drive about the road with haste and fury,
As Jehu drove about all over Jewry.
Just now, while walking slowly, I was all but
Run over by the Lady Emma Talbot,
Whom not long since a lovely babe I knew,
With eyes and cap-ribbons of perfect blue.

J. – Downstairs and upstairs, every blessed minute,
There's each room with pianofortes in it.   70
How can I write with noises such as those?
And, being always discomposed, compose?

E. – Seven Germans through my garden lately strayed,
And all on instruments of torture played;
They blew, they screamed, they yelled: how can I paint
Unless my room is quiet, which it ain't?

J. – How can I study if a hundred flies
Each moment blunder into both my eyes?

E. – How can I draw with green or blue or red,
If flies and beetles vex my old bald head?   80

J. – How can I translate German Metaphys-
ics, if mosquitoes round my forehead whizz?

E. – I've bought some bacon, (though it's much too fat,)
But round the house there prowls a hideous cat:

Once should I see my bacon in her mouth,
What care I if my rooms look north or south?

J. – Pain from a pane in one cracked window comes,
Which sings and whistles, buzzes, shrieks and hums;
In vain amain with pain the pane with this chord
90   I fain would strain to stop the beastly *dis*cord!

E. – If rain and wind and snow and such like ills
Continue here, how shall I pay my bills?
For who through cold and slush and rain will come
To see my drawings and to purchase some?
And if they don't, what destiny is mine?
How can I ever get to Palestine?

J. – The blinding sun strikes through the olive trees,
When I walk out, and always makes me sneeze.

E. – Next door, if all night long the moon is shining,
100   There sits a dog, who wakes me up with whining.

Cath. – Forbear! You both are bores, you've growled enough:
No longer will I listen to such stuff!
All men have nuisances and bores to afflict 'um:
Hark then, and bow to my official dictum!

For you, Johannes, there is most excuse,
(Some interruptions are the very deuce,)
You're younger than the other cove, who surely
Might have some sense – besides, you're somewhat
    poorly.
This therefore is my sentence, that you nurse
110   The Baby for seven hours, and nothing worse.
For you, Edwardus, I shall say no more
Than that your griefs are fudge, yourself a bore:
Return at once to cold, stewed, minced, hashed
    mutton –
To wristbands ever guiltless of a button –

To raging winds and sea, (where don't you wish
Your luck may ever let you catch one fish?) –
To make large drawings nobody will buy –
To paint oil pictures which will never dry –
To write new books which nobody will read –
To drink weak tea, on tough old pigs to feed –   120
Till spring-time brings the birds and leaves and flowers,
And time restores a world of happier hours.

The Owl and the Pussy-cat

The Owl and the Pussy-cat went to sea
   In a beautiful pea-green boat,
They took some honey, and plenty of money,
   Wrapped up in a five-pound note.
The Owl looked up to the stars above,
   And sang to a small guitar,
'O lovely Pussy! O Pussy, my love,
   What a beautiful Pussy you are,
       You are,
10   You are!
What a beautiful Pussy you are!'

Pussy said to the Owl, 'You elegant fowl!
   How charmingly sweet you sing!
O let us be married! too long we have tarried:
   But what shall we do for a ring?'
They sailed away, for a year and a day,
   To the land where the Bong-tree grows,
And there in a wood a Piggy-wig stood,
   With a ring at the end of his nose,
       His nose,
20   His nose,
With a ring at the end of his nose.

'Dear Pig, are you willing to sell for one shilling
  Your ring?' Said the Piggy, 'I will.'
So they took it away, and were married next day
  By the Turkey who lives on the hill.
They dinèd on mince, and slices of quince,
  Which they ate with a runcible spoon;
And hand in hand, on the edge of the sand,
  They danced by the light of the moon,   30
      The moon,
      The moon,
They danced by the light of the moon.

[Mrs Blue Dickey-bird]

Mrs Blue Dickey-bird, who went out a-walking with her six chickey
 birds: she carried a parasol and wore a bonnet of green silk.
The first little chickey bird had daisies growing out of his head, and
 wore boots because of the dirt.
The second little chickey bird wore a hat, for fear it should rain.
The third little chickey bird carried a jug of water.
The fourth little chickey bird carried a muff, to keep her wings warm.
The fifth little chickey bird was round as a ball.
And the sixth little chickey bird walked on his head, to save his feet.

'Some people their attention fixes'

Some people their attention fixes
On 'Istory or Polly=tixes
Some studies French, & some Hastronomy
And others cultivates Heconomy.

The Broom, the Shovel, the Poker, and the Tongs

The Broom and the Shovel, the Poker and Tongs,
    They all took a drive in the Park,
And they each sang a song, Ding-a-dong, Ding-a-dong,
    Before they went back in the dark.
Mr Poker he sate quite upright in the coach,
    Mr Tongs made a clatter and clash,
Miss Shovel was dressed all in black (with a brooch),
    Mrs Broom was in blue (with a sash).
        Ding-a-dong! Ding-a-dong!
        And they all sang a song!   10

'Oh Shovely so lovely!' the Poker he sang,
    'You have perfectly conquered my heart!
Ding-a-dong! Ding-a-dong! If you're pleased with my song,
    I will feed you with cold apple tart!
When you scrape up the coals with a delicate sound,
    You enrapture my life with delight!
Your nose is so shiny! your head is so round!
    And your shape is so slender and bright!
        Ding-a-dong! Ding-a-dong!
        Ain't you pleased with my song?'   20

'Alas! Mrs Broom !' sighed the Tongs in his song,
    'O is it because I'm so thin,
And my legs are so long – Ding-a-dong! Ding-a-dong!
    That you don't care about me a pin?
Ah! fairest of creatures, when sweeping the room,
    Ah! why don't you heed my complaint!
Must you needs be so cruel, you beautiful Broom,
    Because you are covered with paint?
        Ding-a-dong! Ding-a-dong!
30   You are certainly wrong!'

Mrs Broom and Miss Shovel together they sang,
    'What nonsense you're singing to-day!'
Said the Shovel, 'I'll certainly hit you a bang!'
    Said the Broom, 'And I'll sweep you away!'
So the Coachman drove homeward as fast as he could,
    Perceiving their anger with pain;
But they put on the kettle, and little by little,
    They all became happy again.
        Ding-a-dong! Ding-a-dong!
40   There's an end of my song!

There was an old man who said – 'Hum!
I am always a-spraining my Thumb.'
　　When they said 'Tell us how?'
　　He made them a bow, –
And said, 'I've no jints in my Thumb!'

Calico Pie

Calico Pie,
  The little birds fly
Down to the calico tree,
  Their wings were blue,
  And they sang 'Tilly-loo!'
  Till away they flew, –
And they never came back to me!
  They never came back!
  They never came back!
They never came back to me!

10

Calico Jam,
  The little Fish swam,
Over the syllabub sea,
  He took off his hat,
  To the Sole and the Sprat,
  And the Willeby-wat, –

But he never came back to me!
  He never came back!
  He never came back!
He never came back to me!   20

  Calico Ban,
  The little Mice ran,
To be ready in time for tea,
  Flippity flup,
  They drank it all up,
  And danced in the cup, –

But they never came back to me!
  They never came back!
  They never came back!
They never came back to me!   30

  Calico Drum,
  The Grasshoppers come,
The Butterfly, Beetle, and Bee,
  Over the ground,
  Around and round,
  With a hop and a bound, –

But they never came back!
They never came back!
They never came back!
They never came back to me!

The Daddy Long-legs and the Fly

Once Mr Daddy Long-legs,
    Dressed in brown and gray,
Walked about upon the sands
    Upon a summer's day;
And there among the pebbles,
    When the wind was rather cold,
He met with Mr Floppy Fly,
    All dressed in blue and gold.
And as it was too soon to dine,
They drank some Periwinkle-wine,
And played an hour or two, or more,
At battlecock and shuttledore.

Said Mr Daddy Long-legs
    To Mr Floppy Fly,
'Why do you never come to court?
    I wish you'd tell me why.
All gold and shine, in dress so fine,
    You'd quite delight the court.
Why do you never go at all?
        I really think you *ought*!
And if you went, you'd see such sights!

Such rugs! and jugs! and candle-lights!
And more than all, the King and Queen,
One in red, and one in green!'

'O Mr Daddy Long-legs,'
    Said Mr Floppy Fly,
'It's true I never go to court,
    And I will tell you why.
If I had six long legs like yours,
    At once I'd go to court!   30
But oh! I can't, because *my* legs
    Are so extremely short.
And I'm afraid the King and Queen
(One in red, and one in green)
Would say aloud, "You are not fit,
You Fly, to come to court to a bit!"'

'O Mr Daddy Long-legs,'
    Said Mr Floppy Fly,
'I wish you'd sing one little song!
    One mumbian melody!   40
You used to sing so awful well
    In former days gone by,
But now you never sing at all;
    I wish you'd tell me why:
For if you would, the silvery sound
Would please the shrimps and cockles round,
And all the crabs would gladly come
To hear you sing, "Ah, Hum di Hum!"'

Said Mr Daddy Long-legs,
    'I can never sing again!   50
And if you wish, I'll tell you why,
    Although it gives me pain.
For years I cannot hum a bit,
    Or sing the smallest song;
And this the dreadful reason is,
    My legs are grown too long!

My six long legs, all here and there,
Oppress my bosom with despair;
And if I stand, or lie, or sit,
60   I cannot sing one single bit!'

So Mr Daddy Long-legs
    And Mr Floppy Fly
Sat down in silence by the sea,
    And gazed upon the sky.
They said, 'This is a dreadful thing!
    The world has all gone wrong,
Since one has legs too short by half,
    The other much too long!
One never more can go to court,
70   Because his legs have grown too short;
The other cannot sing a song,
Because his legs have grown too long!'

Then Mr Daddy Long-legs
    And Mr Floppy Fly
Rushed downward to the foamy sea
    With one sponge-taneous cry;
And there they found a little boat,
    Whose sails were pink and gray;
And off they sailed among the waves,
80   Far, and far away.
They sailed across the silent main,
And reached the great Gromboolian plain;
And there they play for evermore
At battlecock and shuttledore.

[Nonsense Cookery]

Extract from the *Nonsense Gazette*, for August, 1870.

Our readers will be interested in the following communications from our valued and learned contributor, Professor Bosh, whose labours in the fields of Culinary and Botanical science, are so well known to all the world. The first three Articles richly merit to be added to the Domestic cookery of every family; those which follow, claim the attention of all Botanists, and we are happy to be able through Dr Bosh's kindness to present our readers with Illustrations of his discoveries. All the new flowers are found in the valley of Verrikwier, near the lake of Oddgrow, and on the summit of the hill Orfeltugg.

THREE RECEIPTS FOR DOMESTIC COOKERY

TO MAKE AN AMBLONGUS PIE

Take 4 pounds (say 4 1/2 pounds) of fresh Amblongusses, and put them in a small pipkin.

Cover them with water and boil them for 8 hours incessantly, after which add 2 pints of new milk, and proceed to boil for 4 hours more.

When you have ascertained that the Amblongusses are quite soft, take them out and place them in a wide pan, taking care to shake them well previously.

Grate some nutmeg over the surface, and cover them carefully with powdered gingerbread, curry-powder, and a sufficient quantity of Cayenne pepper.

Remove the pan into the next room, and place it on the floor. Bring it back again, and let it simmer for three-quarters of an hour. Shake the pan violently till all the Amblongusses have become of a pale purple colour.

Then, having prepared the paste, insert the whole carefully, adding at the same time a small pigeon, 2 slices of beef, 4 cauliflowers, and any number of oysters.

Watch patiently till the crust begins to rise, and add a pinch of salt from time to time.

Serve up in a clean dish, and throw the whole out of the window as fast as possible.

TO MAKE CRUMBOBBLIOUS CUTLETS

Procure some strips of beef, and having cut them into the smallest possible slices, proceed to cut them still smaller, eight or perhaps nine times.

When the whole is thus minced, brush it up hastily with a new clothes-brush, and stir round rapidly and capriciously with a salt-spoon or a soup-ladle.

Place the whole in a saucepan, and remove it to a sunny place, – say the roof of the house if free from sparrows or other birds, – and leave it there for about a week.

At the end of that time add a little lavender, some oil of almonds, and a few herring-bones; and then cover the whole with 4 gallons of clarified crumbobblious sauce, when it will be ready for use.

Cut it into the shape of ordinary cutlets, and serve up in a clean tablecloth or dinner-napkin.

TO MAKE GOSKY PATTIES

Take a Pig, three or four years of age, and tie him by the off-hind leg to a post. Place 5 pounds of currants, 3 of sugar, 2 pecks of peas, 18 roast chestnuts, a candle, and six bushels of turnips, within his reach; if he eats these, constantly provide him with more.

Then procure some cream, some slices of Cheshire cheese, four quires of foolscap paper, and a packet of black pins. Work the whole into a paste, and spread it out to dry on a sheet of clean brown waterproof linen.

When the paste is perfectly dry, but not before, proceed to beat the Pig violently, with the handle of a large broom. If he squeals, beat him again.

Visit the paste and beat the Pig alternately for some days, and ascertain if at the end of that period the whole is about to turn into Gosky Patties.

If it does not then, it never will; and in that case the Pig may be let loose, and the whole process may be considered as finished.

[Nonsense Botany – 1]

Baccopipia Gracilis   Bottlephorkia Spoonifolia

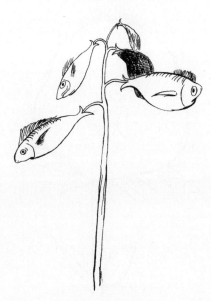

Cockatooca Superba   Fishia Marina

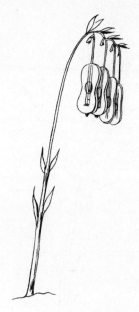

Guittara Pensilis

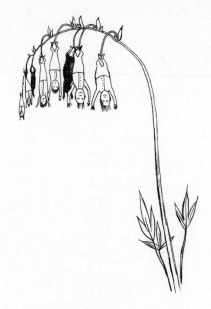

Manypeeplia Upsidownia

Phattfacia Stupenda

Piggiawiggia Pyramidalis

Plumbunnia Nutritiosa   Pollybirdia Singularis

The Jumblies

They went to sea in a Sieve, they did,
    In a Sieve they went to sea:
In spite of all their friends could say,
On a winter's morn, on a stormy day,
    In a Sieve they went to sea!
And when the Sieve turned round and round,

And every one cried, 'You'll all be drowned!'
They called aloud, 'Our Sieve ain't big,
But we don't care a button! we don't care a fig!
    In a Sieve we'll go to sea!'
        Far and few, far and few,
            Are the lands where the Jumblies live;
            Their heads are green, and their hands are blue,
                And they went to sea in a Sieve.

They sailed away in a Sieve, they did,
    In a Sieve they sailed so fast,
With only a beautiful pea-green veil
Tied with a riband by way of a sail,
    To a small tobacco-pipe mast;
And every one said, who saw them go,
'O won't they be soon upset, you know!
For the sky is dark, and the voyage is long,
And happen what may, it's extremely wrong
    In a Sieve to sail so fast!'
        Far and few, far and few,
            Are the lands where the Jumblies live;
            Their heads are green, and their hands are blue,
                And they went to sea in a Sieve.

The water it soon came in, it did,
    The water it soon came in;
So to keep them dry, they wrapped their feet
In a pinky paper all folded neat,
    And they fastened it down with a pin.
And they passed the night in a crockery-jar,
And each of them said, 'How wise we are!
Though the sky be dark, and the voyage be long,
Yet we never can think we were rash or wrong,
    While round in our Sieve we spin!'
        Far and few, far and few,
            Are the lands where the Jumblies live;
            Their heads are green, and their hands are blue,
                And they went to sea in a Sieve.

And all night long they sailed away;
  And when the sun went down,
They whistled and warbled a moony song
To the echoing sound of a coppery gong,
    In the shade of the mountains brown.
'O Timballo! How happy we are,
When we live in a sieve and a crockery-jar,
And all night long in the moonlight pale,   50
We sail away with a pea-green sail,
    In the shade of the mountains brown!'
        Far and few, far and few,
          Are the lands where the Jumblies live;
          Their heads are green, and their hands are blue,
          And they went to sea in a Sieve.

They sailed to the Western Sea, they did,
  To a land all covered with trees,
And they bought an Owl, and a useful Cart,
And a pound of Rice, and a Cranberry Tart,   60
    And a hive of silvery Bees.
And they bought a Pig, and some green Jack-daws,
And a lovely Monkey with lollipop paws,
And forty bottles of Ring-Bo-Ree,
    And no end of Stilton Cheese.
        Far and few, far and few,
          Are the lands where the Jumblies live;
          Their heads are green, and their hands are blue,
          And they went to sea in a Sieve.

And in twenty years they all came back,   70
  In twenty years or more,
And every one said, 'How tall they've grown!
For they've been to the Lakes, and the Torrible Zone,
    And the hills of the Chankly Bore!'
And they drank their health, and gave them a feast
Of dumplings made of beautiful yeast;
And every one said, 'If we only live,

We too will go to sea in a Sieve, –
   To the hills of the Chankly Bore!'
      Far and few, far and few,
         Are the lands where the Jumblies live;
      Their heads are green, and their hands are blue,
         And they went to sea in a Sieve.

80

'The Absolutely Abstemious Ass'

THIS
ALPHABET
was made for
DAISY and ARTHUR TERRY
at
LA CERTOSA DEL PESIO
by their
ADOPTY DUNCLE,

Edward Lear.
August 31. 1870

The Absolutely Abstemious Ass,
who resided in a Barrel, and only lived on
Soda Water and Pickled Cucumbers.

The Bountiful Beetle,
who always carried a Green Umbrella when it didn't rain,
and left it at home when it did.

The Comfortable Confidential Cow,
who sate in her Red Morocco Arm Chair and
toasted her own Bread at the parlour Fire.

The Dolomphious Duck,
who caught Spotted Frogs for her dinner
with a Runcible Spoon.

The Enthusiastic Elephant,
who ferried himself across the water with the
Kitchen Poker and a New pair of Ear-rings.

The Fizzgiggious Fish,
who always walked about upon Stilts
because he had no Legs.

The Goodnatured Grey Gull,
who carried the Old Owl, and his Crimson Carpet-bag
across the river, because he could not swim.

The Hasty Higgeldipiggledy Hen,
who went to market in a Blue Bonnet and Shawl,
and bought a Fish for her Supper.

The Inventive Indian,
who caught a Remarkable Rabbit in a
Stupendous Silver Spoon.

The Judicious Jubilant Jay,
who did up her Back Hair every morning with a Wreath of Roses,
Three Feathers, and a Gold Pin.

The Kicking Kangaroo,
who wore a Pale Pink Muslin Dress
with Blue Spots.

The Lively Learned Lobster,
who mended his own Clothes with
a Needle and Thread.

The Melodious Meritorious Mouse,
who played a Merry Minuet on the
Piano-forte.

The Nutritious Newt,
who purchased a Round Plum-pudding
for his Grand-daughter.

The Obsequious Ornamental Ostrich,
who wore Boots to keep his
Feet quite dry.

The Perpendicular Purple Polly,
who read the Newspaper and ate Parsnip Pie
with his Spectacles.

The Queer Querulous Quail,
who smoked a Pipe of Tobacco on the top of
a Tin Tea-kettle.

The Rural Runcible Raven,
who wore a White Wig and flew away
with the Carpet Broom.

The Scroobious Snake,
who always wore a Hat on his Head for
fear he should bite anybody.

The Tumultuous Tom-tommy Tortoise,
who beat a Drum all day long in the
middle of the Wilderness.

The Umbrageous Umbrella-maker,
whose Face nobody ever saw because it was
always covered by his Umbrella.

The Visibly Vicious Vulture,
who wrote some Verses to a Veal-cutlet in a
Volume bound in Vellum.

The Worrying Whizzing Wasp,
who stood on a Table, and played sweetly on a
Flute with a Morning Cap.

The Excellent Double-extra XX
imbibing King Xerxes, who lived a
long while ago.

The Yonghy-Bonghy-Bo,
whose Head was ever so much bigger than his
Body, and whose Hat was rather small.

The Zigzag Zealous Zebra,
who carried five Monkeys on his Back all
the way to Jellibolee.

'The Uncareful Cow, who walked about'

The Uncareful Cow, who walked about,
But took no care at all;
And so she bumped her silly head
Against a hard stone wall.
And when the Bump began to grow
Into a Horn, they said –
'There goes the Uncareful Cow, – who has
Three Horns upon her head!' –

And when the Bumpy Horn grew large,
'Uncareful Cow!' – they said –
'Here, take and hang this Camphor bottle
Upon your bumpy head! –
And with the Camphor rub the bump
Two hundred times a day.' –
And so she did – till bit by bit
She rubbed the Horn away.

10

[Creatures playing chequers]

The Nutcrackers and the Sugar-tongs

The Nutcrackers sate by a plate on the table,
   The Sugar-tongs sate by a plate at his side;
And the Nutcrackers said, 'Don't you wish we were able
   Along the blue hills and green meadows to ride?
Must we drag on this stupid existence for ever,
   So idle and weary, so full of remorse, –
While every one else takes his pleasure, and never
   Seems happy unless he is riding a horse?

'Don't you think we could ride without being instructed?
   Without any saddle, or bridle, or spur?
Our legs are so long, and so aptly constructed,
   I'm sure that an accident could not occur.
Let us all of a sudden hop down from the table,
   And hustle downstairs, and each jump on a horse!
Shall we try? Shall we go? Do you think we are able?'
   The Sugar-tongs answered distinctly, 'Of course!'

So down the long staircase they hopped in a minute,
   The Sugar-tongs snapped, and the Crackers said 'crack!'
The stable was open, the horses were in it;
   Each took out a pony, and jumped on his back.
The Cat in a fright scrambled out of the doorway,
   The Mice tumbled out of a bundle of hay,
The brown and white Rats, and the black ones from Norway,
   Screamed out, 'They are taking the horses away!'

The whole of the household was filled with amazement,
   The Cups and the Saucers danced madly about,
The Plates and the Dishes looked out of the casement,
   The Salt-cellar stood on his head with a shout,
The Spoons with a clatter looked out of the lattice,
   The Mustard-pot climbed up the Gooseberry Pies,   30
The Soup-ladle peeped through a heap of Veal Patties,
   And squeaked with a ladle-like scream of surprise.

The Frying-pan said, 'It's an awful delusion!'
   The Tea-kettle hissed and grew black in the face;
And they all rushed downstairs in the wildest confusion,
   To see the great Nutcracker–Sugar-tong race.
And out of the stable, with screamings and laughter,
   (Their ponies were cream-coloured, speckled with brown,)
The Nutcrackers first, and the Sugar-tongs after,
   Rode all round the yard, and then all round the town.   40

They rode through the street, and they rode by the station,
   They galloped away to the beautiful shore;
In silence they rode, and 'made no observation,'
   Save this: 'We will never go back any more!'
And still you might hear, till they rode out of hearing,
   The Sugar-tongs snap, and the Crackers say 'crack!'
Till far in the distance their forms disappearing,
   They faded away. – And they never came back!

Mr and Mrs Spikky Sparrow

On a little piece of wood,
Mr Spikky Sparrow stood;
Mrs Sparrow sate close by,
A-making of an insect pie,
For her little children five,
In the nest and all alive,
Singing with a cheerful smile
To amuse them all while,
    Twikky wikky wikky wee,
10   Wikky bikky twikky tee,
      Spikky bikky bee!

Mrs Spikky Sparrow said,
'Spikky, Darling! in my head
Many thoughts of trouble come,
Like to flies upon a plum!
All last night, among the trees,
I heard you cough, I heard you sneeze;
And, thought I, it's come to that
Because he does not wear a hat!
20   Chippy wippy sikky tee!
    Bikky wikky tikky mee!
      Spikky chippy wee!

'Not that you are growing old,
But the nights are growing cold.
No one stays out all night long
Without a hat: I'm sure it's wrong!'
Mr Spikky said, 'How kind,
Dear! you are, to speak your mind!
All your life I wish you luck!
You are! you are! a lovely duck!   30
    Witchy witchy witchy wee!
    Twitchy witchy witchy bee!
      Tikky tikky tee!

'I was also sad, and thinking,
When one day I saw you winking,
And I heard you sniffle-snuffle,
And I saw your feathers ruffle;
To myself I sadly said,
She's neuralgia in her head!
That dear head has nothing on it!   40
Ought she not to wear a bonnet?
    Witchy kitchy kitchy wee?
    Spikky wikky mikky bee?
      Chippy wippy chee?

'Let us both fly up to town!
There I'll buy you such a gown!
Which, completely in the fashion,
You shall tie a sky-blue sash on.
And a pair of slippers neat,
To fit your darling little feet,   50
So that you will look and feel
Quite galloobious and genteel!
    Jikky wikky bikky see,
    Chicky bikky wikky bee,
      Twicky witchy wee!'

So they both to London went,
Alighting on the Monument,
Whence they flew down swiftly – pop,
Into Moses' wholesale shop;
There they bought a hat and bonnet,
And a gown with spots upon it,
A satin sash of Cloxam blue,
And a pair of slippers too.
     Zikky wikky mikky bee,
     Witchy witchy mitchy kee,
        Sikky tikky wee!

Then when so completely drest,
Back they flew, and reached their nest.
Their children cried, 'O Ma and Pa!
How truly beautiful you are!'
Said they, 'We trust that cold or pain
We shall never feel again!
While, perched on tree, or house, or steeple,
We now shall look like other people.
     Witchy witchy witchy wee,
     Twikky mikky bikky bee,
        Zikky sikky tee!'

The Table and the Chair

Said the Table to the Chair,
'You can hardly be aware,
How I suffer from the heat,
And from chilblains on my feet!
If we took a little walk,
We might have a little talk!
Pray let us take the air!'
Said the Table to the Chair.

Said the Chair unto the Table,
'Now you *know* we are not able!   10
How foolishly you talk,
When you know we *cannot* walk!'
Said the Table, with a sigh,
'It can do no harm to try,
I've as many legs as you,
Why can't we walk on two?'

So they both went slowly down,
And walked about the town
With a cheerful bumpy sound,
As they toddled round and round.   20
And everybody cried,
As they hastened to their side,

'See! the Table and the Chair,
Have come out to take the air!'

But in going down an alley,
To a castle in the valley,
They completely lost their way,
And wandered all the day,
Till, to see them safely back,
They paid a Ducky-quack,
And a Beetle, and a Mouse,
Who took them to their house.

Then they whispered to each other,
'O delightful little brother!
What a lovely walk we've taken!
Let us dine on Beans and Bacon!'
So the Ducky, and the leetle
Browny-Mousy and the Beetle
Dined, and danced upon their heads
Till they toddled to their beds.

'A was once an apple-pie'

A

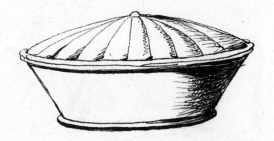

a

A was once an apple-pie,
  Pidy
  Widy
  Tidy
  Pidy
Nice insidy
Apple-Pie!

B

b

B was once a little bear,
  Beary
  Wary
  Hairy
  Beary
Taky cary
Little Bear!

C

C

C was once a little cake,
  Caky
  Baky
  Maky
  Caky
Taky caky
Little Cake!

D

d

D was once a little doll,
  Dolly
  Molly
  Polly
  Nolly
Nursy dolly
Little Doll!

E

e

E was once a little eel,
  Eely
  Weely
  Peely
  Eely
Twirly-tweely
Little Eel!

F

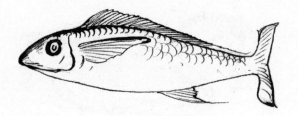

f

F was once a little fish,
  Fishy
  Wishy
  Squishy
  Fishy
In a dishy
Little Fish!

G

g

G was once a little goose,
  Goosy
  Moosy
  Boosey
  Goosey
Waddly-woosy
Little Goose!

H was once a little hen,
  Henny
  Chenny
  Tenny
  Henny
Eggsy-any
Little Hen?

I

i

I was once a bottle of ink,
   Inky
   Dinky
   Thinky
   Inky
Blacky minky
Bottle of Ink!

J was once a jar of jam,
   Jammy
   Mammy
   Clammy
   Jammy
Sweety-swammy
Jar of Jam!

K

k

K was once a little kite,
  Kity
  Whity
  Flighty
  Kity
Out of sighty
Little Kite!

L

l

L was once a little lark,
   Larky
   Marky
   Harky
   Larky
In the parky
Little Lark!

M

m

M was once a little mouse,
  Mousey
  Bousey
  Sousy
  Mousy
In the housy
Little Mouse!

N

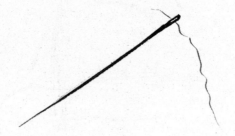

n

N was once a little needle,
 Needly
 Tweedly
 Threedly
 Needly
Wisky-wheedly
Little Needle!

O

O

O was once a little owl,
  Owly
  Prowly
  Howly
  Owly
Browny fowly
Little Owl!

P

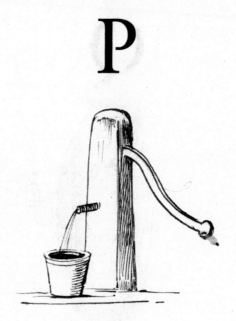

p

P was once a little pump,
   Pumpy
   Slumpy
   Flumpy
   Pumpy
Dumpy thumpy
Little Pump!

Q

q

Q was once a little quail,
　　Quaily
　　Faily
　　Daily
　　Quaily
Stumpy-taily
Little Quail!

R

r

R was once a little rose,
  Rosy
  Posy
  Nosy
  Rosy
Blows-y grows-y
Little Rose!

S

S

S was once a little shrimp,
  Shrimpy
  Nimpy
  Flimpy
  Shrimpy
Jumpy-jimpy
Little Shrimp!

T

t

T was once a little thrush,
    Thrushy
    Hushy
    Bushy
    Thrushy
Flitty-flushy
Little Thrush!

U

u

U was once a little urn,
  Urny
  Burny
  Turny
  Urny
Bubbly-burny
Little Urn!

V

V

V was once a little vine,
   Viny
   Winy
   Twiny
   Viny
Twisty-twiny
Little Vine!

W was once a whale,
  Whaly
  Scaly
  Shaly
  Whaly
Tumbly-taily
Mighty Whale!

X

X

X was once a great king Xerxes,
　Xerxy
　Perxy
　Turxy
　Xerxy
Linxy-lurxy
Great King Xerxes!

Y was once a little yew,
  Yewdy
  Fewdy
  Crudy
  Yewdy
Growdy grewdy
Little Yew!

Z

Z

Z was once a piece of zinc,
   Tinky
   Winky
   Blinky
   Tinky
Tinkly minky
Piece of Zinc!

'A was an Area Arch'

Papa he said, 'My little Boy!
   My little Boy so dear!
This Alphabet was made for you,
   By Mr Edward Lear.
And should you ever meet with him,
   This is his picture here.'
Papa he said, – 'This really does
   Resemble,

Edward Lear.'

A

A was an Area Arch,
Where washerwomen sat;
They made a lot of lovely starch
To starch Papa's cravat.

B

B was a Bottle Blue,
Which was not very small;
Papa he filled it full of beer,
And then he drank it all.

C

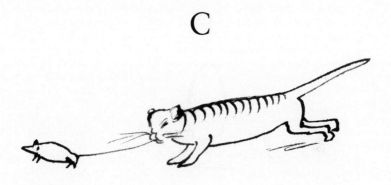

C was Papa's gray Cat,
Who caught a squeaky Mouse;
She pulled him by his twirly tail
All about the house.

D

D was Papa's white Duck,
Who had a curly tail;
One day it ate a great fat frog,
Besides a leetle snail.

E

E was a little Egg,
Upon the breakfast table;
Papa came in and ate it up
As fast as he was able.

F

F was a little Fish,
Cook in the river took it;
Papa said, 'Cook! Cook! bring a dish!
And Cook! be quick and cook it!'

G

G was Papa's new Gun,
He put it in a box;
And then he went and bought a bun,
And walked about the docks.

H

H was Papa's new Hat,
He wore it on his head;
Outside it was completely black,
But inside it was red.

I

I was an Inkstand new,
Papa he likes to use it;
He keeps it in his pocket now,
For fear that he should lose it.

J

J was some Apple Jam,
Of which Papa ate part,
But all the rest he took away,
And stuffed into a tart.

K

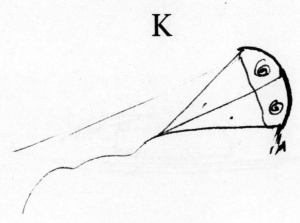

K was a great new Kite,
Papa he saw it fly
Above a thousand chimney pots,
And all about the sky.

L

L was a fine new Lamp,
But when the wick was lit,
Papa he said, 'This light ain't good!
I cannot read a bit!'

M

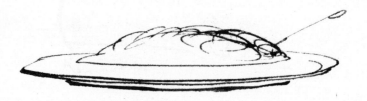

M was a dish of Mince,
It looked so good to eat!
Papa, he quickly ate it up,
And said, 'This is a treat!'

N

N was a Nut that grew
High up upon a tree;
Papa, who could not reach it, said,
'That's much too high for me!'

O

O was an Owl who flew
All in the dark away;
Papa said, 'What an owl you are!
Why don't you fly by day!'

P

P was a little Pig,
Went out to take a walk;
Papa he said, 'If Piggy dead,
He'd all turn into pork!'

Q

Q was a Quince that hung
Upon a garden tree;
Papa he brought it with him home,
And ate it with his tea.

R

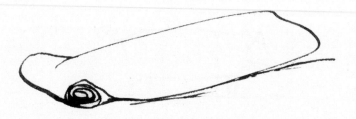

R was a Railway Rug,
Extremely large and warm;
Papa he wrapped it round his head
In a most dreadful storm.

S

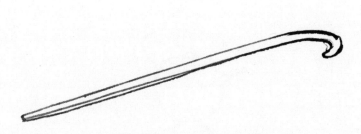

S was Papa's new Stick,
Papa's new thumping Stick,
To thump extremely wicked boys,
Because it was so thick.

T

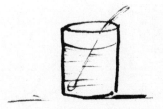

T was a Tumbler full
Of punch all hot and good;
Papa he drank it up, when in
The middle of a wood.

U

U was a silver Urn,
Full of hot scalding water;
Papa said, 'If that Urn were mine,
I'd give it to my daughter!'

V

V was a Villain; once
He stole a piece of beef;
Papa he said, 'O! dreadful man!
That Villain is a thief!'

W

W was a Watch of gold,
It told the time of day,
So that Papa knew when to come,
And when to go away.

X

X was King Xerxes, whom
Papa much wished to know;
But this he could not do, because
Xerxes died long ago.

Y

Y was a Youth, who kicked
And screamed and cried like mad;
Papa he said, 'Your conduct is
Abominably bad!'

Z

Z was a Zebra striped
And streaked with lines of black;
Papa said once, he thought he'd like
A ride upon his back.

[Mr Lear receives a letter from Marianne North]

Mr Lear refuses to pay for a Letter insufficiently stamped and sends it away.

Mr Lear remembers that the handwriting is Miss North's, and stamps with late remorse and rage.

Mr Lear executes a rapid Stampede to the Post Office.

Mr Lear delivers an extampary and affecting discourse to obtain the Letter.

Mr Lear stamps and dances for joy on securing Miss North's letter.

Mr and Mrs Discobbolos

Mr and Mrs Discobbolos
    Climbed to the top of a wall,
  And they sate to watch the sunset sky
  And to hear the Nupiter Piffkin cry
    And the Biscuit Buffalo call.
They took up a roll and some Camomile tea,
And both were as happy as happy could be –
    Till Mrs Discobbolos said –
    'Oh! W! X! Y! Z!
    It has just come into my head –   10
Suppose we should happen to fall!!!!!
        Darling Mr Discobbolos!

'Suppose we should fall down flumpetty
    Just like pieces of stone!
  On to the thorns, – or into the moat!
  What would become of your new green coat?
    And might you not break a bone?
It never occurred to me before –
That perhaps we shall never go down any more!'
    And Mrs Discobbolos said –   20
    'Oh! W! X! Y! Z!
    What put it into your head
To climb up this wall? – my own
        Darling Mr Discobbolos?'

Mr Discobbolos answered, –
    'At first it gave me pain, –
  And I felt my ears turn perfectly pink
  When your exclamation made me think
    We might never get down again!
But now I believe it is wiser far   30
To remain for ever just where we are.' –
    And Mr Discobbolos said,
    'Oh! W! X! Y! Z!

It is just come into my head –
– We shall never go down again –
Dearest Mrs Discobbolos!'

So Mr and Mrs Discobbolos
  Stood up, and began to sing,
 'Far away from hurry and strife
  Here we will pass the rest of life,
   Ding a dong, ding dong, ding!
We want no knives nor forks nor chairs,
No tables nor carpets nor household cares,
  From worry of life we've fled –
  Oh! W! X! Y! Z!
  There's no more trouble ahead,
Sorrow or any such thing –
For Mr and Mrs Discobbolos!'

40

The Courtship of the Yonghy-Bonghy-Bò

On the Coast of Coromandel
　　Where the early pumpkins blow,
　　　In the middle of the woods
　　Lived the Yonghy-Bonghy-Bò.
Two old chairs, and half a candle, –
One old jug without a handle, –
　　　These were all his worldly goods,
　　　In the middle of the woods,
　　　These were all the worldly goods,
　　　Of the Yonghy-Bonghy-Bò,
　　　Of the Yonghy-Bonghy-Bò.

Once, among the Bong-trees walking
　　Where the early pumpkins blow,
　　　To a little heap of stones
　　Came the Yonghy-Bonghy-Bò.
There he heard a Lady talking,
To some milk-white Hens of Dorking, –
　　　'Tis the Lady Jingly Jones!
　　　On that little heap of stones
　　　Sits the Lady Jingly Jones!'
Said the Yonghy-Bonghy-Bò,
Said the Yonghy-Bonghy-Bò.

'Lady Jingly! Lady Jingly!
    Sitting where the pumpkins blow,
        Will you come and be my wife?'
    Said the Yonghy-Bonghy-Bò.
'I am tired of living singly, –
On this coast so wild and shingly, –
    I'm a-weary of my life;
    If you'll come and be my wife,   30
        Quite serene would be my life!' –
    Said the Yonghy-Bonghy-Bò,
    Said the Yonghy-Bonghy-Bò.

'On this Coast of Coromandel,
    Shrimps and watercresses grow,
        Prawns are plentiful and cheap,'
    Said the Yonghy-Bonghy-Bò.
'You shall have my chairs and candle,
And my jug without a handle! –
        Gaze upon the rolling deep   40
        (Fish is plentiful and cheap;)
        As the sea, my love is deep!'
    Said the Yonghy-Bonghy-Bò,
    Said the Yonghy-Bonghy-Bò.

Lady Jingly answered sadly,
    And her tears began to flow, –
        'Your proposal comes too late,
    Mr Yonghy-Bonghy-Bò!
I would be your wife most gladly!'
(Here she twirled her fingers madly,)   50
        'But in England I've a mate!
        Yes! you've asked me far too late,
        For in England I've a mate,
    Mr Yonghy-Bonghy-Bò!
    Mr Yonghy-Bonghy-Bò!'

'Mr Jones – (his name is Handel, –
    Handel Jones, Esquire, & Co.)
        Dorking fowls delights to send,
    Mr Yonghy-Bonghy-Bò!
60 Keep, oh! keep your chairs and candle,
And your jug without a handle, –
        I can merely be your friend!
        – Should my Jones more Dorkings send,
        I will give you three, my friend!
    Mr Yonghy-Bonghy-Bò!
    Mr Yonghy-Bonghy-Bò!

'Though you've such a tiny body,
    And your head so large doth grow, –
        Though your hat may blow away,
70   Mr Yonghy-Bonghy-Bò!
Though you're such a Hoddy Doddy –
Yet I wished that I could modi-
        fy the words I needs must say!
        Will you please to go away?
        That is all I have to say –
    Mr Yonghy-Bonghy-Bò!
    Mr Yonghy-Bonghy-Bò!'

Down the slippery slopes of Myrtle,
    Where the early pumpkins blow,
80   To the calm and silent sea
    Fled the Yonghy-Bonghy-Bò.
There, beyond the Bay of Gurtle,
Lay a large and lively Turtle; –
        'You're the Cove,' he said, 'for me;
        On your back beyond the sea,
        Turtle, you shall carry me!'
    Said the Yonghy-Bonghy-Bò,
    Said the Yonghy-Bonghy-Bò.

Through the silent-roaring ocean
   Did the Turtle swiftly go;   90
      Holding fast upon his shell
   Rode the Yonghy-Bonghy-Bò.
With a sad primæval motion
Towards the sunset isles of Boshen
      Still the Turtle bore him well.
      Holding fast upon his shell,
      'Lady Jingly Jones, farewell!'
   Said the Yonghy-Bonghy-Bò,
   Said the Yonghy-Bonghy-Bò.

From the Coast of Coromandel,   100
   Did that Lady never go;
      On that heap of stones she mourns
   For the Yonghy-Bonghy-Bò.
On that Coast of Coromandel,
In his jug without a handle,
      Still she weeps, and daily moans;
      On that little heap of stones
      To her Dorking Hens she moans,
   For the Yonghy-Bonghy-Bò,
   For the Yonghy-Bonghy-Bò.   110

[Limericks published in *More Nonsense*]

There was a Young Person of Bantry,
Who frequently slept in the pantry;
When disturbed by the mice, she appeased them with rice
That judicious Young Person of Bantry.

There was an Old Man at a Junction,
Whose feelings were wrung with compunction;
When they said, 'The Train's gone!' he exclaimed 'How forlorn,'
But remained on the rails of the Junction.

There was an Old Man, who when little,
Fell casually into a kettle;
But, growing too stout, he could never get out,
So he passed all his life in that kettle.

There was an Old Man whose despair
Induced him to purchase a hare;
Whereon one fine day, he rode wholly away,
Which partly assuaged his despair.

There was an Old Person of Minety,
Who purchased five hundred and ninety
Large apples and pears, which he threw unawares,
At the heads of the people of Minety.

There was an Old Man of Thermopylæ,
Who never did anything properly;
But they said, 'If you choose to boil eggs in your shoes,
You shall never remain in Thermopylæ.'

There was an Old Person of Deal,
Who in walking used only his heel;
When they said, 'Tell us why?' – he made no reply;
That mysterious Old Person of Deal.

There was an Old Man on the Humber,
Who dined on a cake of Burnt Umber;
When he said, 'It's enough!' – they only said, 'Stuff!
You amazing Old Man on the Humber!'

There was an Old Man of Blackheath,
Whose head was adorned with a wreath
Of lobsters and spice, pickled onions and mice,
That uncommon Old Man of Blackheath.

There was an Old Man of Toulouse,
Who purchased a new pair of shoes;
When they asked, 'Are they pleasant?' he said, 'Not at present!'
That turbid Old Man of Toulouse.

There was an Old Person in black,
A Grasshopper jumped on his back;
When it chirped in his ear, he was smitten with fear,
That helpless Old Person in black.

There was an Old Man in a barge,
Whose nose was exceedingly large;
But in fishing by night, it supported a light,
Which helped that Old Man in a barge.

There was an Old Man of Dunrose,
A parrot seized hold of his nose;
When he grew melancholy, they said, 'His name's Polly,'
Which soothed that Old Man of Dunrose.

There was an Old Person of Bromley,
Whose ways were not cheerful or comely;
He sate in the dust, eating spiders and crust,
That unpleasing Old Person of Bromley.

There was an Old Man of Dunluce,
Who went out to sea on a goose;
When he'd gone out a mile, he observ'd with a smile,
'It is time to return to Dunluce.'

There was an Old Person of Pinner,
As thin as a lath, if not thinner;
They dressed him in white, and roll'd him up tight,
That elastic Old Person of Pinner.

There was an Old Man in a Marsh,
Whose manners were futile and harsh;
He sate on a log, and sang songs to a frog,
That instructive Old Man in a Marsh.

There was an Old Man of Dee-side,
Whose hat was exceedingly wide;
But he said, 'Do not fail, if it happened to hail,
To come under my hat at Dee-side!'

There was an Old Person of Bree,
Who frequented the depths of the sea;
She nurs'd the small fishes, and washed all the dishes,
And swam back again into Bree.

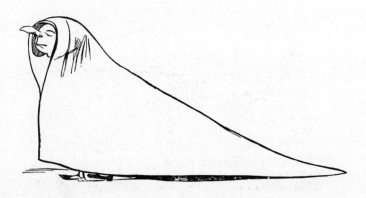

There was a Young Person in green,
Who seldom was fit to be seen;
She wore a long shawl, over bonnet and all,
Which envelloped that Person in green.

There was an Old Person of Wick,
Who said, 'Tick-a-Tick, Tick-a-Tick,
Chickabee, Chickabaw.' And he said, nothing more,
That laconic Old Person of Wick.

There was an Old Man at a Station,
Who made a promiscuous oration;
But they said, 'Take some snuff! – You have talk'd quite enough,
You afflicting Old Man at a Station!'

There was an Old Man of Three Bridges,
Whose mind was distracted by midges;
He sate on a wheel, eating underdone veal,
Which relieved that Old Man of Three Bridges.

There was an Old Person of Woking,
Whose mind was perverse and provoking;
He sate on a rail, with his head in a pail,
That illusive Old Person of Woking.

There was an Old Person of Fife,
Who was greatly disgusted with life;
They sang him a ballad, and fed him on salad,
Which cured that Old Person of Fife.

There was an Old Person of Shields,
Who frequented the vallies and fields;
All the mice and the cats, and the snakes and the rats,
Followed after that Person of Shields.

There was an Old Person of China,
Whose daughters were Jiska and Dinah,
Amelia and Fluffy, Olivia and Chuffy,
And all of them settled in China.

There was an Old Man of the Dargle,
Who purchased six barrels of Gargle;
For he said, 'I'll sit still, and will roll them downhill,
For the fish in the depths of the Dargle.'

There was an Old Man who screamed out
Whenever they knocked him about;
So they took off his boots, and fed him with fruits,
And continued to knock him about.

There was an Old Person of Brill,
Who purchased a shirt with a frill;
But they said, 'Don't you wish you mayn't look like a fish,
You obsequious Old Person of Brill?'

There was an Old Person of Slough,
Who danced at the end of a bough;
But they said, 'If you sneeze, you might damage the trees,
You imprudent Old Person of Slough.'

There was a Young Person in red,
Who carefully covered her head
With a bonnet of leather, and three lines of feather,
Besides some long ribands of red.

There was a Young Person in pink,
Who called out for something to drink;
But they said, 'O my daughter, there's nothing but water!'
Which vexed that Young Person in pink.

There was a Young Lady in white,
Who looked out at the depths of the night;
But the birds of the air, filled her heart with despair,
And oppressed that Young Lady in white.

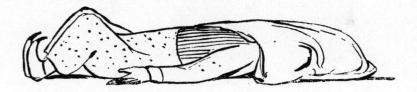

There was an Old Man of Hong Kong,
Who never did anything wrong;
He lay on his back, with his head in a sack,
That innocuous Old Man of Hong Kong.

There was an Old Person of Putney,
Whose food was roast spiders and chutney,
Which he took with his tea, within sight of the sea,
That romantic Old Person of Putney.

There was an Old Lady of France,
Who taught little ducklings to dance;
When she said, 'Tick-a-tack!' – they only said, 'Quack!'
Which grieved that Old Lady of France.

There was a Young Lady in blue,
Who said, 'Is it you? Is it you?'
When they said, 'Yes, it is,' – she replied only, 'Whizz!'
That ungracious Young Lady in blue.

There was an Old Man in a garden,
Who always begged everyone's pardon;
When they asked him, 'What for?' – he replied, 'You're a bore!
And I trust you'll go out of my garden.'

There was an Old Person of Loo,
Who said, 'What on earth shall I do?'
When they said, 'Go away!' – she continued to stay,
That vexatious Old Person of Loo.

There was an Old Person of Pisa,
Whose daughters did nothing to please her;
She dressed them in gray, and banged them all day,
Round the walls of the city of Pisa.

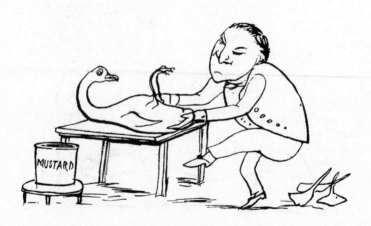

There was an Old Person of Florence,
Who held mutton chops in abhorrence;
He purchased a Bustard, and fried him in Mustard,
Which choked that Old Person of Florence.

There was an Old Person of Sheen,
Whose expression was calm and serene;
He sate in the water, and drank bottled porter,
That placid Old Person of Sheen.

There was an Old Person of Ware,
Who rode on the back of a bear;
When they ask'd, 'Does it trot?' – he said, 'Certainly not!
He's a Moppsikon Floppsikon Bear!'

There was an Old Person of Dean,
Who dined on one pea and one bean;
For he said, 'More than that would make me too fat,'
That cautious Old Person of Dean.

There was a Young Person of Janina,
Whose uncle was always a-fanning her;
When he fanned off her head, she smiled sweetly, and said,
'You propitious Old Person of Janina!'

There was an Old Person of Down,
Whose face was adorned with a frown;
When he opened the door, for one minute or more,
He alarmed all the people of Down.

There was an Old Person of Cassel,
Whose nose finished off in a tassel;
But they call'd out, 'Oh well! – don't it look like a bell!'
Which perplexed that Old Person of Cassel.

There was an Old Man of Cashmere,
Whose movements were scroobious and queer;
Being slender and tall, he looked over a wall,
And perceived two fat ducks of Cashmere.

There was an Old Person of Hove,
Who frequented the depths of a grove
Where he studied his books, with the wrens and the rooks,
That tranquil Old Person of Hove.

There was an Old Man of Spithead,
Who opened the window, and said, –
'Fil-jomble, fil-jumble, fil-rumble-come-tumble!'
That doubtful Old Man of Spithead.

There was an Old Man on the Border,
Who lived in the utmost disorder;
He danced with the cat, and made tea in his hat,
Which vexed all the folks on the Border.

There was an Old Person of Dundalk,
Who tried to teach fishes to walk;
When they tumbled down dead, he grew weary, and said,
'I had better go back to Dundalk!'

There was an Old Man of Dumbree,
Who taught little owls to drink tea;
For he said, 'To eat mice is not proper or nice',
That amiable Man of Dumbree.

There was an Old Person of Jodd,
Whose ways were perplexing and odd;
She purchased a whistle, and sate on a thistle,
And squeaked to the people of Jodd.

There was an Old Person of Shoreham,
Whose habits were marked by decorum;
He bought an Umbrella, and sate in the cellar,
Which pleased all the people of Shoreham.

There was an Old Man whose remorse,
Induced him to drink Caper Sauce;
For he said, 'If mixed up with some cold claret-cup,
It will certainly soothe your remorse!'

There was an Old Person of Wilts,
Who constantly walked upon stilts;
He wreathed them with lilies and daffy-down-dillies,
That elegant Person of Wilts.

There was an Old Person of Newry,
Whose manners were tinctured with fury;
He tore all the rugs, and broke all the jugs
Within twenty miles' distance of Newry.

There was an Old Person of Pett,
Who was partly consumed by regret;
He sate in a cart, and ate cold apple tart,
Which relieved that Old Person of Pett.

There was an Old Man of Port Grigor,
Whose actions were noted for vigour;
He stood on his head, till his waistcoat turned red,
That eclectic Old Man of Port Grigor.

There was an Old Person of Bar,
Who passed all her life in a jar,
Which she painted pea-green, to appear more serene,
That placid Old Person of Bar.

There was an Old Man of West Dumpet,
Who possessed a large nose like a trumpet;
When he blew it aloud, it astonished the crowd,
And was heard through the whole of West Dumpet.

There was an Old Person of Grange,
Whose manners were scroobious and strange;
He sailed to St Blubb, in a waterproof tub,
That aquatic Old Person of Grange.

There was an Old Person of Nice,
Whose associates were usually Geese;
They walked out together, in all sorts of weather,
That affable Person of Nice!

There was a Young Person of Kew,
Whose virtues and vices were few;
But with blameable haste, she devoured some hot paste,
Which destroyed that Young Person of Kew.

There was an Old Person of Sark,
Who made an unpleasant remark;
But they said, 'Don't you see what a brute you must be!
You obnoxious Old Person of Sark.'

There was an Old Person of Filey,
Of whom his acquaintance spoke highly;
He danced perfectly well, to the sound of a bell,
And delighted the people of Filey.

There was an Old Man of El Hums,
Who lived upon nothing but crumbs,
Which he picked off the ground, with the other birds round,
In the roads and the lanes of El Hums.

There was an Old Man of Dunblane,
Who greatly resembled a crane;
But they said, – 'Is it wrong, since your legs are so long,
To request you won't stay in Dunblane?'

There was an Old Person of Hyde,
Who walked by the shore with his bride,
Till a Crab who came near, fill'd their bosoms with fear,
And they said, 'Would we'd never left Hyde!'

There was an Old Man of Ancona,
Who found a small dog with no owner,
Which he took up and down all the streets of the town,
That anxious Old Man of Ancona.

There was an Old Person of Rimini,
Who said, 'Gracious! Goodness! O Gimini!'
When they said, 'Please be still!' she ran down a hill,
And was never more heard of at Rimini.

There was an Old Person of Cannes,
Who purchased three fowls and a fan;
Those she placed on a stool, and to make them feel cool
She constantly fanned them at Cannes.

There was an Old Person of Bude,
Whose deportment was vicious and crude;
He wore a large ruff, of pale straw-colored stuff,
Which perplexed all the people of Bude.

There was an Old Person of Ickley,
Who could not abide to ride quickly;
He rode to Karnak, on a tortoise's back,
That moony Old Person of Ickley.

There was an Old Person of Barnes,
Whose garments were covered with darns;
But they said, 'Without doubt, you will soon wear them out,
You luminous Person of Barnes!'

There was an Old Person of Blythe,
Who cut up his meat with a scythe;
When they said, 'Well! I never!' – he cried, 'Scythes for ever!'
That lively Old Person of Blythe.

There was an Old Person of Ealing,
Who was wholly devoid of good feeling;
He drove a small gig, with three Owls and a Pig,
Which distressed all the people of Ealing.

There was an Old Person of Bray,
Who sang through the whole of the day
To his ducks and his pigs, whom he fed upon figs,
That valuable Person of Bray.

There was an Old Person of Bow,
Whom nobody happened to know;
So they gave him some soap, and said, coldly, 'We hope
You will go back directly to Bow!'

There was an Old Person in gray,
Whose feelings were tinged with dismay;
She purchased two parrots, and fed them with carrots,
Which pleased that Old Person in gray.

There was an Old Person of Crowle,
Who lived in the nest of an owl;
When they screamed in the nest, he screamed out with the rest,
That depressing Old Person of Crowle.

There was an Old Person of Brigg,
Who purchased no end of a wig,
So that only his nose, and the end of his toes,
Could be seen when he walked about Brigg.

There was a Young Lady of Greenwich,
Whose garments were border'd with Spinach;
But a large spotty Calf, bit her shawl quite in half,
Which alarmed that Young Lady of Greenwich.

There was an Old Person of Rye,
Who went up to town on a fly;
But they said, 'If you cough, you are safe to fall off!
You abstemious Old Person of Rye!'

There was an Old Man of Messina,
Whose daughter was named Opsibeena;
She wore a small wig, and rode out on a pig,
To the perfect delight of Messina.

There was a Young Lady whose nose,
Continually prospers and grows;
When it grew out of sight, she exclaimed in a fright,
'Oh! Farewell to the end of my nose!'

There was an Old Person of Sestri,
Who sate himself down in the vestry;
When they said, 'You are wrong!' – he merely said, 'Bong!'
That repulsive Old Person of Sestri.

There was an Old Man in a tree,
Whose whiskers were lovely to see;
But the birds of the air pluck'd them perfectly bare,
To make themselves nests in that tree.

There was a Young Lady of Corsica,
Who purchased a little brown saucy-cur
Which she fed upon ham, and hot raspberry jam,
That expensive Young Lady of Corsica.

There was a Young Lady of Firle,
Whose hair was addicted to curl;
It curled up a tree, and all over the sea,
That expansive Young Lady of Firle.

There was an Old Lady of Winchelsea,
Who said, 'If you needle or pin shall see
On the floor of my room, sweep it up with the broom!' –
That exhaustive Old Lady of Winchelsea!

There was a Young Person whose history
Was always considered a mystery;
She sate in a ditch, although no one knew which,
And composed a small treatise on history.

There was an Old Man of Boulak,
Who sate on a Crocodile's back;
But they said, 'Tow'rds the night, he may probably bite,
Which might vex you, Old Man of Boulak!'

There was an Old Man of Ibreem,
Who suddenly threaten'd to scream;
But they said, 'If you do, we will thump you quite blue,
You disgusting Old Man of Ibreem!'

There was an Old Person of Stroud,
Who was horribly jammed in a crowd;
Some she slew with a kick, some she scrunched with a stick,
That impulsive Old Person of Stroud.

There was an Old Man of Thames Ditton,
Who called out for something to sit on;
But they brought him a hat, and said, 'Sit upon that,
You abruptious Old Man of Thames Ditton!'

There was an Old Person of Skye,
Who waltz'd with a Bluebottle fly;
They buzz'd a sweet tune, to the light of the moon,
And entranced all the people of Skye.

There was a Young Person of Ayr,
Whose head was remarkably square;
On the top, in fine weather, she wore a gold feather,
Which dazzled the people of Ayr.

[Extra limericks prepared for *More Nonsense*]

There was an Old Person of Brussels,
Who lived upon Brandy and Mussels;
When he rushed through the town, he knocked most people down,
Which distressed all the people of Brussels.

There was an Old Man of the hills,
Who lived upon Syrup of Squills;
Which he drank all night long, to the sound of a gong,
That persistent Old Man of the hills.

There was an Old Person of Twickenham,
Who whipped his four horses to quicken 'em;
When they stood on one leg, he said faintly, 'I beg
We may go back directly to Twickenham.'

There was an Old Person of Bradley,
Who sang all so loudly and sadly;
With a poker and tongs, he beat time to his songs,
That melodious Old Person of Bradley.

There was an Old Man of Carlisle,
Who was left in a desolate isle;
Where he fed upon cakes, and lived wholly with snakes,
Who danced with that Man of Carlisle.

There was an Old Person of Diss,
Who said, 'It is this! It is this!'
When they said, 'What? or which?' – he jumped into a ditch,
Which absorbed that Old Person of Diss.

There was an Old Person of Harrow,
Who bought a mahogany barrow;
For he said to his wife, 'You're the joy of my life!
And I'll wheel you all day in this barrow!'

There was an Old Person of Cheam,
Who said, 'It is just like a dream,
When I play on the drum, and wear rings on my thumb
In the beautiful meadows of Cheam!'

There was an Old Man of Girgenti,
Who lived in profusion and plenty;
He lay on two chairs, and ate thousands of pears,
That susceptible Man of Girgenti.

[Nonsense Botany – 2]

Barkia Howlaloudia

Enkoopia Chickabiddia

Jinglia Tinkettlia

Nasticreechia Krorluppia

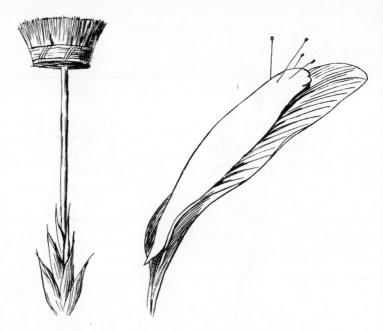

Arthbroomia Rigida   Sophtsluggia Glutinosa

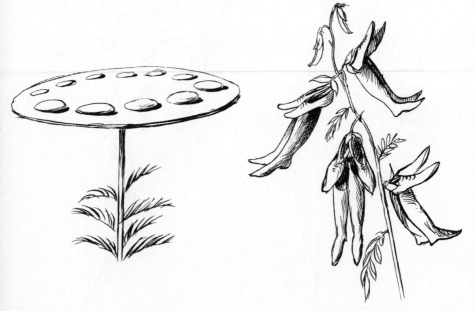

Minspysia Deliciosa   Shoebootia Utilis

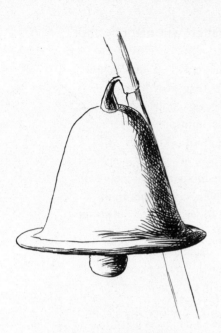

Stunnia Dinnerbellia

Tickia Orologica

Washtubbia Circularis

Tigerlillia Terribilis

'Cold are the crabs that crawl on yonder hill'

Cold are the crabs that crawl on yonder hill,
Colder the cucumbers that grow beneath
And colder still the brazen chops that wreath
The tedious gloom of philosophic pills!
For when the tardy film of nectar fills
The ample bowls of demons and of men,
There lurks the feeble mouse, the homely hen,
And there the Porcupine with all her quills.
Yet much remains; – to weave a solemn strain
That lingering sadly – slowly dies away,
Daily departing with departing day
A pea-green gamut on a distant plain.
Where wily walruses in congress meet –
Such such is life –
Where early buffaloes in congress meet
Than salt more salt, than sugar still more sweet,
And pearly centipedes adjust their feet
Where buffaloes bewail the loss of soap
Where frantic walruses in clouds elope,
And early pipkins bid adiew to hope.

The Scroobious Pip

The Scroobious Pip went out one day
When the grass was green, and the sky was gray,
Then all the beasts in the world came round
When the Scroobious Pip sate down on the ground.
The Cats and the Dog and the Kangaroo,
The Sheep and the Cow and the Guinea Pig too –
The Wolf he howled, the Horse he neighed,
The little Pig squeaked and the Donkey brayed,
And when the Lion began to roar
There never was heard such a noise before,   10
And every beast he stood on the tip
Of his toes to look at the Scroobious Pip.

At last they said to the Fox – 'By far
You're the wisest beast – you know you are!
Go close to the Scroobious Pip and say,
"Tell us all about yourself we pray! –
For as yet we can't make out in the least
If you're Fish or Insect, or Bird or Beast."'

The Scroobious Pip looked vaguely round
And sang these words with a rumbling sound –
    'Chippetty Flip – Flippetty Chip –
    My only name is the Scroobious Pip.'

The Scroobious Pip from the top of a tree
Saw the distant Jellybolee, –
And all the birds in the world came there,
Flying in crowds all through the air.
The Vulture and Eagle – the Cock and the Hen,
The Ostrich, the Turkey, the Snipe and Wren,
The Parrot chattered, the Blackbird sung,
And the Owl looked wise but held his tongue,
And when the Peacock began to scream,
The hullabaloo was quite extreme.
And every bird he fluttered the tip
Of his wing as he stared at the Scroobious Pip.

At last they said to the Owl, – 'By far
You're wisest Bird – you know you are!
Fly close to the Scroobious Pip and say,
"Explain all about yourself we pray! -
For as yet we have neither seen nor heard
If you're Fish or Insect, Beast or Bird!"'

The Scroobious Pip looked gaily round
And sang these words with a chirpy sound –
    'Flippetty chip – Chippetty flip –
    My only name is the Scroobious Pip.'

The Scroobious Pip went into the sea
By the beautiful shore of the Jellybolee –
All the Fish in the world swam round
With a splashy squashy spluttery sound,
The Sprat, the Herring, the Turbot too,
The Shark, the Sole, and the Mackerel blue,
The ——————— spluttered, the Porpoise puffed
———Flounder ———————————-

And when the Whale began to spout –

And every Fish he shook the tip
Of his tail as he gazed on the Scroobious Pip.

At last they said to the Whale – 'By far
You're the biggest Fish – you know you are!
Swim close to the Scroobious Pip and say,
"Tell us all about yourself we pray! –   60
For to know from yourself is our only wish –
Are you Beast or Insect, Bird or Fish?"'

The Scroobious Pip looked softly round
And sang these words with a liquid sound -
       'Plifatty flip – Pliffity flip –
       My only name is the Scroobious Pip.'

The Scroobious Pip sate under a tree
By the silent shores of the Jellybolee,
All the Insects in all the world
About the Scroobious Pip fluttered and twirled.   70
Beetles and ——— with purple eyes
Gnats and buzztilential Flies –
Grasshoppers, Butterflies, Spiders too,
Wasps and Bees and Dragonfly blue,
And when the Gnats began to hum
——— bounced like a dismal drum –
And every insect curled the tip
Of his snout, and looked at the Scroobious Pip.

At last they said the Ant, – 'By far
You're the wisest Insect – you know you are!   80
Creep close to the Scroobious Pip and say,
"Tell us all about yourself we pray! –
For we can't find out, and we can't tell why –
If you're Beast or Fish or a Bird or a Fly. –"'

The Scroobious Pip turned quickly round
And sang these words with a whistly sound –
    'Wizziby wip – wizziby wip –
    My only name is the Scroobious Pip.'

90   Then all the Beasts that walk on the ground
Danced in a circle round and round,
And all the Birds that fly in the air
Flew round and round in a circle there,
And all the Fish in the Jellybolēe
Swam in a circle about the sea,
And all the Insects that creep or go
Buzzed in a circle to and fro –
And they roared and sang and whistled and cried
Till the noise was heard from side to side –
100   'Chippetty Tip! Chippetty Tip!
    Its only name is the Scroobious Pip.'

The Quangle Wangle's Hat

On the top of the Crumpetty Tree
   The Quangle Wangle sat,
But his face you could not see,
   On account of his Beaver Hat.
For his Hat was a hundred and two feet wide,
With ribbons and bibbons on every side,
And bells, and buttons, and loops, and lace,
So that nobody ever could see the face
      Of the Quangle Wangle Quee.

The Quangle Wangle said   10
   To himself on the Crumpetty Tree, –
'Jam; and jelly; and bread;
   Are the best of food for me!
But the longer I live on this Crumpetty Tree,
The plainer than ever it seems to me
That very few people come this way
And that life on the whole is far from gay!'
      Said the Quangle Wangle Quee.

But there came to the Crumpetty Tree,
   Mr and Mrs Canary;   20
And they said, – 'Did ever you see

Any spot so charmingly airy?
May we build a nest on your lovely Hat?
Mr Quangle Wangle, grant us that!
O please let us come and build a nest
Of whatever material suits you best,
          Mr Quangle Wangle Quee!'

And besides, to the Crumpetty Tree
    Came the Stork, the Duck, and the Owl;
The Snail, and the Bumble-Bee,
    The Frog, and the Fimble Fowl;
(The Fimble Fowl, with a Corkscrew leg;)
And all of them said, – 'We humbly beg,
We may build our homes on your lovely Hat, –
Mr Quangle Wangle, grant us that!
          Mr Quangle Wangle Quee!'

And the Golden Grouse came there,
    And the Pobble who has no toes, –
And the small Olympian bear, –
    And the Dong with a luminous nose.
And the Blue Baboon, who played the flute, –
And the Orient Calf from the Land of Tute, –
And the Attery Squash, and the Bisky Bat, –
All came and built on the lovely Hat
          Of the Quangle Wangle Quee.

And the Quangle Wangle said
    To himself on the Crumpetty Tree, –
'When all these creatures move
    What a wonderful noise there'll be!'
And at night by the light of the Mulberry moon
They danced to the Flute of the Blue Baboon,
On the broad green leaves of the Crumpetty Tree,
And all were as happy as happy could be,
          With the Quangle Wangle Quee.

[Receipt for George Scrivens, Esq.]

[Received August 2 1872   From George Scrivens Esqre.   The sum of
Ten Pounds, for a drawing of the Seeders of Lebanon.   Edward Lear.]

'Papa once went to Greece'

Papa once went to Greece,
And there I understand
He saw no end of lovely spots
About that lovely land.
He talks about these spots of Greece
To both Mama and me
Yet spots of Greece upon my dress
He can't abear to see!
I cannot make it out at all –
If ever on my frock
They see the smallest spot of Greece
It gives them quite a shock!
Henceforth, therefore, – to please them both
These spots of Greece no more
Shall be upon my frock at all –
Nor on my Pinafore.

The Story of the Pobble, who has no toes, and the Princess Bink

The Pobble who has no toes,
    Had once as many as we; –
When they said – 'Some day you may lose them all!' –
    He replied – 'Phum, phiddle de dee!' –
And his Aunt Jobiska made him drink
Lavender-water, tinged with pink,
For she said, – 'The world in general knows
There's nothing so good for a Pobble's toes!'

The Pobble who has no toes
    Swam across the Bristol Channel,
But before he went he swaddled his nose
    In a piece of scarlet flannel,

For his Aunt Jobiska said, – 'No harm
Can come to his toes if his nose is warm;
And it's perfectly known that a Pobble's toes
Are safe – provided he minds his nose!'

The Pobble swam fast and well,
    And when boats or ships came near him,
He tinkelty-binkelty-winkl'd a bell,
    So that all the world could hear him.
And all the Sailors and Admirals cried
When they saw him land on the farther side, –
'He has gone to fish for his Aunt Jobiska's
Runcible cat with crimson whiskers!'   20

The Pobble went gaily on,
    To a rock on the edge of the water,
And there, – a-eating of crumbs and cream,
    Sat King Jampoodle's daughter.
Her cap was a root of Beetroot red,
With a hole cut out to insert her head;   30
Her gloves were yellow; her shoes were pink,
Her frock was green; and her name was Bink.

Said the Pobble, – 'Oh Princess Bink,
    A-eating of crumbs and cream!
Your beautiful face has filled my heart
    With the most profound esteem!
And my Aunt Jobiska says, Man's life
Ain't worth a penny without a wife,
Whereby it will give me the greatest pleasure
If you'll marry me now, or when you've leisure!'   40

Said the Princess Bink – 'O! Yes!
    I will certainly cross the Channel
And marry you then if you'll give me now
    That lovely scarlet flannel!
And besides that flannel about your nose
I trust you will give me all your toes,

To place in my Pa's Museum collection,
As proof of your deep genteel affection.'

The Pobble unwrapped his nose,
      And gave her the flannel so red,
Which, throwing her Beetroot cap away, –
      She wreathed around her head.
And one by one he unscrewed his toes
Which were made of the beautiful wood that grows
In his Aunt Jobiska's roorial park,
When the days are short and the nights are dark.

Said the Princess – 'O Pobble! my Pobble!
      I'm yours for ever and ever!
I never will leave you my Pobble! my Pobble!
      Never, and never, and never!'
Said the Pobble – 'My Binky! O bless your heart! –
But say – would you like at once to start
Without taking leave of your dumpetty Father?
Jampoodle the King?' – Said the Princess – 'Rather!'

They crossed the Channel at once
      And when boats and ships came near them
They winkelty-binkelty-tinkled their bell
      So that all the world could hear them.
And all the Sailors and Admirals cried
When they saw them swim to the farther side, –
'There are no more fish for his Aunt Jobiska's
Runcible Cat with crimson whiskers!'

They danced about all day,
      All over the hills and dales;
They danced in every village and town
      In the North and the South of Wales.
And their Aunt Jobiska made them a dish
Of Mice and Buttercups fried with fish
For she said, – 'The World in general knows,
Pobbles are happier without their toes!'

The Pobble who has no Toes

The Pobble who has no toes
  Had once as many as we;
When they said, 'Some day you may lose them all;' –
  He replied, –'Fish fiddle de-dee!'
And his Aunt Jobiska made him drink,
Lavender water tinged with pink,
For she said, 'The World in general knows
There's nothing so good for a Pobble's toes!'

The Pobble who has no toes,
  Swam across the Bristol Channel;   10
But before he set out he wrapped his nose,
  In a piece of scarlet flannel.
For his Aunt Jobiska said, 'No harm
Can come to his toes if his nose is warm;
And it's perfectly known that a Pobble's toes
Are safe, – provided he minds his nose.'

The Pobble swam fast and well,
  And when boats or ships came near him
He tinkledy-binkledy-winkled a bell,
  So that all the world could hear him.   20

And all the Sailors and Admirals cried,
When they saw him nearing the further side, –
'He has gone to fish for his Aunt Jobiska's
Runcible Cat with crimson whiskers!'

But before he touched the shore,
    The shore of the Bristol Channel,
A sea-green Porpoise carried away
    His wrapper of scarlet flannel.
And when he came to observe his feet,
Formerly garnished with toes so neat,
His face at once became forlorn
On perceiving that all his toes were gone!

And nobody ever knew
    From that dark day to the present,
Whoso had taken the Pobble's toes,
    In a manner so far from pleasant.
Whether the shrimps or crawfish gray,
Or crafty Mermaids stole them away –
Nobody knew; and nobody knows
How the Pobble was robbed of his twice five toes!

The Pobble who has no toes
    Was placed in a friendly Bark,
And they rowed him back, and carried him up,
    To his Aunt Jobiska's Park.
And she made him a feast at his earnest wish
Of eggs and buttercups fried with fish; –
And she said, – 'It's a fact the whole world knows,
That Pobbles are happier without their toes.'

The Akond of Swat

Who, or why, or which, or *what*, Is the Akond of SWAT?

Is he tall or short, or dark or fair?
Does he sit on a stool or a sofa or chair   or SQUAT,
                                    The Akond of Swat?

Is he wise or foolish, young or old?
Does he drink his soup and his coffee cold   or HOT,
                                    The Akond of Swat?

Does he sing or whistle, jabber or talk,
And when riding abroad does he gallop or walk   or TROT,
                                    The Akond of Swat?   10

Does he wear a turban, a fez, or a hat?
Does he sleep on a mattress, a bed, or a mat   or a COT,
                                    The Akond of Swat?

When he writes a copy in round-hand size,
Does he cross his T's and finish his I's   with a DOT,
                                    The Akond of Swat?

Can he write a letter concisely clear
Without a speck or a smudge or smear   or BLOT,
                                    The Akond of Swat?

Do his people like him extremely well?   20
Or do they, whenever they can, rebel   or PLOT,
                                  At the Akond of Swat?

If he catches them then, either old or young,
Does he have them chopped in pieces or hung   or SHOT,
                                    The Akond of Swat?

Do his people prig in the lanes or park?
Or even at times, when days are dark   GAROTTE,
                                  O the Akond of Swat!

Does he study the wants of his own dominion?
Or doesn't he care for public opinion   a JOT,   30
                                    The Akond of Swat?

To amuse his mind do his people show him
Pictures, or anyone's last new poem   or WHAT,
                                  For the Akond of Swat?

At night if he suddenly screams and wakes,
Do they bring him only a few small cakes   or a LOT,
                                For the Akond of Swat?

Does he live on turnips, tea, or tripe?
Does he like his shawl to be marked with a stripe or a DOT,
40   The Akond of Swat?

Does he like to lie on his back in a boat
Like the lady who lived in that isle remote,   SHALOTT,
                                The Akond of Swat?

Is he quiet, or always making a fuss?
Is his steward a Swiss or a Swede or a Russ   or a SCOT,
                                The Akond of Swat?

Does he like to sit by the calm blue wave?
Or to sleep and snore in a dark green cave   or a GROTT,
                                The Akond of Swat?

50 Does he drink small beer from a silver jug?
Or a bowl? or a glass? or a cup? or a mug?   or a POT,
                                The Akond of Swat?

Does he beat his wife with a gold-topped pipe,
When she lets the gooseberries grow too ripe   or ROT,
                                The Akond of Swat?

Does he wear a white tie when he dines with friends,
And tie it neat in a bow with ends   or a KNOT,
                                The Akond of Swat?

Does he like new cream, and hate mince-pies?
60 When he looks at the sun does he wink his eyes   or NOT,
                                The Akond of Swat?

Does he teach his subjects to roast and bake?
Does he sail about on an inland lake   in a YACHT,
                                The Akond of Swat?

Someone, or nobody, knows I wot
Who or which or why or what   Is the Akond of Swat!

'The Attalik Ghaz*ee*'

The Attalik Ghaz*ee*
Had a wife whose name was Jee
And a Lady proud was she,
While residing by the sea.

Said the Attalik Ghaz*ee*
(Who resided by the sea,)
'My own beloved Jee!
I am suffering from a flea
Which has settled on my knee.'

Said the Begum Lady Jee
(Who resided by the sea,)
'Why! What is that to me?
Do you think I'll catch a flea
That has settled on your knee?'

[Indian limericks]

There was an old man of Narkūnder,
Whose voice was like peals of loud thunder;
It shivered the hills into Colocynth Pills,
And destroyed half the trees of Narkūnder.

There lived a small puppy at Nārkunda,
Who sought for the best tree to bārk under;
Which he found, and said, 'Now, I can call out Bow wow
Underneath the best Cedar in Nārkundar.'

There was a small child at Narkūnda,
Who said, 'Don't you hear! That is thunder!'
But they said, 'It's the Bonzes, a-making responses,
In a temple eight miles from Narkūnda.'

There was an old man of Teōg,
Who purchased that Nārkunder dog,
Whom he fed on the hills, with those Colocynth pills,
Till he wholly ran off from Teōg.

There was an old man of Mahasso,
Who sang both as Tenor and Basso;
His voice was that high, it went into the sky,
And came down again quite to Mahasso.

There was an old person of Fágoo,
Who purchased a ship and its Cargo;
    When the Sails were all furled,
    He sailed all round the world,
And returned all promiscuous to Fágoo.

There was an old man in a Tonga,
Who said, 'If this ride lasts much longer, –
    Between shaking and dust,
    I shall probably bust,
And never ride more in a Tonga.'

'O! Chichester, my Carlingford!'

O! Chichester, my Carlingford!
O! Parkinson, my Sam!
O! SPQ, my Fortescue!
How awful glad I am!

For now you'll do no more hard work
Because by sudden=pleasing jerk
You're all at once a peer, –
Whereby I cry, 'God bless the Queen!
As was, and is, and still has been.'
Yours ever, Edward Lear.

The Cummerbund

An Indian Poem

She sate upon her Dobie,
　　To watch the Evening Star,
And all the Punkahs as they passed,
　　Cried, 'My! how fair you are!'
Around her bower, with quivering leaves,
　　The tall Kamsamahs grew,
And Kitmutgars in wild festoons
　　Hung down from Tchokis blue.

Below her home the river rolled
　　With soft meloobious sound,   10
Where golden-finned Chuprassies swam,
　　In myriads circling round.
Above, on tallest trees remote,
　　Green Ayahs perched alone,
And all night long the Mussak moan'd
　　Its melancholy tone.

And where the purple Nullahs threw
　　Their branches far and wide, –
The silvery Goreewallahs flew
　　In silence, side by side, –   20
The little Bheesties' twittering cry
　　Rose on the flagrant air,
And oft the angry Jampan howled
　　Deep in his hateful lair.

She sate upon her Dobie, –
　　She heard the Nimmak hum, –
When all at once a cry arose, –
　　'The Cummerbund is come!'
In vain she fled: – with open jaws
　　The angry monster followed,   30

And so, (before assistance came,)
    That Lady Fair was swollowed.

They sought in vain for even a bone
    Respectfully to bury, –
They said, – 'Hers was a dreadful fate!'
    (And Echo answered 'Very.')
They nailed her Dobie to the wall,
    Where last her form was seen,
And underneath they wrote these words,
    In yellow, blue, and green: –

'Beware, ye Fair! Ye Fair, beware!
    Nor sit out late at night, –
Lest horrid Cummerbunds should come,
    And swollow you outright.'

Letter to Lady Wyatt

Dear Lady Wyatt,

If I a*m int*errupting you please excuse me
as I *mint* to have asked you a question the other day
but forgot to *mint*=ion it. Can you tell me how to make
preserved or dry *mint*? I have got a
mint of
mint in my garden, but although I
a*m int*=erested in getting some of it dried for
pea-soup, I a*m in t*errible ignorance of how to dry it,
and a*m in t*orture till I know how. On cutting the
leaves, should they be *mint*'sd up small like   10
mint'sd meat? – or should I put
the*m int*o Gin & Tarragon vinegar? Or place them
in a jar of *Mint*on pottery, & expose them to the
ele*mint*s in a
her*mint*ically sealed bottle? If Mr Disraeli,
who is now Prime *mint*=stir, could teach us how to stir
the *mint*,
I a*m int*ernally convinced we could manage it.
This is as plain as that the *Mint*cio is a large River in Italy, or that
Lord *Mint*o was once Governor Genl. of India. Perhaps   20
at the rising of Palia*mint*, he may help us. After all would the
success be com*mint*surate with the trouble?
What com*mint* can be made on this except
that Mrs Wyatt should send To*m int*o the country if he is unwell in town?
One thing is sure, all ver*mint* must be carefully excluded
from the bottle, & I a*m int*ending to get one really well
made, for I a*m int*oxicated with the idea of getting good dry
mint. Please if you have a receipt, give it me
which will be a monu*mint* of your good nature.
*Mint*ime I   30
a*m in t*oo much haste to write any
more, so will leave off im*mint*iately.

Yours sincerely,
Edward Lear

Poona Observer, May 1875.

We are able to present our readers with an inaccurate misrepresenta-
tion of the well known Author & Artist Mr Edward Lear, who has late-
ly caused so much sensation in our city by having become a Fakeer. He
may be seen any day beneath the 18th Banyan tree on the wrong hand
as you descend the level road entering and leaving Poonah from
Peshawar and Madras. He is constantly attended by a tame crow & a
large dog of the Grumpsifactious species, & passes his days in placid
conkimplation of the surrounding scenery. –

The New Vestments

There lived an old man in the Kingdom of Tess,
Who invented a purely original dress;
And when it was perfectly made and complete,
He opened the door, and walked into the street.

By way of a hat, he'd a loaf of Brown Bread,
In the middle of which he inserted his head; –
His Shirt was made up of no end of dead Mice,
The warmth of whose skins was quite fluffy and nice; –
His Drawers were of Rabbit-skins; – so were his Shoes; –
His Stockings were skins, – but it is not known whose; –   10
His Waistcoat and Trowsers were made of Pork Chops; –
His Buttons were Jujubes, and Chocolate Drops; –
His Coat was all Pancakes with Jam for a border,
And a girdle of Biscuits to keep it in order;
And he wore over all, as a screen from bad weather,
A Cloak of green Cabbage-leaves stitched all together.

He had walked a short way, when he heard a great noise,
Of all sorts of Beasticles, Birdlings, and Boys; –
And from every long street and dark lane in the town
Beasts, Birdles, and Boys in a tumult rushed down.   20
Two Cows and a Calf ate his Cabbage-leaf Cloak; –
Four Apes seized his Girdle, which vanished like smoke; –
Three Kids ate up half of his Pancaky Coat, –
And the tails were devour'd by an ancient He Goat; –
An army of Dogs in a twinkling tore *up* his
Pork Waistcoat and Trowsers to give to their Puppies; –
And while they were growling, and mumbling the Chops,
Ten Boys prigged the Jujubes and Chocolate Drops. –
He tried to run back to his house, but in vain,
For Scores of fat Pigs came again and again; –   30
They rushed out of stables and hovels and doors, –
They tore off his stockings, his shoes, and his drawers; –

And now from the housetops with screechings descend,
Striped, spotted, white, black, and gray Cats without end,
They jumped on his shoulders and knocked off his hat, –
When Crows, Ducks, and Hens made a mincemeat of that; –
They speedily flew at this sleeves in a trice,
And utterly tore up his Shirt of dead Mice; –
They swallowed the last of his Shirt with a squall, –
Whereon he ran home with no clothes on at all.

And he said to himself as he bolted the door,
'I will not wear a similar dress any more,
Any more, any more, any more, never more!'

The Pelican Chorus

King and Queen of the Pelicans we;
No other Birds so grand we see!
None but we have feet like fins!
With lovely leathery throats and chins!
    Ploffskin, Pluffskin, Pelican jee!
    We think no Birds so happy as we!
    Plumpskin, Ploshkin, Pelican jill!
    We think so then, and we thought so still!

We live on the Nile. The Nile we love.
By night we sleep on the cliffs above;
By day we fish, and at eve we stand
On long bare islands of yellow sand.
And when the sun sinks slowly down
And the great rock walls grow dark and brown,
When the purple river rolls fast and dim
And the Ivory Ibis starlike skim,
Wing to wing we dance around, –
Stamping our feet with a flumpy sound, –
Opening our mouths as Pelicans ought,
And this is the song we nightly snort; –

Ploffskin, Pluffskin, Pelican jee!
We think no Birds so happy as we!
Plumpskin, Ploshkin, Pelican jill!
We think so then, and we thought so still!

Last year came out our Daughter, Dell;
And all the Birds received her well.
To do her honour, a feast we made
For every bird that can swim or wade.
Herons and Gulls, and Cormorants black,
Cranes, and Flamingos with scarlet back,   30
Plovers and Storks, and Geese in clouds,
Swans and Dilberry Ducks in crowds.
Thousands of Birds in wondrous flight!
They ate and drank and danced all night,
And echoing back from the rocks you heard
Multitude-echoes from Bird and Bird, –
    Ploffskin, Pluffskin, Pelican jee!
    We think no Birds so happy as we!
    Plumpskin, Ploshkin, Pelican jill!
    We think so then, and we thought so still!   40

Yes, they came; and among the rest,
The King of the Cranes all grandly dressed.
Such a lovely tail! Its feathers float
Between the ends of his blue dress-coat;
With pea-green trowsers all so neat,
And a delicate frill to hide his feet, –
(For though no one speaks of it, every one knows,
He has got no webs between his toes!)

As soon as he saw our Daughter Dell,
In violent love that Crane King fell, –   50
On seeing her waddling form so fair,
With a wreath of shrimps in her short white hair.
And before the end of the next long day,
Our Dell had given her heart away;

For the King of the Cranes had won that heart,
With a Crocodile's egg and a large fish-tart.
She vowed to marry the King of the Cranes,
Leaving the Nile for stranger plains;
And away they flew in a gathering crowd
Of endless birds in a lengthening cloud.
    Ploffskin, Pluffskin, Pelican jee!
    We think no Birds so happy as we!
    Plumpskin, Ploshkin, Pelican jill!
    We think so then, and we thought so still!

And far away in the twilight sky,
We heard them singing a lessening cry, –
Farther and farther till out of sight,
And we stood alone in the silent night!
Often since, in the nights of June,
We sit on the sand and watch the moon; –
She has gone to the great Gromboolian plain,
And we probably never shall meet again!
Oft, in the long still nights of June,
We sit on the rocks and watch the moon; –
– She dwells by the streams of the Chankly Bore,
And we probably never shall see her more.
    Ploffskin, Pluffskin, Pelican jee!
    We think no Birds so happy as we!
    Plumpskin, Ploshkin, Pelican jill!
    We think so then, and we thought so still!

The Two Old Bachelors

Two old Bachelors were living in one house;
One caught a Muffin, the other caught a Mouse.
Said he who caught the Muffin to him who caught the Mouse, –
'This happens just in time! For we've nothing in the house,
Save a tiny slice of lemon and a teaspoonful of honey,
And what to do for dinner – since we haven't any money?
And what can we expect if we haven't any dinner,
But to lose our teeth and eyelashes and keep on growing thinner?'

Said he who caught the Mouse to him who caught the Muffin, –
'We might cook this little Mouse, if we only had some Stuffin'!   10
If we had but Sage and Onion we could do extremely well,
But how to get that Stuffin' it is difficult to tell!' –

Those two old Bachelors ran quickly to the town
And asked for Sage and Onions as they wandered up and down;
They borrowed two large Onions, but no Sage was to be found
In the Shops, or in the Market, or in all the Gardens round.

But someone said, – 'A hill there is, a little to the north,
And to its purpledicular top a narrow way leads forth; –
And there among the rugged rocks abides an ancient Sage, –
An earnest Man, who reads all day a most perplexing page.   20

Climb up, and seize him by the toes! – all studious as he sits, –
And pull him down, – and chop him into endless little bits!
Then mix him with your Onion, (cut up likewise into Scraps,) –
When your Stuffin' will be ready – and very good: perhaps.'

Those two old Bachelors without loss of time
The nearly purpledicular crags at once began to climb;
And at the top, among the rocks, all seated in a nook,
They saw that Sage, a-reading of a most enormous book.

'You earnest Sage!' aloud they cried, 'your book you've read
    enough in! –
We wish to chop you into bits to mix you into Stuffin'!' –

But that old Sage looked calmly up, and with his awful book,
At those two Bachelors' bald heads a certain aim he took; –
And over crag and precipice they rolled promiscuous down, –
At once they rolled, and never stopped in lane or field or town, –
And when they reached their house, they found (beside their want
    of Stuffin')
The Mouse had fled; – and, previously, had eaten up the Muffin.

They left their home in silence by the once convivial door.
And from that hour those Bachelors were never heard of more.

[Nonsense Botany – 3]

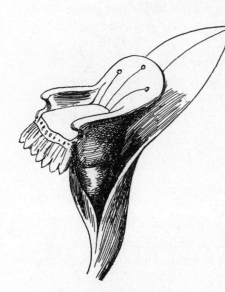

Armchairia Comfortabilis

Bassia Palealensis

Bubblia Blowpipia

Bluebottlia Buzztilentia

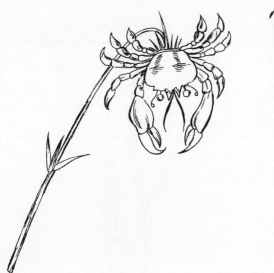

Crabbia Horrida

Smalltoothcombia Domestica

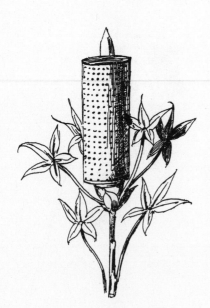

Knutmigrata Simplice

Tureenia Ladlecum

Puffia Leatherbéllowsa   Queeriflora Babyöides

'A tumbled down, and hurt his Arm, against a bit of wood'

A tumbled down, and hurt his Arm, against a bit of wood.

B said, 'My Boy, O! do not cry; it cannot do you good!'

C said, 'A Cup of Coffee hot can't do you any harm.'

D said, 'A Doctor should be fetched, and he would cure the arm.'

E said, 'An Egg beat up with milk would quickly make him well.'

F said, 'A Fish, if broiled, might cure, if only by the smell.'

G said, 'Green Gooseberry fool, the best of cures I hold.'

H said, 'His Hat should be kept on, to keep him from the cold.'

I said, 'Some Ice upon his head will make him better soon.'

J said, 'Some Jam, if spread on bread, or given in a spoon!'

K said, 'A Kangaroo is here, – this picture let him see.'

L said, 'A Lamp pray keep alight, to make some barley tea.'

M said, 'A Mulberry or two might give him satisfaction.'

N said, 'Some Nuts, if rolled about, might be a slight attraction.'

O said, 'An Owl might make him laugh, if only it would wink.'

P said, 'Some Poetry might be read aloud, to make him think.'

Q said, 'A Quince I recommend, – a Quince, or else a Quail.'

R said, 'Some Rats might make him move, if fastened by their tail.'

S said, 'A Song should now be sung, in hopes to make him laugh!'

T said, 'A Turnip might avail, if sliced or cut in half!'

U said, 'An Urn, with water hot, place underneath his chin!'

V said, 'I'll stand upon a chair, and play a Violin!'

W said, 'Some Whisky-Whizzgigs fetch, some marbles and a ball!'

X said, 'Some double XX ale would be the best of all!'

Y said, 'Some Yeast mixed up with salt would make a perfect plaster!'

Z said, 'Here is a box of Zinc! Get in, my little master!
We'll shut you up! We'll nail you down! We will, my little master!
We think we've all heard quite enough of this your sad disaster!'

The Dong with a Luminous Nose

When awful darkness and silence reign
  Over the great Gromboolian plain,
    Through the long, long wintry nights; –
When the angry breakers roar
As they beat on the rocky shore; –
    When Storm-clouds brood on the towering heights
Of the Hills of the Chankly Bore: –

Then, through the vast and gloomy dark,
There moves what seems a fiery spark,
    A lonely spark with silvery rays
    Piercing the coal-black night, –
    A Meteor strange and bright: –
Hither and thither the vision strays,
    A single lurid light.

Slowly it wanders, – pauses, – creeps, –
Anon it sparkles, – flashes and leaps;
And ever as onward it gleaming goes
A light on the Bong-tree stems it throws.
And those who watch at that midnight hour
From Hall or Terrace, or lofty Tower,

10

20

Cry, as the wild light passes along, –
    'The Dong! – the Dong!
      The wandering Dong through the forest goes!
      The Dong! the Dong!
      The Dong with a luminous Nose!'

    Long years ago
    The Dong was happy and gay,
Till he fell in love with a Jumbly Girl
    Who came to those shores one day.
For the Jumblies came in a sieve, they did, –   30
Landing at eve near the Zemmery Fidd
    Where the Oblong Oysters grow,
    And the rocks are smooth and gray.
And all the woods and the valleys rang
With the Chorus they daily and nightly sang, –
    'Far and few, far and few,
    Are the lands where the Jumblies live;
    Their heads are green, and their hands are blue,
    And they went to sea in a sieve.'

Happily, happily passed those days!   40
    While the cheerful Jumblies staid;
    They danced in circlets all night long,
    To the plaintive pipe of the lively Dong,
    In moonlight, shine, or shade.
For day and night he was always there
By the side of the Jumbly Girl so fair,
With her sky-blue hands, and her sea-green hair.
Till the morning came of that hateful day
When the Jumblies sailed in their sieve away,
And the Dong was left on the cruel shore   50
Gazing – gazing for evermore, –
Ever keeping his weary eyes on
That pea-green sail on the far horizon, –
Singing the Jumbly Chorus still
As he sate all day on the grassy hill, –

'Far and few, far and few,
Are the lands where the Jumblies live;
Their heads are green, and their hands are blue,
And they went to sea in a sieve.'

60   But when the sun was low in the West,
          The Dong arose and said; –
          – 'What little sense I once possessed
          Has quite gone out of my head!' –
And since that day he wanders still
By lake and forest, marsh and hill,
Singing – 'O somewhere, in valley or plain
Might I find my Jumbly Girl again!
For ever I'll seek by lake and shore
Till I find my Jumbly Girl once more!'

70   Playing a pipe with silvery squeaks,
               Since then his Jumbly Girl he seeks,
               And because by night he could not see,
               He gathered the bark of the Twangum Tree
                    On the flowery plain that grows.
                    And he wove him a wondrous Nose, –
               A Nose as strange as a Nose could be!
Of vast proportions and painted red,
And tied with cords to the back of his head.
               – In a hollow rounded space it ended
80   With a luminous Lamp within suspended,
                    All fenced about
                    With a bandage stout
                    To prevent the wind from blowing it out; –
               And with holes all round to send the light,
               In gleaming rays on the dismal light.

And now each night, and all night long,
Over those plains still roams the Dong;
And above the wail of the Chimp and Snipe
You may hear the squeak of his plaintive pipe

While ever he seeks, but seeks in vain   90
To meet with his Jumbly Girl again;
Lonely and wild – all night he goes, –
The Dong with a luminous Nose!
And all who watch at the midnight hour,
From Hall or Terrace, or lofty Tower,
Cry, as they trace the Meteor bright,
Moving along through the dreary night, –
      'This is the hour when forth he goes,
      The Dong with a luminous Nose!
      Yonder – over the plain he goes;   100
          He goes!
          He goes;
      The Dong with a luminous Nose!'

'Finale Marina! If ever you'd seen her!'

Finale Marina! If ever you'd seen her!
Your heart had been quickly enslaved.
Her eyes were pea-green, and her bonnet was greener,
And wonderful fine she behaved!

In medio Tutorissimus ibis
'Thou shalt walk in the midst of thy Tutors'

Once on a time a youthful cove
  As was a cheery lad
Lived in a Willa by the sea. –
  The cove was not so bad;

The dogs and cats, the cow and ass,
  The birds in cage or grove,
The rabbits, hens, ducks, pony – pigs
  All loved that cheery cove.

Some folk, – one female and six male, –
   Seized on that youthful cove;
They said, – 'To edjukate this chap
   Us seven it doth behove.'

The first his parient was, – who taught
   The cove to read and ride,
Latin, and Grammarithmetic,
   And lots of things beside.

Says Pa, 'I'll spare no pains or time
   Your school hours so to cut,
And square and fit, that you will make
   No end of progress – *but* –'

Says Mrs Grey, – 'I'll teach him French,
   Pour parler dans cette pays, –
Je crois qui'il parlerà bien;
   Même comme un Français – *mais*, –'

Says Signor Gambinossi, – 'Si;
   Progresso si farà,
Lo voglio insegnare qui,
   La Lingua mia – *ma* –'

Says Mr Crump, – 'Geology,
   And Matthewmatics stiff,
I'll teach the cove, who's sure to go
   Ahead like blazes, – *if* –'

Says James, – 'I'll teach him every day
   My Nastics; – now and then
To stand upon his 'ed; and make
   His mussels harder, – *when* –'

Says Signor Blanchi, ' – Lascia far; –
  La musica da me,
Ben insegnata gli sarà; –
  Farà progresso, – *se* –'   40

Says Edward Lear, – 'I'll make him draw
  A Palace, or a hut,
Trees, mountains, rivers, cities, plains,
  And prapps to paint them, – *but* – '

So all these seven joined hands and sang
  This chorus by the sea; –
'O! Ven his edjukation's done,
  Vy! Vot a cove he'll be!'

'O dear! how disgusting is life!'

O dear! how disgusting is life!
To improve it O what can we do?
Most disgusting is hustle and strife,
And of all things an ill fitting shoe –
  Shoe
    O bother an ill fitting shoe!

'How pleasant to know Mr Lear!'

From a Photograph.

'How pleasant to know Mr Lear!'
    Who has written such volumes of stuff!
Some think him ill-tempered and queer,
    But a few think him pleasant enough.

His mind is concrete and fastidious; –
    His nose is remarkably big; –
His visage is more or less hideous; –
    His beard it resembles a wig.

He has ears, and two eyes, and ten fingers, –
    (Leastways if you reckon two thumbs;)
Long ago he was one of the singers,
    But now he is one of the dumms.

He sits in a beautiful parlour,
    With hundreds of books on the wall;
He drinks a great deal of Marsala,
    But never gets tipsy at all.

10

He has many friends, laymen and clerical;
   Old Foss is the name of his cat;
His body is perfectly spherical; –
   He weareth a runcible hat.   20

When he walks in a waterproof white
   The children run after him *so*!
Calling out, – 'He's come out in his night-
   gown, that crazy old Englishman, – O!'

He weeps by the side of the ocean,
   He weeps on the top of the hill;
He purchases pancakes and lotion,
   And chocolate shrimps from the mill.

He reads, but he cannot speak, Spanish;
   He cannot abide ginger-beer. –   30
Ere the days of his pilgrimage vanish, –
   'How pleasant to know Mr Lear!'

Mr and Mrs Discobbolos
Second Part

Mr and Mrs Discobbolos
    Lived on the top of the wall,
    For twenty years, a month and a day,
    Till their hair had grown all pearly gray,
    And their teeth began to fall.
They never were ill, or at all dejected, –
By all admired, and by some respected,
    Till Mrs Discobbolos said,
    'O W! X! Y! Z!
    It is just come into my head –
    We have no more room at all –
        Darling Mr Discobbolos!

'Look at our six fine boys!
    And our six sweet girls so fair!
    Up on this wall they have all been born,
    And not one of the twelve has happened to fall,
    Through my maternal care!
Surely they should not pass their lives
Without any chance of husbands or wives!'
    And Mrs Discobbolos said,
    'O W! X! Y! Z!
    Did it never come into your head
    That our lives must be lived elsewhere,
        Dearest Mr Discobbolos?

'They have never been at a Ball,
    Nor have even seen a Bazaar!
    Nor have heard folks say in a tone all hearty, –
    "What loves of girls (at a garden party)
    Those Misses Discobbolos are!"
Morning and night it drives me wild
To think of the fate of each darling child, – ! –'
    But Mr Discobbolos said,

'O – W! X! Y! Z!
What has come into your fiddledum head!
What a runcible goose you are!
        Octopod Mrs Discobbolos!'

Suddenly Mr Discobbolos
    Slid from the top of the wall;
And beneath it he dug a dreadful trench, –
And filled it with Dynamite gunpowder gench, –   40
    And aloud began to call, –
'Let the wild bee sing and the blue bird hum!
For the end of our lives has certainly come!'
    And Mrs Discobbolos said,
      'O! W! X! Y! Z!
    We shall presently all be dead,
On this ancient runcible wall, –
        Terrible Mr Discobbolos!'

Pensively, Mr Discobbolos
    Sate with his back to the wall; –   50
He lighted a match, and fired the train, –
    And the mortified mountains echoed again
    To the sounds of an awful fall!
And all the Discobbolos family flew
 In thousands of bits to the sky so blue,
    And no one was left to have said,
      'O! W! X! Y! Z!
    Has it come into anyone's head
That the end has happened to all
        Of the whole of the Clan Discobbolos?' 60

'O Brother Chicken! Sister Chick!'

O Brother Chicken! Sister Chick!
    O gracious me! O my!
This broken Eggshell was my home!
    I see it with my eye!
However did I get inside? Or how did I get out?
And must my life be evermore, an atmosphere of doubt?

Can no one tell? Can no one solve, this mystery of Eggs?
Or why we chirp and flap our wings, – or why we've all two legs?
And since we cannot understand, –
    May it not seem to me,
That we were merely born by chance,
    Egg-nostics for to be?

'Dear Sir, Though many checks prevent'

Dear Sir, Though many checks prevent
More tours in Isle or Continent,
(Checks once I minded not a pin, –
Advancing years, or want of tin, –)
Yet of all checks the best is found,
A Cheque for Five and Thirty Pound.

So for such cheque upon your *Bank, you*
Sent me just now, I beg to *thank you*;
(Besides your letter – and for *this 'tis in*
εγὼ προσφέρω εὐχαρίστησιν.–
And so I sign me – your sincere
Obliged admirer, *Edward Lear.*

(As for the Picture, that will *quick and soon*
Be sent to Messrs Foord and *Dickenson.*)

Remminissenciz of Orgust 14 Aitnundrednaity

There was a great Person of Stratton,
Who fell fast asleep with his Hat=on.
    He slept for one hour,
    And awoke with more power
To leave Micheldéver for Stratton.

'I am awfull aged in apierance lately
and am exactly like this.'

There was an old man with a ribbon,
Who found a large volume of Gibbon,
Which he tied to his nose –
And said – 'I suppose
This is quite the best use for my ribbon.'

Letter to Mrs Stuart Wortley [The Moon Journey]

My dear Mrs Stuart Wortley,

In the first place observe the Envellope, for the appearance of which an oppology is kneaded, the fact being that there was only this one in the house large enough, & so, though it was originally addressed to the Hon. J. Warren, I altered it to what it now is. Secondly, I thought it so kind of you to have purchased the Mte Generoso drawing, that I wanted you to have 2 scraps to remind you of 'Simla', and 'Ravenna forest'. Which two I enclose, hoping you may think them worth a corner in some Album. I also send 2 still smaller, – one for each of the young Ladies.

These are of singular – I may say bingular value, – as they were done in the Moon, to which I lately went one night, returning next morning on a Moonbeam. As the Signorine Blanche & Katherine appreciate nonsense, I will add some few notes concerning the 2 subjects which I got with great rapidity during my visit, nothing being easier in that wonderful country than to travel thousands of miles in a minute. And these journeys are all done by means of Moonbeams, which, far from being mere portions of light, are in reality living creatures, endowed with considerable sogassity, & a long nose like the truck of a Nelliphant, though this is quite imperceptible to the naked eye. You have only to whisper to the Moonbeam what you wish to see, & you are there in a moment, & its nose or trunk being placed round your body, you cannot by any possibility fall.

The first view it is of the Jizzdoddle rocks, with 2 of the many remarkable planets which surround the moon rising or riz in the distance; these orange-coloured & peagreen orbs leaving a profound impression of sensational surprise on the mind of the speckletator who first beholds them. The second view represents the Rumbytumby ravine, with the crimson planet Buzz and its 5 Satanites on the horizon. In the foreground on the left is a Blompopp tree, so called from the Blompopp, a gigantic and gorgeous bird which builds on its summit. To the left are the tall Vizzikilly trees, the most common vegetation of the
10 Lunar hummysphere. These trees grow to an immense height, & bloom only once in 15 years, when they produce a large crop of immemorial soapbubbles, submarine sucking-pigs, songs of sunrise, & silver sixpences, – which last are ground into powder by the Lunar population, & drunk in warm water without any sugar.

So little is known of the inhabitants of the moon, that a few descriptive but accurate notices relating to them may be interesting. They do not in the least resemble the people of our world, – as for instance they are all much broader than they are high; they have no hair on their heads, – but on the contrary a beautiful crest of yellow feathers which
20 they can raise or depress at will, like that of the ordinary Cockatoo. And from the tip of their nose depends an elegant and affecting bunch of hair, sometimes extending to as much as 20 miles in length, and as it is considered sacrilegious to cut it, it is gradually wound round a silvergilt post firmly placed in the ground, but removable at pleasure. The faces of the more educated classes have a pensively perverse and placid expression, – not unlike the countenance of an Oyster, while frequently a delicately doubleminded semi-visual obliquity adds a pathos to their pungent physiognomy.

These remarkable people, so unlike ourselves, pass 18 months of
30 their year (which consists of 22) in the strictest seclusion, – suspended with their heads downwards, and held carefully in crimson silk bags, – which are severely & suddenly shaken from time to time by select servants. Thus, – exempt from the futile & fluctuating fatuity of fashion, these estimable creatures pass an indigenous life of indefinite duration surrounded by their admiring ancestors, & despised by their incipient posterity. Their servants are not natives of the Moon, but are brought at great expense from a negative although nutritious star at a remote distance, and are wholly of a different species from the Lunar popula-

tion, having 8 arms & 8 legs each, but no head whatever; – only a chin in the middle of which are their eyes, – their mouths, (of which each individual possesses 8,) being one in each little toe, & with these they discourse with an overpowering volubility & an indiscriminating alacrity surprising to contemplate. The conduct of these singular domestics is usually virtuous & voluminous, & their general aspic highly mucilaginous & meritorious.

I have no time at present to dilate further on other particulars of Lunar Natural History; – the prevalence of 2 sorts of gales, gales of wind and nightingales; – the general inebriety of the Atmosphere; – or   10
the devotional functions of the inhabitants, consisting chiefly in the immense consumption of Ambleboff pies.

Hoping that I may see you & the 2 two young ladies on Wednesday,
    Believe me,
        Yours sincerely,
          Edward Lear.

[Chichester Fortescue is appointed Lord Privy Seal]

A curious circumstance and one worthy of note must also be recorded, because a similar fact is not found in the ceremonies of any other Royal Court whatsoever.

Before the guests go to their rooms, – after the Queen has left the Gallery, – the President of the Privy Council is seen entering, followed by 10 servants in livery, not however as President, but as Guardian of the Great Seal, – a post of the greatest importance and significance, and only given to the most trustworthy, learned, clever, and amiable gentlemen of the Court.

By the side of the Lord Guardian, and held by him by means of a chain, the Seal – which has no feet – makes its progress all through the Gallery, and is so to speak, taken to make the acquaintance of all the guests. One cannot well describe the motion of this enormous animal, as Italian is lacking in words that adequately translate 'Wallop' or 'Flump', verbs that well suit its motion, but that are unknown to us Italians. Many ladies are a good deal frightened the first time that they see the Great Seal, but they are strictly forbidden to scream. When it has been all round the Gallery, this amiable beast withdraws again with a Wallop-flump, with the Lord Guardian; – and before retiring, the latter gives the Seal more that 37 pounds of macaroni, 18 bottles of Champagne, 2 beefsteaks, and a ball of scarlet worsted – all of which are brought by 10 servants in livery.

[Nonsense Trees]

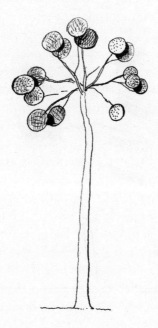

The Biscuit Tree

This remarkable vegetable production has never yet been described or delineated. As it never grows near rivers, nor near the sea, nor near mountains, or vallies, or houses, – its native place is wholly uncertain. When the flowers fall off, and the tree breaks out in biscuits, the effect is by no means disagreeable, especially to the hungry. – If the Biscuits grow in pairs, they do not grow single, and if they ever fall off, they cannot be said to remain on. –

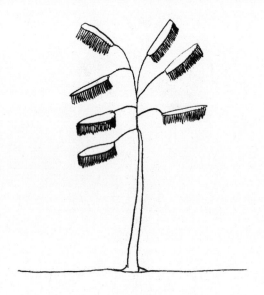

The Clothes-Brush Tree

This most useful natural production does not produce many clothes-brushes, which accounts for those objects being expensive. The omsquombious nature of this extraordinary vegetable it is of course unnecessary to be diffuse upon.

The Fork Tree

This pleasing and amazing Tree never grows above four hundred and sixty-three feet in height, – nor has any specimen hitherto produced above forty thousand silver forks at one time. If violently shaken it is most probable that many forks would fall off, – and in a high wind it is highly possible that all the forks would rattle dreadfully, and produce a musical tinkling to the ears of the happy beholder.

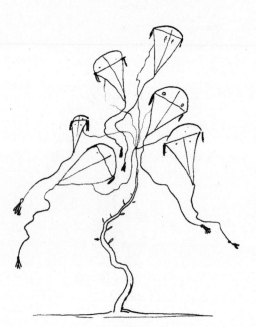

The Kite Tree

The Kite Tree is a fearful and astonishing vegetable when all the Kites are agitated by a tremendous wind, and endeavour to escape from their strings. The tree does not appear to be of any particular use to society, but would be frequented by small boys if they knew where it grew.

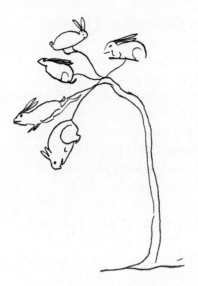

The Rabbit Tree

The Clomjombimbilious Tree   The Dish Tree

'The Octopods and Reptiles'

The Octopods and Reptiles
They dine at six o'clock,
And having dined, rush wildly out
　Like an electric shock.
They hang about the bannisters,
The corridors they block,
　And gabbling bothering,
A most unpleasant flock.

They hang about the bannisters,
　Upon the stairs they flock,
And howly-gabbling all the while
　The corridors they block.

[The Heraldic Blazons of Foss the Cat]

Foss Couchant

Foss, a untin.

Foss rampant

Foss dansant

Foss, regardant

Foss Pprpr.

Foss, Passant

'Mrs Jaypher found a wafer'

Mrs Jaypher found a wafer
Which she stuck upon a note;
This she took and gave the cook.
Then she went and bought a boat
Which she paddled down the stream
Shouting, 'Ice produces cream,
Beer when churned produces butter!
Henceforth all the words I utter
Distant ages thus shall note –
From the Jaypher Wisdom-Boat.'

Mrs Jaypher said, 'It's safer,
If you've Lemons in your head,
First to eat a pound of meat,
And then to go at once to bed.
Eating meat is half the battle,
Till you hear the Lemons rattle!
If you don't, you'll always moan;
In a Lemoncolly tone;
For there's nothing half so dread=
=ful, as Lemons in your head!'

From a letter to the Hon. Mrs Augusta Parker

– And my garden is now admirably beautiful, & were it not for the Slugs & Snails would be inimitable. But these melancholy muciliginous Molluscs have eaten up all my Higher-cynths & also my Lower-cynths & I have only just now found a mode of getting rid of these enemies: – which is by flattering their vanity in taking them friendly walks up & down the garden, – an inganno which blinds them to ulterior consequences. And thus, (they being of a monstrous size as you may see by the sketch below,) when I get them near the cistern, I pitch them into the water, where they justly expiate their unpleasant & greedy sins.

[The Later History of the Owl and the Pussy-cat]

My dear Miss Violet,

Your brother Jack goodnaturedly came here yesterday & dined with me, & he brought me a collar from your sister for the Pussy-cat. It was very good of her to think of this, but she evidently has not known, what it is very painful for me to elude to, that the Owl has long been a widower, & that the Pussy I now have is the maternal Uncle of the original Pussy who went to the Bongtree Land.

That party all eventually settled in the North East coast of New Guinea, – the Owl and the Pussy-cat & their 6 children, who are still
10 living & are most lovely & subsequeamish and reprehensible animals, & their subsqueakious history=mystery will some day be exotically & hysterically known to the Public.

The exact details of the death of the original Pussy can now, it seems to me, never be perfectly known. It is certain that she & the Owl staid for more than a month on the Coast of Coromandel with Lady Jingly Jones in a rocky cave, where they led a very happy & hippsipombious life. The next accounts which reached Europe of this estimable creature were that she & her husband the Owl had established themselves in New Guinea, after a vacillating tour to the Seychelles & Madagascar,
20 Mecca, the sauce of the Nile, Amsterdam, Winnipeg, the river Congo & Japan. At New Guinea the whole didactic family were living peaceably, when some savages are said by some of my informants to have suddenly visited their retreat, & to have had long conferences with the Pussy-cat in French, a language which she indiscriminately understood. These visitors went away, but soon afterwards were succeeded by a larger party of persons, who threatened the Pussy-cat most violently with a pair of Tongs & a Pepperbox. In the greatest perplexity she then ran up a tree in company with the Owl, carrying with them a sealed paper, & she was overheard distinctly praying her husband to swallow
30 the document, inasmuch as if found upon them the discovery would insuredly lead to acrostic results. But, – continued my informant, – the Owl positively declined to eat the Paper, whereon the Pussy-cat swallowed it in a rage, and finally – busting into Tears idle Tears, said to her unfortunate husband, – 'My Pœtus! it is not painful!' – (for latterly the Pussy-cat had diligently studied the Roman Bistorians.) Shortly after

mutter-uttering these words, she fell off the tree and instantly perspired & became a Copse. It is difficult to imagine the grief of the poor Owl, who immediately disembarked in a sailing vessel & left New Guinea for ever & above: – his grief however was such that it was not possible to get a sufficiently large quantity of Pocket handkerchiefs to wipe his eyes, & they had to cut up the Mainsail & all the other sails for that purpose, – by which untoward fact the vessel could not sail any more, but was wrecked felicitously on the Coast of Cornwall, where the Owl & his children still live though in a bereaved & bohemian condition.

There are however other accounts of the death of the Pussy-cat   10 which are quite different from what I have belated above. For it is said that at New Guinea the brooms with which the family used to sweep out the hole of the tree they inhabited were furnished with handles made of a mellifluous & mucilaginous but highly poisonous sort of wood: & that the Pussy-cat had indulged in a habit of sucking the end of these Broomhandles during intervals of work, & thus imbibed the infectious accusative which ultimately occasioned her dolorific death.

Please to read this letter to your sister Maria, – as slowly & oppro-briously as you can in order to save her feelings from a too sudden shock.   20

    Believe me,
        Yours sincerely,
            Edward Lear.

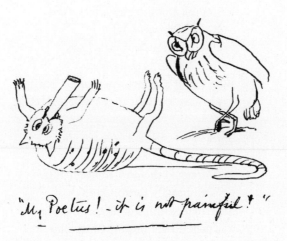

"My Poeticus! – it is not painful!"

'When "grand old men" persist in folly'

When 'grand old men' persist in folly
    In slaughtering men and chopping trees,
What art can soothe the melancholy
    Of those whom futile 'statesmen' teaze?

The only way their wrath to cover
    To let mankind know who's to blame ō –
Is first to rush by train to Dover
    And then straight onward to Sanremo.

'He lived at Dingle Bank – he did'

He lived at Dingle Bank – he did; –
    He lived at Dingle Bank;
And in his garden was one Quail,
    Four tulips, and a Tank:
And from his windows he could see
    The otion and the River Dee.

His house stood on a cliff, – it did,
    Its aspic it was cool;
And many thousand little boys
    Resorted to his school,
Where if of progress they could boast
    He gave them heaps of butter'd toast.

But he grew rabid-wroth, he did,
    If they neglected books,
And dragged them to adjacent cliffs
    With beastly Button Hooks,
And there with fatuous glee he threw
    Them down into the otion blue.

And in the sea they swam, they did, –
    All playfully about,
And some eventually became
    Sponges, or speckled trout: –
But Liverpool doth all bewail
    Their fate; – likewise his Garden Quail.

20

'And this is certain; if so be'

And this is certain; if so be
You could just now my garden see,
The aspic of my flowers so bright
Would make you shudder with delight.

And if you voz to see my roziz
As is a boon to all men's noziz, –
You'd fall upon your back and scream –
'O Lawk! o criky! it's a dream!'

Edward Lear
Archbishop of Canterbury
1886

Eggstrax from The Maloja Gazette

It is our painful duty to denounce to a repugnant public, a most fearful clamity which has just occurred to the excellent Mr A. J. Mundella, lately secretary of The Minister of Public destruction. Whatever objections may have been made to some of Mr Mundella's Theories it is impossible to deny that for energy and activity of porpoise, as well as of courtesy and kindliness, he [has] been universally and justly commended. All the more therefore do we egret what has occurred. On quitting his lonerous position, Mr Mundella, with a kindness which those who know him will fully opreciate, proposed to give a substantial proof of his interest in the Bore'd Children, by taking them [on] an excursion to Maloja, and having selected 83 of the most surreptitious and balsamic scholars, he accordingly arrived here at the Grand Hotel, accompanied by Mrs and Miss Mundella, and the 83 little boys. The extreme cold of this exalted situation, did not perfectly agree with the systematic stomachs of the children, but Mr and Mrs Mundella took them all out daily on sledges drawn by poodles, – the snow at Maloja being at present over six feet deep. Mr M. was however constantly warned of the danger arising from the pestilent proclivity of the numerous Polar Bears that infect the neighbourhood, a warning – alas! unheeded. For on Friday last, at some distance from the hotel, a drove of Bolar Pares were seen advancing, and there was no prospik of safety but in flight. Mr, Mrs, and Miss Mundella, we are renowned to say, reached the Hotel in contiguous security, – but the whole 83 'bored children' were all snatchell'd up rapidly and destructively devoured. The boots of one little boy alone have been left to Bear witness to the subsistence of the unfortunate scholars: – and these, with a beautiful feeling of simplicity and pathos, Mr Mundella has had stuffed and placed in a blue glass case embellished with gold stars and surmounted by the figures of a sucking pig and a silver stethoscope, and the letters QED as a mucilaginous but merited motto, worked in periwinkle shells.

'When leaving this beautiful blessed Briánza'

When leaving this beautiful blessed Briánza,
  My trunks were all corded and locked except one;
But that was unfilled, through a dismal mancanza,
  Nor could I determine on what should be done.

For out of *three* volumes (all equally bulky),
  Which – travelling, I constantly carry about, –
There was room but for two. So that angry and sulky,
  I had to decide as to which to leave out.

A Bible! A Shakespeare! A Tennyson! – stuffing
  And stamping and squeezing were wholly in vain!   10
A Tennyson! a Shakespeare! a Bible! – all puffing
  Was useless, and one of the three *must* remain.

And this was the end, – (and it's truth and no libel;) –
  A-weary with thinking I settled my doubt,
As I packed and sent off both the Shakespeare and Bible,
  And finally left the 'Lord Tennyson' out.

Some Incidents in the Life of my Uncle Arly

O my agèd Uncle Arly! –
Sitting on a heap of Barley
    All the silent hours of night, –
Close beside a leafy thicket: –
On his nose there was a Cricket, –
In his hat a Railway Ticket; –
    (But his shoes were far too tight.)

Long ago, in youth, he squander'd
All his goods away, and wander'd
    To the Timskoop Hills afar.
There, on golden sunsets blazing
Every evening found him gazing, –
Singing, – 'Orb! you're quite amazing!
    How I wonder what you are!'

Like the ancient Medes and Persians,
Always by his own exertions
    He subsisted on those hills; –
Whiles, – by teaching children spelling, –
Or at times by merely yelling, –
Or at intervals by selling
    'Propter's Nicodemus Pills'.

Later, in his morning rambles
He perceived the moving brambles
    Something square and white disclose; –
'Twas a First-class Railway-Ticket
But in stooping down to pick it
Off the ground, – a pea-green Cricket
    Settled on my uncle's Nose.

Never – never more, – oh! never,
Did that Cricket leave him ever, –   30
　　Dawn or evening, day or night; –
Clinging as a constant treasure, –
Chirping with a cheerious measure, –
Wholly to my uncle's pleasure, –
　　(Though his shoes were far too tight.)

So, for three-and-forty winters,
Till his shoes were worn to splinters,
　　All those hills he wander'd o'er, –
Sometimes silent; – sometimes yelling; –
Till he came to Borly-Melling,   40
Near his old ancestral dwelling;–
　　– And he wander'd thence no more.

On a little heap of Barley
Died my agèd Uncle Arly,
　　And they buried him one night; –
Close beside the leafy thicket; –
There, – his hat and Railway Ticket; –
There, – his ever faithful Cricket; –
　　(But his shoes were far too tight.)

'He only said, "I'm very weary'

He only said, 'I'm very weary.'
The rheumatiz he said,
He said, 'It's awful dull and dreary.
I think I'll go to bed.'

I must stop now, as the little gold watch
said when the fat blue-beetle got into his inside.

I think human nature is pretty much the same all along.
On the whole perhaps Pussycat nature is the best.

Appendix

Examples of Lear's Nonsense Similes

What *is* the use of all these revolutions which lead to nothing? – as the displeased turnspit said to the angry cookmaid. Fort. 16.x.47

Now I am at the end of replying to your letter – & a very jolly one it is. – So I must e'en turn over another stone as the sandpiper said when he was alooking for vermicules. Fort. 12.ii.48

I find my effort vain – all vain – as the mouse said when she climbed up as far as the top of the church steeple. HH 16.i.53

Now my dear boy I must close this as the Cyclopses used to say of their one eye. Fort. 11.i.57

... that is quite uncertain, as the tadpole observed concerning his future prospects and occupations, – when his tail fell off and his feet came forth and he was altogether in a spasmodic rhapsody of arrangement fit to throw him into a fever. ET 12.ix.57

Cheer up – as the limpet said to the weeping willow. Fort. 6.i.60

I'll make up for lost time as the Tadpole said when he lost his tail & found he could jump about. Fort. 29.iv.60

... it can't be helped as the Rhinoceros said when they told him he had a thick skin. ET 15.viii.60

... my thread of thought is broken as the spider said to the housemaid. Fort. 14.iv.62

Never mind. They will be useful when I am dead – those pictures; – as the reflective & expiring bear thought when he considered that his skin would become muffs. Bruce 31.vii.63

Concentrate your ideas if you want to do anything well & don't run about – as the Tortoise said to the Armadillo. Fort. 14.viii.63

... as the obstinate spider said when the amiable Bee offered to make part of his web, – 'I *must* do it myself.' Prescott 17.xi.63

This is my tale as the pertinacious peacock said aloud when he spread his in the radiant sumbeans. Bruce 8.ix.66

I must stop, as the watch said when a beetle got into his wheels. Fort. 26.xii.67

I am in a very unsettled condition, as the oyster said when they poured melted butter all over his back. Fort. 13.ix.71

... my eyes ache my Isaac! – as Rebekah said when she had the opthalmia. *diary* 28.v.72

... there is as yet but little advance made in this affair, as the snail said when he crawled up the Monument. Edgar 21.vii.78

It is unpleasant to feel prickly spiny pains in one's eyelids, as the – o dear! – I had such a beautiful nonsense simile – but the excellent cat Foss has just most improperly upset the biscuit box (I believe with a view of gain in the scramble) & all has gone out of my head. Miss Penrhyn 11.xi.79

What will happen to me, as the oyster said when he very inadvertently swallowed the gooseberry bush, nobody can tell. Marianne North 16.ii.80

I do not know what I may do, as the Oyster said when they asked him if he could fly. Fort. 5.iv.80

Time will show as the Lobster said when they assured him he would become red if he fell into the boiler. Fort. 4.ix.80

O cricky! – here's a go! as the Flea said when he jumped into the middle of the plate of apricots & found nothing to eat. HT 16.ix.80

I will leave off talking as the frog said when the pike swallowed him. ibid.

... truth is truth, as the Guineapig said when they told him he had no tail, & he didn't care a button whether he had or not. Drummond 13.x.80

I have had so much to be thankful for in a longish life, that one ought to check any tendency to growl – as the well-bred cat said to her irascible kitten. G. W. Curtis 1.i.81

On the whole, as the morbid & mucilaginous monkey said when he climbed up to the top of the Palm-tree & found no fruit there – one can't depend upon dates. Fort. 12.ii.82

I suppose everything will come right some day, as the Caterpillar said when he saw all his legs fall off as he turned into a Chrysalis. ET 12.iii.82

I have a vast deal to be thankful for as the tadpole said when his tail fell off, but a pair of legs grew instead. Fort. 30.iii.82

... regarding this matter there seems a little misunderstanding between us, as the fly said to the spider when the latter bit 4 of his legs off. R. R. Bowker, 16.vi.82

So after all one has much to be thankful for as the Centipede said when the rat bit off 97 of his hundred legs. Fort. 2.vii.82

When you have fully digested my proposal – as the stag said when he offered to jump down the Boa Constrictor's throat – please let me know. Selwyn 22.viii.82

Che so io? as the fly said – he was an Italian fly – when the Hippopotamus asked him what the moon was made of. Fort. 14.x.82

... what is done is done as the tadpole said when his tail fell off. Selwyn 15.x.82

Let us hope for 'lucidity' as the Elephant said when they told him to get out of the light, because he was opaque. ibid.

I am glad to find you writing in better spirits. It is a good thing to be in spirits, as the wise but spotted Lizard observed when they put him into a bottle of spirits of wine and shunted him onto the 45th shelf of the 8th Compartment in the Natural History Gallery at Pekin. F. T. Underhill 14.xii.82

... all is well as ends well, as the tadpole said when he became a phrogg. Selwyn 19.xii.82

I feel better, as the old Lady said after she had brought forth twins. Fort. 25.xii.82

... it was not my turn – as the cartwheel said to the Vindmill, – for I wrote last. Selwyn 9.iv.83

I will now look over your last letter & make ozbervatims on its points, as the monkey said when he casually sate down on the pincushion. Selwyn 17.v.83

I have done well to come to a new place, & that I find it 'agrees with me' as the snake said when he swallowed the ox. Evelyn Baring 19.viii.83

It has just come into my head – as the little charity boy said of the unexpected advent of an undesirable parasite. Fort.i.84

... sufficient to the day is the weevil thereof, as the hazelnut said when the caterpillar made a hole in his shell. Selwyn 1.i.84

'Een in our hashes live their wanted fires' – as the poetical cook said when they said her hashed mutton was not hot enough. Fort. 16.iv.84

I am not sure as the Tadpole said when the mouse asked him if he were going to walk or swim. Fort. 1.v.84

I suppose however, as the Caterpillar said when he became a Chrysalis, – time will show what will happen. Fort. 13.ix.84

Hence onward, my letter will be confused & indicative of my mucilaginous & morose mind – all more or less queer & upside down as the mouse said when he bit off his grandmother's tail – having mistaken it for a Barley Straw. Fort. 30.iv.85

I can't write much. Am all over eduneyyers in my AT illustrations, which I hope to bubblish some day – in a series of 10 or 20, but to be had separately, – as the centipede said of his 100 legs when they kept dropping off as he walked through the raspberry jam dish and the legs stuck in the juice. Mundella 27.x.85

As for myself, I am sitting up today for the first time – partly dressed as the cucumber said when oil & vinegar were poured over him salt & pepper being omitted. Fort. 18.i.86

I may not have thyme later, as the busy bee said when the snail urged him to lie in bed. Selwyn. 19.v.86

... one oughtn't to judge harshly, as the chaffinch said when he heard the snail call the Hedgehog a cursed old pincushion. Selwyn 7.vii.86

I fear I have only the alternative before me of beginning & executing the whole 200 over again, or of giving up my 40 years work, altogether a disgust & humiliation I shrink from, as the snail said when they showed him the salt cellar. Fort. 22.v.87

Work Erroneously Attributed to Lear

NSSBA, drawings to 'A was an Area Arch'.

QLN (p. 64), 'Beneath these high Cathedral stairs'. Lear copied this epitaph into his diary for 20 April 1887, during a visit from Lord Northbrook and his daughter, Emma, when he wrote: 'We had great fits of laughter about the Welsh epitaphs, making lots of others for fun', but he does not say if this one was composed by him or not.

OF (p. 158), fourteen lines written in an inserted fly-leaf in a copy of *NSSBA*: 'Not strange so blithesome I appear! ... For he felt for all Germans a natural repulsion'.

T&Q (p. 48), 'There was a young man of Iowa'.

(p. 59), Nonsense botanies 'Ourbeerdsia Socherishdah' and 'Cheenyoneena Falsaria'.

Edward Lear 1812–1888, catalogue of the Arts Council Exhibition (1958), p. 50: 'L was Mr Lear', a caricature of Lear sitting at a piano. This, together with a drawing of Lear as a bird entitled 'The Spectacled Owl', was first published in *QLN*, where they were correctly ascribed to Ward Braham. They were sold at Sotheby's on 8 October 1960, lot 218, as the work of Lear.

Edward Lear's Flora Nonsensica, Harvard College Library (1963).

St Kiven and the Gentle Kathleen (New Haven, CT, 1973). The poem, to which Lear made illustrations, is by Thomas Moore.

A Book of Learned Nonsense, ed. Peter Haining (1987). Much of Lear's prose has been substantially rewritten by the editor.

Susan Chitty, *That Singular Person Called Lear* (1988). Facing contents page is an extract purporting to come from Lear's diary. 'I see life as basically tragic and futile and the only thing that matters is making little jokes.' This error is perpetuated in Jackie Wullschläger's *Inventing Wonderland* (1995), p. 65.

Notes

The source of the texts is given in bold.

[Title-page]
Illustration from a letter to the American publisher James Fields of Boston of 15 October 1879 (**Huntington**). Pub. *VN*.

[Contents]
Illustration from a letter to Chichester Fortescue of 9 October 1856 (**Taunton**). Pub. *LEL*.

See headnote to 'There was a Young Girl of Majorca' in [Limericks for the 1846 and 1855 editions of *A Book of Nonsense*].

Eclogue: *Vide* Collins 'Hassan – or the Camel Driver'
Written on 23 August 1825. **TS** *Bowen*.

The Lear family lived in an elegant Georgian house called Bowman's Lodge in Highgate; it was here that Edward Lear was born (see also Introduction). In 1816 his father, Jeremiah Lear, became a defaulter in the recently opened Stock Exchange, of which he was one of the original proprietors. Family tradition says that he was bankrupted, and Lear later wrote that his father had served a short prison sentence for fraud and debt, but the evidence is not clear. The family appears to have suffered continuing financial difficulties, and this may be why they left Bowman's Lodge for a while.

Title *Collins 'Hassan – or the Camel Driver'*: William Collins (1721–59) published *Persian Eclogues*, including 'Hassan – or the Camel Driver', in 1742.

5 *Hackney-coach*: a horse-drawn coach available for hire.

7 *the turnpike gate*: toll gate.

17–18 *Bethink thee ... behind?*: Lear used to tease his mother about her pretensions (see 'The Shady Side of Sunnyside'). In contrast, the worldly goods of his own autobiographical character, the Yonghy-Bonghy-Bò, were no more than 'Two old chairs, and half a candle, – / One old jug without a handle', and in 'Mr and Mrs Discobbolos' the characters proclaim: 'We want no knives nor forks nor chairs, / No tables nor carpets nor household cares, / From worry of life we've fled'.

51–6 *the mobs ... they cry*: the years following the Napoleonic wars saw widespread unemployment leading to violent political and social unrest.

72 *The large sidegarden*: when Lear revisited the Highgate house in 1863 he noted that the garden had been sold to make way for buildings and new roads.

To Miss Lear on her Birthday

Written on 17 January 1826 in a letter for the thirty-fifth birthday of Lear's sister Ann. TS *Bowen*. Pub. *SL*.

Ann was born in 1791, the oldest of the twenty-one children; Edward was the twentieth. She was responsible for his upbringing: see Introduction.

Compare Lewis Carroll's 'Rules and Regulations', in *Useful and Instructive Poetry*, ed. Derek Hudson (1954): written for his younger siblings in about 1845, it has twenty lines ending in '-tion'.

4 *recubation*: reclining.

5 *respiration*: the original MS has not survived; in the typed transcript a possible alternative reading '(recuperation?)' is also given.

12 *glomeration*: heaping together.

20 *gratulation*: congratulation.

21 *peragration*: travelling or passing through.

23 *indagation*: investigation. A possible alternative reading is given as '(indication?)'.

33 *improbation*: reproach.

36 *dication*: a formal declaration.

50 *lunation*: lunar month.

56 *fomentation*: the application of warm or medicated lotions to the skin.

59 *adumbration*: shadowing.

63 *Sanguification*: formation of blood.

   defalcation: cutting away.

65 *Rhabarbaration*: treatment with the salt of rhabarbaric acid.

   scarification: making a number of small incisions.

70 *trucidation*: cutting into pieces.

71 *malversation*: corrupt behaviour in employment, or position of trust.

75 *discalceation*: taking off her shoes.

78 *obtrectation*: slander or disparagement.

85–8 *You … elevation*: Ann never married.

91 *advesperation*: a Lear neologism, meaning moving towards evening.

94 *deliquation*: melting down.

95 *conquassation*: shaking violently.

100 *refullerlation*: either a neologism meaning replenishment, or a misreading in the typed transcript; the typist, Eleanor Bowen, has crossed through a first possible reading.

The Shady Side of Sunnyside
Written on 24 July 1826. **TS** *Bowen*.

Lear's maternal great-great-great-great-grandfather, called Brignall (his first name is not known) owned Sunnyside, an estate in County Durham. His daughter, Alice, married John Grainger, Gentleman. Lear's mother, Ann, was descended from their youngest daughter, Eleanor. It seems that Ann felt that she had married beneath herself, and that her frequent reminders of her more elevated origins and the glory which could (and should) have been hers became something of a family joke. See also 'Eclogue: *Vide* Collins "Hassan – or the Camel Driver"', note to ll. 17–18.

2 *Hymen*: the Greek and Roman god of marriage.

3 *'Hurrum, – Scurrum'*: harum-scarum. Here, a reckless or careless person.

22 *'Figs on it'*: not to care a fig, to treat with contempt.

   Granny Skerritt: Lear's maternal grandmother, Florence Brignall Usher, married Edward Skerritt. According to family legend, she left Durham some time after the 1745 rebellion, and came south to settle in London.

Journal
Written on 7 November 1829. **TS** *Bowen*. Pub. *SL*.

Written while Lear was staying with his second sister, Sarah, who in 1822 had married Charles Street and moved to Arundel, in Sussex. They had two sons, Charles and Frederick. Lear spent some of his happiest childhood days there, and in the nearby village of Burpham. The poem is written in the style of Thomas Moore's 'The Fudge Family in Paris', in *Thomas Brown, the Younger*, 5th edn (1818). It has not been possible to identify all the people and places named by Lear.

9 *White Horse cellar*: a post coach left the New White Horse Cellar in the City of London daily at 8 a.m. Its route took it west down the Strand, then through the villages of Chelsea and Fulham before crossing the River Thames at Putney and across Surrey into Sussex.

10 *stage and four*: a coach drawn by four horses.

13 *mudscrapers*: street urchins, particularly those who scavenged the river mud of the Thames at low tide.

34 *Petworth*: Petworth House, about twelve miles from Arundel, was the home of the earls of Egremont. Lord Egremont (1751–1837) was a patron of J. M.W. Turner (1775–1851), and Lear, who admired Turner's work above that of any other painter, would have seen his work there when he visited Petworth as a boy and young man.

36 *globose as a harvest moon*: the image of globular rotundity may have been suggested to Lear by Ann, who would tease her brother Frederick by likening him to a large round cooking apple the Norfolk biffin. The image returned to Lear when he was travelling in Calabria in 1847. On 18 August he stayed with Baron Rivettini, and in his *Journals of a Landscape Painter in Southern Calabria, &c.* he wrote: 'In a spacious salone on the first floor sate a party playing at cards, and one of them a minute gentleman, with a form more resembling that of a sphere than any person I ever remember to have seen, was pointed out to me as the Baron.' He later described him in the *Journals* as 'the globose little Baron' and 'the globular Baron'. It was an image to which he returned in his nonsense, for example in the limerick 'That globular person of Hurst'. From July 1860, in his nonsense self-portraits Lear habitually drew himself as completely round (see e.g. pp. 154 and 155), and in 'How pleasant to know Mr Lear' he wrote that 'His body is perfectly spherical'.

39 *Bury Hill side*: see headnote to 'When the light dies away on a calm summer's eve'.

44 *the Bank*: Charles Street managed a bank in Arundel.

46 *Peppering*: Peppering House, rebuilt in 1824, adjoins the village of Burpham, in the downs near Arundel. It was the home of the Drewitt family whom Lear first met in 1823. The father, Robert, was an amateur naturalist and ornithologist. There were three children: Fanny, who married George Coombe and whom Lear called Mrs George, Eliza and Robert. Many of the poems that have survived from Lear's boyhood were written for the Drewitt family.

47 *the hard chalk*: see headnote to 'Peppering Roads'.

54 *my friends*: the Drewitts.

56 *Goliath*: the Philistine giant who was killed by David using a shepherd boy's sling and stone (Samuel 15.24–54).

69 *syllabub*: a pudding made of flavoured whipped cream.

77 *Lyminster*: Batworth Park, Lyminster, near Arundel, was the home of another Jeremiah Lear, a friend of Lear's father but not related. His youngest son, George Lear, was articled in 1827 to the solicitors Ellis and Blackmore of Gray's Inn. Working with him was a young office boy called Charles Dickens.

78 *Roger's Italy*: Samuel Roger's poem *Italy* was first published in two parts in 1822 and 1828; an illustrated edition appeared in 1830, and copies were available at the end of 1829.

79 *Talked ... Brougham*: Henry Peter Brougham (1778–1868), Lord Chancellor, was at this time involved in a scheme of common-law reform.

91 *Wardropers*: James Wardroper was a subscriber to Lear's *Views in Rome and its Environs* (1841), and in a letter of 15 July [1832] Lear writes of a W. Wardroper.

93 *gammoned*: beaten at backgammon by a score equal to two hits or games.

101 *Capsicums*: red peppers.

135 *multiply – like Widow's oil*: This refers to the widow and the cruse of oil (I Kings 17.10–16), where a small supply is made, by good management, to go a long way or to be inexhaustible.

Turkey Discipline
Written in the late autumn of 1829. **TS** *Bowen*.

This incident took place at Peppering House, the home of the Drewitt family (see 'Journal', note to l. 46).

Subtitle '*Shades of Evening*': a popular song of the day.
1 *pother*: commotion or uproar.

'When the light dies away on a calm summer's eve'
Written in November 1829 on Bury Hill. **MS** *Edin*. Published in *Poetry Review*, April 1950, pp. 82–3.

Bury Hill is part of the South Downs in West Sussex above Arundel from which there are wide views across the valley of the River Arun.

'From the pale and the deep'
Written on 3 December 1829. MS *Edin*. Pub. *Poetry Review*, April 1950, p. 83.

Peppering Roads
Written on 12 December 1829. MS *Warne*. Pub. *Sussex County Magazine*, 10:1 (January 1936) pp. 69–70.

For Peppering, see 'Journal', note to l. 46. Until the late nineteenth century there was only a very rough track to Burpham from Warningcamp, north of Arundel.

10 *within side*: passengers could either travel inside the coach, or take seats outside which were cheaper but exposed to the weather.
after 16] ~~Then we passed through a deluge of water~~
25 *gig*: a light, two-wheeled, one-horse carriage.
27 *a gibbetted thief*: at Blakehurst, near Warningcamp, there had stood a gibbet where a local man Jack Upperton was hanged for robbing a coach carrying mail from the south coast through Storrington to London.
37 *sartin*: certain.
39 *Day and Martin*: a patent boot-blacking.
47 *the inmates*: the Drewitt family.

Miss Fraser's Album
The **fair copy** was written in about 1830 on the opening pages of a leather-bound autograph volume which Lear presented as a '1st Drawing Prize' to a Miss Fraser, who lived near his home in Highgate (*private collection*). See Vivien Noakes, *The Painter Edward Lear* (1991), pp. 34–5.

Lear began to earn his living as an artist at the age of fifteen-and-a-half, and part of his income came from teaching drawing and painting: see Introduction.

23 *Zephyr's sighs*: Zephyr, the west wind, was the son of Astraeus the Titan and Eos the goddess of dawn, the parents of the winds and the stars. His sighs are a soft, gentle wind.

Ruins of the Temple of Jupiter Aegina, Greece
The **fair copy** in Miss Fraser's album is subscribed 'E. Lear. 28th September / Gray's Inn Road': see headnote to 'Miss Fraser's Album'. There is a draft (*Edin.* 1), and a fair copy (*Edin.* 2) which is dated 23 October 1829.

Aegina, one of the Greek islands in the Saronic group, was at the height of its glory in the fifth century BC. After this it suffered various fortunes, before declining into poverty. It was part of the Ottoman Empire until 1826, and between 1826 and 1828 was the temporary capital of the newly independent Greece. Although Lear later travelled widely in Greece, he did not visit Aegina. The temple was probably that of Aphaia, explored by German archaeologists in 1811, which was attributed first to Zeus Panhellenios and later to Athena.

7 souls] Edin.1, 2 hearts
41–4 And on ... liberty] Edin.1 these lines come after ll. 45–8.

The Bride's Farewell
The date of composition is unknown, but probably written in the late 1820s or early 1830s. MS Edin.
39 Ianthe: Cretan girl, in Ovid's Metamorphoses, who married Iphis who had been transformed from a girl into a young man.

Ruby
Written in 1829 or 1830. MS Warne.

A watercolour drawing of Ruby by Lear, dated 1830, is mounted separately. The dog belonged to the Drewitt family.

18 in both thou didst shine: these words are added in pencil. They are possibly, but not certainly, in Lear's hand.

Miss Maniac
Written in the late 1820s or early 1830s. MS Houghton. Accompanying the poem and illustrations is a slip inscribed 'for Miss Drewitt with EL's respects. Illustrations for Miss Maniac. E. Lear'.

Miss Drewitt is probably Fanny Drewitt. This may be a sentimental poem of the day, but if so it has not been traced.

Lear made similar absurd illustrations to poems by Lady Anne Lindsay (1750–1825), Robert Burns (1759–96), Thomas Moore (1779–1852) and Thomas Haynes Bayly (1797–1839). They reflect an important stage in his development as a nonsense writer, where the illustrations combine with the words to create an extra dimension, here bathos and absurdity. They also show the influence of George Cruikshank (1792–1878) on Lear's early nonsense drawing.

2 *A darkness ... stole*: the gloom of the Jews exiled in slavery in Egypt.
47 *sate*: sat. Although in his writings Lear uses both 'sate' and 'sat', 'sate' occurs more frequently.

'I slept, and back to my early days'
The date of composition is unknown. **MS** *PM*.

This may be a parody of a poem or song that has not been traced.

Resignation
Written in July 1830. **TS** *Bowen*.

'I've just seen Mrs Hopkins – and read her the lines'
The date of composition is unknown, but probably written in 1830, for Eliza Drewitt. **MS** *Houghton*. There is also a TS *Bowen*, and the punctuation follows it. Pub. *SL*.

1 *Mrs Hopkins*: listed among Lear's subscribers to *Parrots* (see headnote to Letter to Harry Hinde), where her address is given as Bank, Arundel. Nothing more is known of her.
7 *Houghton*: a village north of Arundel.
9 *Robert*: Eliza Drewitt's brother.

Ode to the little China Man
Part of the same **MS** as '"I've just seen Mrs Hopkins"', which it follows. Pub. *SL*.

13–14 *But ev'ry one ... way*: 'à chacun son goût', each one to his own taste.
15 *pipkin*: a small earthenware cooking pot.

Peppering Bell
Written on 15 July 1830. **MS** *Texas*. There is also a TS *Bowen*.

Miss D— was Fanny Drewitt. In 1834 a new bell for Burpham church was cast by T. Mears of London. This, in its turn, was replaced in 1922 by four new bells, each bearing the name of a member of the Drewitt family.

Title *Peppering*] *Bowen* Burpham

2 *The*] *Bowen* Its
5 *whack*] *Bowen* crack
9 *horrid*] *Bowen* noisy
12 *And ... bell?*] *Bowen* Take down that horrid dumb bell!
14–15 *Nor ... soon*] *Bowen* Your old cracked bell bestowing, – / For soon I fear, with grief

Letter to Harry Hinde
Written in December 1830. **TS** *Bowen*. Pub. *SL*.

Lear was working on *Illustrations of the Family of Psittacidæ, or Parrots*, which he published in folios to subscribers between November 1830 and April 1832. Nothing is known of Harry Hinde.

18 *flute*: as a young man, Lear played the flute, the lute, the guitar and the accordion, as well as the piano. He took a flute with him when he travelled in Italy in 1837, but there is no further mention of this instrument until April 1876, when he bought a new one. It is the instrument most frequently played by his nonsense characters. See, for example, 'The Quangle Wangle's Hat', l. 51; 'There was an Old Person of Bute'; and The Worrying Whizzing Wasp in the alphabet 'The Absolutely Abstemious Ass'. On Lear's guitar, see 'The Owl and the Pussy-cat', note to l. 6.
21 *Dask*: no MS has survived, so it is impossible to tell if this is a version of the mild expletive 'Dash', or a misreading of 'Dusk'.
27 *museum*: the museum of the Zoological Society in Bruton Street in London's West End, where Lear made some of his drawings of parrots.
Illustration: the date of the parrot drawing is unknown, but it is between June 1830 and early 1832 (**Houghton**).

Scrawl
Written on 5 April 1831. **TS** *Bowen*.

Lear was a sickly child and young man: see Introduction. He was staying in Sussex to recover after a bout of illness.

21 *the Castle*: Arundel Castle, home of the Dukes of Norfolk.
21–2 *Sidi Mahommed*: in Western India, a title of honour given to African Muslims, used in Lear's time as an exclamation.
24 *wap*: a blow or fall.
25 *my drawings*: Lear was making drawings for Sir William Jardine's *The Naturalists' Library*, Vol. V, *Pigeons* (1835).

33 *malad*: ill.

50 *I'll try to remember the text*: Ann had trained Edward to learn a biblical text each Sunday.

Letter to Fanny Jane Dolly Coombe
Written on 15 July 1832. **MS** *Houghton*. Pub. *SL*.

p. 49 l. 1 *Niece – par adoption*: Fanny was the daughter of George and Fanny Coombe (see 'Journal', note to l. 46). In 1870 Lear again called himself an 'Adopty Duncle', to two small American children, Daisy and Arthur Terry (see headnote to 'The Absolutely Abstemious Ass').

p. 50 l. 10 *my old complaint in the head*: possibly a reference to the epilepsy from which Lear suffered from the age of 5 or 6, and which he referred to in his diaries as 'the Demon'.

p. 50 l. 19 *British Quadrupeds*: Thomas Bell's *A History of British Quadrupeds* (1837), to which Lear contributed at least four drawings, including a hedgehog, a ferret weasel and two of a Greater Horseshoe bat.

p. 50 l. 26 *Gallinaceous*: of the family Gallinae, which includes domestic poultry, pheasants and partridges.

p. 50 l. 35 *John Sayres*: Lear later recalled visiting Uppark with John Sayres in 1828, and walking with him on Compton Down in 1829. Sayres lived first in Midhurst and then in Chichester, but nothing more is known of him.

p. 50 ll. 37–8 *Paganini*: Niccolo Paganini (1782–1840), Italian violinist and composer, made a highly successful tour of England in 1832.

'Oh! Pan!'
The date of composition is unknown. **MS** *Koch*. Pub. *Kraus*.

5 *Pantheon*: in Oxford Street, London, opened in 1772 as a place of winter entertainment with card rooms, and tea and supper rooms. After a chequered career, it was converted in 1833–4 into a covered bazaar.

8 *coup de soleil*: sun-stroke.

Letter to George Coombe
Written on 4 March 1834. **MS** *Warne*.

4 *Argyllshire sister*: Lear's sister, Mary Boswell.

7 *Mr Curtis*: mutual friend who was an entymologist.

10 *an aperient pill*: a laxative.

22 *distich*: a couplet.

26 *at Rotterdam*: Lear had visited Rotterdam in 1833, with John Gould (1804–81), the ornithological draughtsman for whom Lear did many drawings in the 1830s.

The Nervous Family

The first three stanzas are part of an old song recalled by Lear; he wrote the last three at Knowsley in 1836. MS *Beinecke*. A second MS (of ll. 25–30) was written for Fanny Coombe, on paper watermarked 1834 (*Warne*); a third for a Mrs Way on 10 November 1869 (*Princeton*); and a fourth for Lady Emma Baring (unlocated), daughter of Lear's friend Lord Northbrook, on 31 August 1877.

Lear lived and worked at Knowsley between 1830/31 and 1837, drawing the animals and birds of Lord Derby, the thirteenth earl (1775–1851), who was president of the Zoological Society of London and a celebrated natural historian. See also headnote to [Limericks for the 1846 and 1855 editions of *A Book of Nonsense*]. Lear noted on the Beinecke MS that the verses are to be sung to the tune of 'We're a'noddin, nod, nod, noddin, and we're a'noddin at our house at home'. In the Princeton MS, stanzas 2 and 3 are reversed.

12 *She ... on*] *Princeton* It's spilt upon
25 *We're getting ... to*] *Warne, Princeton* We now very seldom
27 *I'm ... I'm*] *Princeton* We're ... We're
28 *I*] *Princeton* We
29 *Aunt*] *Warne* wife
36 *shaky*] *Princeton* nervous

The Nervous Family: Alternative version

The date of composition is unknown. Written on paper watermarked 1834, on the same sheet as the draft of ll. 25–30 of 'The Nervous Family', for Fanny Coombe. MS *Warne*.

'The gloom that winter casts'

The date of composition is unknown. Written on the same sheet as 'The Nervous Family: Alternative version'. MS *Warne*.

'My dear Mrs Gale – from my leaving the cradle'
Written on 19 June 1835 in a letter to Fanny Coombe. **MS** *Warne.*

In the letter, Lear describes his preparations, at his lodgings in 28 South-ampton Row, London, for his annual bachelor party for 'old cronies – and people to whom one is under an obligation of some sort'. It was planned for seven but at the last minute came news of three extra guests:

Conceive – for they can't be described – the momentous cogitations with my landlady which ensued – the cleanings – the hurryings – the widening of table and multiplication of dishes, – and above all – add the misery of an Irish servant who almost always mis-understands whatever you say – I only thank St Peter that I am speaking of the Past! – The Gales very kindly – as usual – sent me in some very old fine Arrack for Punch. *Of course* I had no punch bowl – but I borrowed one from them. Yet when the multitude are just coming – up rushed Jane with a face of horror – 'Please – serr – Messes Smith has found out all her ladles – booter ladles and all have been *smished*' – Misfortune helps Genius I suppose – for a sudden fit of the muse came upon me and I instantly sent round the following pathetic stanzas ...

8 *She ... all*] Are all ~~of them~~ she vows

Portraites of the inditchenous beestes of New Olland
The date of composition is unknown, but this sheet of drawings may have been inspired by the 1838 visit to Australia of John Gould. **MS** *PM.* Pub. *RA.*

On 17 October 1839 Lear wrote to Gould: 'Do not fancy ... that I should not be much entertained by an account of your novelties abroad for I still know an Opposum from a Frogon.'

'My Sweet Home is no longer mine'
In a letter of 1 December 1838 to Fanny Coombe, written from Rome. **MS** *Warne.*

In the letter Lear says that he feels homesick for England: 'Have you got a lit-tle song – "My Sweet Home is no longer mine"? – It has only one verse, but before I left England I composed 2 more which I shall write – I often sing them nowadays.'

[Illustrations for 'Kathleen O'More']
Date of drawings unknown, but probably done in 1841. **MS** *Houghton.*

'Kathleen O'Moore', a popular song of the day, was written by George Nugent Reynolds (1770–1802).

As well as making drawings for popular songs, Lear illustrated nursery rhymes. Drawings survive for 'Sing a song of sixpence', 'Hey diddle diddle', 'One, two, three, four, five', 'Goosy goosy gander', 'Humpty Dumpty' and 'Dumpling dumpling dee'. In October 1841 he also made for the Phipps Hornby family (see headnote to [Lear's adventures on horseback]), a set of twenty-two drawings illustrating 'The tragical life and death of Caius Marius – Esqre – late her Majesty's Consul=general in the Roman States: illustrated from authentic sauces by Edward Lear'. Pub. for Justin Schiller (New York, 1983).

Scene in the Campagna of Rome
Drawn in 1842. **MS** *BL.* Pub. *VN.*

The drawing is in a common-place book put together in Rome by Isabella Knight. Lear lived in Rome between 1837 and 1848.

As well as placing absurdities in conventional landscape, Lear also drew nonsense figures in the margins of some of the drawings he made in preparation for *Parrots.* See parrot drawing on p. 47.

[Lear's adventures on horseback]
Drawn in July 1842, or shortly after. **MS** *BL.* Pub. nos. 2, 8, 26, 27, *RA;* nos. 3, 4, 5, 10, 12, 14, 21, 25, 33, *Edward Lear in the Levant,* ed. Susan Hyman (1988).

The drawings are in a common-place book put together by Isabella Knight (see headnote to 'Scene in the Campagna of Rome'), and show the adventures of Lear and her brother, Charles, during a visit to the Abruzzi. In preparation for this, Knight had given Lear riding lessons, and for the tour he lent Lear his arab, Gridiron. Lear described this in *Illustrated Excursions in Italy,* Vol. 1 (1846). Some of the drawings, e.g. 16–20, have not survived.

Lear made many such sets of drawings describing his adventures. The earliest to have survived is of eight drawings dating from 1841, and relates to a visit to Geoffrey Phipps Hornby at Greenwich Naval Base (pub. *Kraus*). Others to have survived, include twenty-six drawings done during a journey to Scotland in 1842 with Phipps Hornby, twenty drawings illustrating travels in Sicily in

1847 with John Proby (pub. *Lear in Sicily* (1938)) and eight drawings done in Switzerland in 1854 (pub. *Ye long Nite in ye Wonderfull Bedde* (Cambridge, 1972)). Admiral Sir Phipps Hornby (1785–1867) was related to Lord Derby. His son Geoffrey (1825–95), who also became an admiral, was a particular friend of Lear.

[Limericks for the 1846 and 1855 editions of *A Book of Nonsense*]
The dates of composition are unknown. Lear rarely mentioned his limericks in his diary or his letters, and it is impossible to date the seventy-three poems (including the title-page) that make up the 1st and 2nd editions of *A Book of Nonsense*. A number of MS sets of some of the limericks have survived. Of these, the set that Lear gave to the Phipps Hornby family (MS *Koch*) was published in *Kraus*, and that for Lady Duncan (MS *Duncan*) (see headnote to Letters to Anna Duncan and Lady Duncan) in *Warne*. Pub. *BN* (1846).

Both editions were printed by lithography by Thomas McLean, of 26 Haymarket, London, and published at Lear's expense. The 1st edition appeared on 10 February 1846; the 2nd edition in late 1854 or early 1855.

The 1st edition was published in two volumes, each containing 36 verses and a title-page (repeated in the second volume) and each costing 3/6. The verses were set out in three lines, and the text was printed in capitals. It is not known how many copies were printed, but very few have survived. Because of the quality of glue, the unnumbered pages soon became detached. The limericks have been printed in the probable order in which they were bound.

In the 2nd edition the limericks were published in a single volume, the verses were arranged on five lines and the text was printed in italics. In the surviving copies, even where these have not been rebound, there is no consistency in the order, suggesting that they were published in a haphazard arrangement. From slight, but significant, differences it would appear that the drawings were retraced for this edition.

Lear published the first two editions anonymously as by 'old Derry down Derry', although an advertisement for *A Book of Nonsense* which appears in Volume 2 of Lear's *Illustrated Excursions in Italy* (1846), also printed by McLean, gave an early clue to the authorship. Many people ascribed authorship to Lear's patron, Lord Derby, and even when Lear's name was printed on the title-page of the 3rd edition (1861) it was thought that Edward Lear was an anagram of Edward Earl.

Although Lord Derby had no direct part in the creation of the book, most of the limericks were written and drawn when Lear was living at his house at Knowsley, and in the 3rd and later editions there is a dedication 'To the great-grandchildren, grand-nephews, and grand-nieces of Edward, 13th Earl of Derby, this book of drawings and verses (the greater part of which were originally made and composed for their parents,) is dedicated by the author, Edward Lear.'

Lear himself never used the word 'limerick', dated in *OED* to 1898. He called them his 'Nonsenses' or 'Old Persons'. Lear did not invent the verseform whose origins are obscure (see Introduction), but was introduced to it when he was shown 'There was a sick man of Tobago' from *Anecdotes and Adventures of Fifteen Gentlemen* (1823). He made his own illustrations to this limerick, and to two others in the volume – 'There was an old soldier of Bicester' and 'As a little fat man of Bombay' (pub. *Kraus*) – and realized that he had discovered 'a form of verse lending itself to limitless variety for Rhymes and Pictures' (Preface to *MN*).

Sources: Justin G. Schiller, *Nonsensus: cross-referencing Edward Lear's original 116 limericks with eight holograph manuscripts and comparing them to printed texts from the 1846, 1855 and 1861 versions; together with a census of known copies of the genuine first edition* (Stroud: Catalpa Press Ltd, 1988), and Howard Nixon, 'The Second Lithographic Edition of Lear's Book of Nonsense', *British Museum Quarterly* 28 (1964), 7–8.

There was an old Derry down Derry

This limerick was on the cover and title-page. Derry down Derry was one of the fools of the traditional English mummers' plays, and is found in the refrains of some early folk songs. In 1840, and possibly earlier, Lear sometimes used what he called his 'long nonsense name'. This varied, but an example is 'Mr Abebika Kratoponoko Prizzikalo Kattefello Ablegorabalus Ableborintophashyph or Chakonoton the Cozovex Dossi Fossi Sini Tomentilla Coronilla Polentilla Battledore & Shuttlecock Derry down Derry Dumps, otherwise Edward Lear'. The name is derived from *Aldiborontiphoskyphorniostikos: A Round Game, for Merry Parties*, by R. Stennett (*c.* 1822), in which the players read aloud the tonguetwisting names and descriptions of the characters, and 'Rapidity of utterance, and gesticulation, are essential.' See headnote to 'The Absolutely Abstemious Ass'.

There was an Old Man of the Hague

3 *built*] *Koch* bought
4 *That deluded*] *Koch* This distracted

There was an Old Man of Leghorn

4 *Who devoured*] *Duncan* Which finished

There was a Young Lady of Bute

4 *amusing*] *Duncan* melodious

There was an Old Man of Kilkenny

3 *He spent all*] *Duncan* And he laid out
4 *That wayward Old*] *Duncan* Which pleased that old *NYPL* That prodigal

There was an Old Man of Kamschatka

4 *fat dogs in*] *Duncan* young dogs of

There was an Old Man of the Cape

3 *on a light*] *Duncan* all alight

There was an Old Person of Burton

4 *distressing*] *Duncan* uncivil

There was an Old Man of th' Abruzzi

3 *replied*] *Duncan* exclaimed
4 *doubtful*] *Duncan* unpleasant

There was an Old Man of Corfu

3 *rushed*] *Koch* walked
4 *That bewildered*] *Duncan* That uneasy *Koch* And distressed that

There was an Old Man of Nepaul
The second picture is **MS** *Koch*. Pub. *Kraus*.

See Rudolph Raspe's *The Travels and Surprising Adventures of Baron Mun-chausen* (1785), pp. 33–4, where the baron's horse is cut in two by a falling portcullis and the 'farrier contrived to bring both parts together while hot. He sewed them up with sprigs and young shoots of laurels that were at hand.'

3 *But, though split*] *Koch* Yet though broken

There was an Old Man of the Isles

3 *high dum diddle*] *Duncan* highdiddlediddle
4 *amiable*] *Duncan* lively old

There was an Old Man of Moldavia

2 *curious*] *NYPL* funny
4 *funny Old*] *Duncan* singular *Koch* curious Old *NYPL* silly Old

There was an Old Man of Vesuvius

2 *Vitruvius*: appears to be a fictional author.
4 *That morbid*] *Duncan* Which destroyed that

There was an Old Person of Rheims

4 *Which amused that*] *Duncan* That afflicted

There was a Young Lady of Hull

3 *seized on*] *Duncan* caught up
4 *Which ... Bull*] *Duncan* That remarkable Lady of Hull

There was an Old Man of the West

In some copies of the 2nd edition the illustrations for the two versions of this limerick were reversed.

There was an Old Man of Peru

There are two versions of this limerick in *Duncan*. In the second, the illustration is quite different and ll. 3–4 read: So he ran up & down till the sun turned him brown / That uneasy old man of Peru.

3 *tore off his hair*] *Duncan* sate in a chair
4 *intrinsic*] *Duncan* unhappy

There was a Young Lady of Clare

This limerick was reproduced on the final page of the 3rd edition. In the first American edition (1863) it was moved to the outside back cover, and was omitted from all subsequent American editions. See headnote to [Additional limericks for the 1861 edition of *A Book of Nonsense*].

There was an Old Man of the South

3 *But in swallowing*] *Koch* Till he swallowed

There was an Old Person of Ischia

3 *danced … figs*] *Koch* ate thousands of figs, and danced hornpipes and jigs *Duncan* danced several jigs, and fed on green figs
4 *lively Old*] *Duncan* indigenous *Koch* susceptible

There was an Old Man of the Coast

3 *But when it was*] *Duncan* When the weather grew

There was an Old Person of Buda

3 *at last*] *Duncan* one day

There was an Old Person of Sparta

2–4 *twenty-five … Person*] *Duncan* 21 sons and one darter – / He weighed them in scales, and fed them with snails – / That oppressive old person

There was an Old Sailor of Compton

This limerick was dropped from the 3rd and later editions.

4 *singular*] *Duncan* funny old

There was an Old Man of Apulia

2 *very*] *Duncan* rather
3 *twenty*] *Duncan* 15
4 *whimsical*] *Duncan* corrosive *Koch* distracting old

There was a Young Lady of Turkey

3 *day turned out*] *Duncan* weather grew

There was an Old Person of Rhodes

3 *several cousins, to catch*] *Duncan* some old cousins to kill
4 *futile*] *Duncan* fearful

There was an Old Man of Cape Horn

3 *So he ... despair*] *Koch* He sate on a chair and behaved like a bear
4 *dolorous*] *Koch* intrinsic

There was an Old Man of Jamaica

4 *distressed*] *Duncan* confused

There was an Old Man of the West

See headnote to first version of 'There was an Old Man of the West'.

4 *cured that Old Man*] *Koch* demolished that man

There was an Old Man of the East

3 *they ... such*] *Duncan* their conduct was such – and they all ate so much (3rd and subsequent editions have 'eat')

There was a Young Lady of Poole

2 *excessively*] *Koch* uncommonly
3 *put*] *Duncan, Koch* set

There was an Old Man of Dundee

4 *exclaimed*] *Duncan* said

There was an Old Man of New York

This limerick was dropped from the 3rd and later editions.

4 *For that silly*] *Duncan* That unlucky

There was an Old Man of the North

3 *fished*] *Duncan* twitched

There was a Young Lady of Wales

1 *Lady*] *Duncan* Person
3–4 *When she … Lady*] *Duncan* She cried – 'Only look – at the end of my hook! – ! – / That lively young person

There was an Old Man of Bohemia

2 *Euphemia*] *Duncan* Skrokemia
3 *married*] *Duncan* ran off with
4 *Which grieved that*] *Duncan* That unhappy *Koch* Which annoyed that

There was an Old Person of Cheadle

3–4 *stealing … Person*] *Koch* running his rigs, and stealing some pigs, / This iniquitous person

There was an Old Lady of Prague

2 *language was*] *Duncan* answers were
4 *oracular Lady*] *Duncan* ambiguous old creature

There was an Old Person of Cadiz

When retracing the drawing for lithography, Lear seems to have misread the tails of the coat as arms. In one of the preliminary drawings there is a single set of arms and the tails of the coat, and in another a single set of arms, but in all the published editions the coat-tails have become a second set of arms.

2 *always*] *Duncan* very

There was a Young Lady of Parma

4 *provoking*] *Duncan* unpleasant

There was a Young Girl of Majorca

Writing to Chichester Fortescue from Corfu on 11 January 1863, Lear said:

Bye the bye – talking of fools – there is an old man here partly by nature – partly by drink – a seafaring man who has formerly been in the Balearic Isles. He has taken a kind of monomaniac fancy to my Nonsense book, & declares that he *knew personally* the Aunt of the Girl of Majorca!! I hear it is more than humanity can bear to hear him point out how exactly like she is – & how she used to jump the walls in Majorca with flying leaps!!!!!!

Fortescue (1823–98) had met Lear in Rome in 1845, and became one of his closest friends. See also 'O! Mimber for the County Louth' note to ll. 1–2 and headnote to 'Oh! Chichester, my Carlingford!'

3 *seventy*] *Duncan* 50

There was an Old Man of Kildare

This limerick was dropped from the 3rd and later editions.

[Other early limericks]

There was an old man who forgot; There was an old man of Orleans; There was an old man of the Dee; There was an old person of Leith
MS *Koch*. Pub. *Kraus*.
These were given to the Phipps Hornby family.

There was an old person whose legs – There was an old man who made bold
(pp. 110–17)
MS *Koch*. Pub. *B&N*.
These were given to the Duncan family.

There was an old man whose Giardino – There was an old person whose tears
(pp. 118–20)
MS *NYPL*.

The Hens of Oripò

Written on 16 June 1848 in Lear's diary of his Greek tour, transcribed by Charles Church who substituted lines of dots for the missing lines of the poem. TS *Westminster School* Pub. *Edward Lear in the Levant*, ed. Hyman.

Lear was travelling in Euboea with Church, who later became Dean of Wells. In his journal for that day, Lear wrote: 'After a long long road, arrived at the Scala di Oripò. Khan. Mice. Fleas. Tea – eggs with a fish-like flavour. Much laughter at impromptu verses.'

1 *Oripò*: the Euripos, the narrow waterway between Euboea and mainland Greece.

'A was an Ant'

Lear's earliest recorded alphabet dates from about 1846, and was prepared for Samuel Sandbach. Accompanying it is a note: 'My dear Sam, I send these alphabetic nonsenses for the future amusement of your little boy. If pasted on linen they will last a long time, till Derry Down Derry comes again to make some more.' The earliest alphabet that is known to have survived dates from 1848, and was prepared for the de Tabley children. One prepared in about 1849 for the Tatton children was published in 1926 as *Facsimile of a Nonsense Alphabet*. During the next twenty years, Lear prepared more than fifteen further alphabets which followed the same format; the one reproduced here was made for his goddaughter, Gertrude Lushington, in 1867 (**MS** *Houghton*). These, with the name of the families for whom they were drawn, were: September 1851, Massingberd; December 1855, Tennyson; November 1857, Crake; March 1858, Gage; March 1858, Shakespeare; March 1858, Reid; May 1859, Blencow; August 1860, Braham; February 1862, Craven; August 1862, Prescott (published in 1988 as *A New Nonsense Alphabet*); December 1862, De Vere; February 1865, Fitzwilliam; April 1866, Williams; June 1866, Rawlinson; and October 1866, Drummond. There are three surviving undated alphabets for unknown recipients, one of which was published as *ABC* (1965); two ('A was an ant' and 'A was an ape') were published in *NSSBA*.

The objects for each of the letters in these alphabets were: A – ass, ape, ant, ants; B – bee, bird, bat, butterfly, broom, book, bat; C – crow, coal, cat, camel, cobweb; D – dish, duck, dove; E – eagle, elephant, eel; F – fire, frog, fox, fan, fish, feather; G – gull, gate, goat, grasshopper, gooseberry; H – hat, hive, heron; I – ice, inkstand, ink; J – jug, jar, jackdaw, jujubes; K – kite, key, kingfisher; L – lyre, lark, light, lily, letter, lady, lamp; M – mouse, mill, man; N – needle, note, nuts, net; O – owl, ostrich, omnibus, orange, oyster; P – pig, punch, polly, puppy, pudding; Q – quail, quill; R – rabbit, ring, rattlesnake; S – snail, spider, shoe, swallow, sugartongs, slipper, spoon, soup, screw; T – toad, thrush, tortoise, trumpet, tower, top, thimble; U – ukase, uppercoat, urn; V – villa, veil, vine; W – whale, watch; X – Xerxes; Y – yew, yak; Z – zinc, zebra.

From about July 1870 Lear began to vary the format of his alphabets (see headnote to 'The Absolutely Abstemious Ass'). An alphabet following the earlier format, made in 1880 for Charles Geffrard Pirouet, was published in 1952 as *A Nonsense Alphabet*. Between 1881 and 1885 Lear made at least six further alphabets which do not appear to have survived. Of these, five probably followed the earlier format, and he described the sixth as 'alphabetic incidents' (diary, 23 July 1885), which probably followed the format of 'A tumbled down'.

'Ribands and pigs'

The date of composition is unknown, but ll. 1–24 are done on paper watermarked 1849 and ll. 25–84 on paper watermarked 1850. **MS** *Houghton*. Pub. *T&Q*.

The order of the verses follows Lear's numbering of the MS sheets, and differs from that in *T&Q*.

Ye poppular author & traveller in Albania & Calabrià, keepinge his feete warme

The date of composition is unknown, but probably drawn in the early 1850s. **MS** *PM*. Pub. *VN*.

In 1851 Lear published an account of his travels in Albania in 1848 and 1849, and the following year that of his travels in Calabria in 1847.

[Lear at the Royal Academy Schools]

Drawn on 20 January 1850 in a letter to Fortescue. **MS** *Duke*. Pub. *LEL*.

Although Lear had attended an evening academy in Rome, he was largely self-taught as a landscape painter, and in January 1850 he applied and was accepted as a student at the Royal Academy Schools.
Illustration (bottom): Pub. *LEL* (MS unlocated).

'There was an old person of Ramleh'

The date of composition is unknown. Lear was in Ramleh in March 1858, and the limerick was done for the Francis family who lived there. Pub. *Sotheby's catalogue*, 10 December 1985.

'O! Mimber for the County Louth'

Written on 4 November 1859 in a letter to Fortescue. MS *Taunton*. Pub. *LEL*.

1–2 *Mimber … Ardee*: Fortescue was Member of Parliament for County Louth in Ireland. He lived in Red House, Ardee.

3 *before I wander South*: Lear was planning to winter in Rome.

6 *I've left the Sussex shore*: Lear had spent several weeks staying at St Leonard's, a seaside resort on the south coast of Sussex.

8 *Do cough for evermore*: with the onset of the English winter, Lear's asthma returned.

14 *My well-developed nose*: Lear made great play of having a large nose, although surviving photographs do not indicate this. See 'How pleasant to know Mr Lear!', l. 6.

19 *my last picture*: Lear was working on a number of paintings at this time, but the one to which he refers is probably a large painting of Petra.

24 *England's Northern part*: during November Lear made an extensive tour, visiting friends in the north-west and west of England before leaving from Folkestone on 17 December.

33 *Blue Posts*: the hostelry in St James's, London, which Fortescue frequented. It had long been a fashionable meeting-place, patronized earlier in the century by Byron.

'Washing my rose-coloured flesh
and brushing my beard with a hairbrush'

Written on 9 July 1860 to Fortescue. MS *Taunton*. Pub. *LEL*.

The poem is written in the style of Arthur William Clough's 'Amours de Voyage' (1858) which, with its unusual metre, was popular at the time.

3–4 *Twickenham station … establishment*: Lear had been staying with Lady Waldegrave at Strawberry Hill, Twickenham, the neo-Gothic house built by Horace Walpole. Lear was introduced to Lady Waldegrave (1821–79) by Fortescue, who in 1871 married her as her fourth husband.

6 *England's metropolis*: London.

13 *Nuneham*: Nuneham Park, near Oxford, was the home of Lady Walde-grave's third husband, George Granville Harcourt, MP. She had commissioned Lear to do two paintings of Nuneham.

15 *Ireland*: later in the summer Lear went to stay with Fortescue at Red House, Ardee.

17 *the Blue Posts*: see 'O! Mimber for the County Louth', note to l. 33.

18 *Mrs Clive*: the wife of George Clive, MP, whom Lear had met in Rome in the winter of 1846–7. The painting of the Dead Sea was one of four oils which the Clives commissioned from Lear between 1852 and 1861.

20 *Bother all painting*: although Lear enjoyed the travel involved in collecting his watercolour sketches, he found studio work increasingly irksome.

200: £200.

26 *Charles Braham's little one*: Constance Braham (later Lady Strachey), for whom Lear made an alphabet in August 1860. She would edit *The Letters of Edward Lear* (1907), *The Later Letters of Edward Lear* (1911), *Queery Leary Nonsense* (1911) and *The Complete Nonsense Book* (1912) at a time when Lear's reputation was at its lowest. Her father was Lady Waldegrave's brother.

27 *accounts of the Lebanon*: in the civil war in Lebanon, it was reported that the Druse had carried out acts of barbarism against the Christians unrestrained by the local authorities, which led to a suggestion that there was a government-backed conspiracy to exterminate the Christians.

Illustration The Bowl of Peace: for some months Lear had been warning his friends of his increasing girth. This illustration is the first in which he adopted the convention of drawing himself as 'perfectly spherical' (see 'Journal', note to l. 36).

From a letter to George Grove

Written on 15 November 1860. Pub. Charles Larcom Graves, *The Life and Letters of Sir George Grove* (1903).

Grove (1820–1900), who had developed a sudden interest in collecting mush-rooms, later edited the *Dictionary of Music and Musicians* (4 vols., 1878–89) and was the first Director of the Royal College of Music. At this time he was secretary to the Crystal Palace Company, where F. Penrose was the head of one of the departments.

The description is reminiscent of Lear's long name (see note to [Limericks for the 1846 and 1855 editions of *A Book of Nonsense*], 'There was an old Derry down Derry').

'But ah! (the Landscape painter said,)'
Written on 16 November 1861 as the conclusion of a letter to Fortescue. MS
Taunton. Pub. *LEL*.

Illustration: the self-portrait was included in a letter to Fortescue on 26 July
1860. MS *Taunton*. Pub. *LEL*.

[Additional limericks for the 1861 edition of *A Book of Nonsense*]
Dates of composition unknown. The text of the limericks is from the 3rd edi-
tion of 1861. It contains seventy of the seventy-three limericks from the first
three editions (Compton, New York and Kildare were dropped), with forty-
three new limericks. It was the first edition to have Lear's name on the title-
page. Pub. *BN* (1861).

The first mention of the new edition is on 26 October 1860, when Lear wrote
to Lady Waldegrave: 'I have been making some new nonsenses in my old age.'
He wanted to make this a cheaper, more available edition, and he decided to
reproduce the drawings by woodcut rather than lithography. In February 1861
he asked the Dalziel brothers to prepare two sample woodcuts. Hoping to sell
the book outright to a publisher, he proposed to Dalziel that they buy the rights
for £100. They declined, and in October 1861 he approached Routledge who
also declined, but who offered to buy 1,000 copies when they were printed.
Writing to Edgar Drummond on 10 October, he said: 'My new Book of Non-
sense progresses. It is the old one, with 42 [*sic*] new and enchanting subjects.'
Lear met Drummond in Rome in the winter of 1858–9; he was a member of the
banking family with whom Lear had his account. On 2 November 1861, Lear
asked Dalziel to print 1,000 copies, and the book was published early in
December 1861. Lear had wanted to sell it at 2/6, but Routledge, whom Lear
described as a 'wary Scotchman', thought this too little and proposed 3/6. By
the following June 4,000 copies had been sold, with a further 2,000 printed.
But Routledge had paid him nothing, and as Dalziel was pressing him for pay-
ment it was with relief that he finalized the outright sale of the book to Rout-
ledge on 4 November 1862 at a price of £200. Writing to Lady Waldegrave that
day, Lear said: 'I went into the city today, to put the 125£ I got for the Book of
Nonsense into the funds. It is doubtless a very unusual thing for an Artist to put
by money, for the whole way from Temple Bar to the Bank was *crowded* with
carriages & people, – so immense a sensation did this occurrence make. And all
the way back it was the same, which was very gratifying.' The book was to go
into twenty-four editions in Lear's lifetime, and has never been out of print.

The popularity was not immediate, for on 21 January 1862 Lear wrote to

Fortescue: 'I was disgusted at the Saty. Review – Decr 21 – talking of the Non-sense *verses* being "anonymous, & a reprint of old nursery rhymes," – tho' they gave "Mr Lear credit for a persistent absurdity." I wish I could have all the cred-it due to me, small as that may be … If you are asked ever about that Book of Nonsense, remember I made *all* the verses: except 2 lines of two of them – Abruzzi & Nile. I wish someone would review it properly & funnily.' However, an undated newspaper fragment spoke of its 'originating quite a new class of prose rhymes that for a good twelvemonth were the rage in all societies', and *Punch* proposed to publish a limerick for every town and city in the country.

The first American edition was published by Willis P. Hazard in Philadel-phia in 1863, and was taken from the 10th London edition.

There was an Old Man with a flute

See 'Letter to Harry Hinde', note to l. 18.

2 *sarpint*: serpent.

There was a Young Lady of Portugal

2 *ideas*] *Duncan* tastes
3–4 *climbed … leave*] *Duncan* felt deep emotion, on viewing the Ocean, / & sighed to be gone out of

There was a Young Person of Crete

4 *ombliferous*: a neologism.

There was an Old Person of Dover

2 *rushed*] *Duncan* ran
4 *very soon*] *Duncan* suddenly

There was an Old Person of Philæ

This is the only example of Lear using a formal landscape background in his limericks. He visited Philæ on the Nile in 1854 and again in 1867, writing to his sister Ann on 7 February 1854: 'It is impossible to describe the place to you, any further than by saying it is more like a real *fairy-island* than anything else I can compare it to.' He made numerous drawings and at least fifteen oil paint-ings of the island with its temples.

2 *scroobious*: the first appearance of one of Lear's most frequently used neologisms. He applied it also to a bird, dubious doubtfulness, existence, movements, a pig, a snake, an unpleasant sound, a state of anxiety, a strong wind and, as runcible=scroobious, to a generally praiseworthy way of life. See also 'The Scroobious Pip'.

There was an Old Man on some rocks

3–4 *said, 'Let ... box.'*] *Duncan* cried – 'let me go!' – He merely said – 'Bo! – / Don't make such a noise in that box!' –

There was an Old Man who said, 'How

Franklin Lushington (1823–1901), Lear's closest friend, later recalled:
[Lear's] indefatigable devotion to his work in no way interfered with the volatile fun which in his youth was always ready to bubble over. The 'Book of Nonsense' is the off-spring of an always fresh and fertile humour. I remember one night in Greece [in 1848] when, after scrambling for fifteen hours on horseback over the roughest mountain paths, we had dismounted and were waiting in black darkness for our guide to find among a few huts a tolerable weather-tight shelter for us to sleep in, Lear, who was thoroughly tired, sat down upon what he supposed to be a bank; but an instant grunt and heave convinced him of error as a dark bovine quadruped suddenly rose up under him and tilted him into the mud. As Lear regained his feet he cheerily burst into song: There was an old man who said, 'Now / I'll sit down on the horns of that cow!' ('A Leaf from the Journals of a Landscape Painter', *Macmillan's Magazine*, 75 (April 1897), p. 410)
3 *continue*] *Duncan* endeavour

There was an Old Person of Dutton

2 *so*] *Duncan* as

There was an Old Man who said, 'Hush!

2 *young*] *Duncan* small
3–4 *'Is it ... as the*] *Duncan* 'does it sing?' – He replied – 'No such thing! – / It's a'building a nest in this

There was an Old Person of Bangor

4 *borascible*: a neologism.

There was an Old Man who said, 'Well!

2–3 *Will nobody ... white*] *Duncan* This *is* a remarkable bell! / I have pulled night and day – till my hair has grown grey

There was an Old Man at a casement

4 *incipient*] *Duncan* astucious

'General appearance of a distinguished Landscapepainter'
Written on 29 May 1862 in a letter to Fortescue. **MS** *Taunton*. Pub. *LEL*.

Lear had visited Malta on his way back to England after wintering in Corfu.

Eggstracts from the Roehampton Chronicle
Written on 16 August, 28 September and 1 November 1862 and 11 July 1863. **MS** *Farq*. 'Object discovered in Beta' pub. *RA*; all four Objects pub. *Edward Lear: A New Nonsense Alphabet*, ed. Susan Hyman (1988).

These household objects were discovered by Lear on successive visits to the William Prescott family in Roehampton, where the rooms of their house were named after the letters of the Greek alphabet.
    Lear met William Prescott and his wife in Rome in the winter of 1859–60. He subsequently realized that Prescott's father had been banker to his father during the financial crisis of 1816 (see headnote to 'Eclogue: *Vide* Collins "Hassan – or the Camel Driver"').

Letter to Ruth Decie
Written on 9 September 1862. **MS** *Farq*. Pub. *SL*.

Ruth Decie, born on 8 September 1862, was a granddaughter of William Prescott.

7 *One of the old Greek Tragedians*: Sophocles' *Oedipus at Colonus*.

'There was an old person of Páxo'
Written on 23 March 1863 in a letter to Fortescue, from Corfu. MS *Taunton*. Pub. *LEL*.

Like Corfu, Paxos is one of the Ionian Islands, which were ceded to the Greeks in 1862. Lear had made his home in Corfu for a number of years, and, before the English left, he wanted to visit the other islands in the group in preparation for a book, *Views in the Seven Ionian Islands*. He had been uncertain whether he could afford to go, but in this letter he wrote: 'The sklimjimfiousness of the situation increases: Sir H. Drummond Wolff has been & gone & bought 2 of my drawings – and Capt. Strachan is to buy another, so that I shall have enough tin to pay rent & shut up house for 8 weeks or thereabouts. Whereupon, I shall first make some studies of what Lady Young used to call "Awnge" trees – & then I shall go to Paxo.' This was followed by the limerick.

'She sits upon her Bulbul'
Written on 4 April 1863 in Lear's **diary**, as he was preparing to leave Corfu. Pub. *VN*.

For a similar use of words, see 'The Cummerbund'.

1 *Bulbul*: an oriental bird admired for its song, sometimes called the nightingale of the East.
4 *Yashmack's*: the veil, concealing the lower part of the face, worn by Muslim women.
5 *Yaourt*: yoghurt.
8 *Asphodel*: a succulent-leaved plant which grows widely around the Mediterranean.

'O Digby my dear'
Written on 14 November 1863 to Matthew Digby Wyatt. MS *Vivien Noakes*. Pub. *RA*.

Wyatt (1820–77), whom Lear had met in Rome, was an architect and first Slade Professor of Fine Arts at Cambridge .

8 *Mrs T Wyatt*: the wife of the architect Thomas Wyatt (1807–80), who was Matthew's brother.

'There was an old man with a Book'

Written in December 1863 to accompany a letter to Prescott. MS *Farq*. Pub. *VN*.

The book is *Views in the Seven Ionian Islands* (see headnote to 'There was an old person of Páxo'). Prescott had ordered a copy and had asked Lear, who was about to leave for Corfu, to leave it to be collected from the Cloakroom at Waterloo station.

Letters to Evelyn Baring

Evelyn Baring (1841–1917) was ADC to Sir Henry Storks, High Commissioner for the Ionian Islands, and it was here that Lear met him at the end of 1863. In 1872 he was appointed secretary to his cousin Lord Northbrook, then Viceroy of India (see 'The Cummerbund', note to l. 1).

p. 186 Written on 12 January 1864. Pub. *QLN*.

p. 186 l. 3 *His Excellency*: the High Commissioner.

p. 186 ll. 4–5 *De Vere's*: Aubrey De Vere (1814–1902), Irish poet, and his wife.

p. 187 Written on 4 February 1864. Pub. *QLN*.

p. 187 l. 4 *Strahan*: like Baring, Strahan was Aide-de-Camp to the High Commissioner.

p. 187 Written on 19 February 1864. Pub. *QLN*.

p. 187 l. 3 *of Hood to Wade Brown*: Captain Wade Brown was part of the garrison in Corfu. The poems of Thomas Hood (1799–1845) had been published in two volumes in 1846.

p. 188 Date of composition unknown, but written early in 1864. Pub. *QLN*.

Letter to Nora Decie

Written on 3 April 1864. MS *Farq*. Pub. *SL*.

Nora Decie, born in 1864, was a granddaughter of William Prescott.

p. 189 l. 5 *Captn. Deverill's*: Captain Deverill was part of the garrison in Corfu.

[Lear's adventures in Crete]

Drawn on 5 July 1864. Lear travelled in Crete in April and May 1864. MS *Farq*. Plate 1 pub. *VN*; Plate 2 and 3 pub. *Edward Lear: The Cretan Journey*, ed. Rowena Fowler (Athens, 1984).

In fact the Cretan mountain goat is the agrimi. Lear did encounter moufflons in Corsica, and in the entry for 1 June 1864 in *Journal of a Landscape Painter in Corsica* (1870) he writes: 'Enquiring after that very exclusive beast, the transitory "Moufflon", I hear he is really returned to his mountain home at Serraggio, and on reaching that place at 8 A.M. I proceed to ascertain the dwelling of his Moufflonship.'

Letters to Anna Duncan and Lady Duncan
Written on 3 and 7 January 1865. MS *Koch*. Pub. *B&N*.

Lear first met Lady Duncan, and her invalid daughter Anna, in Rome, and then again in Malta during the winter of 1865–6. It was for Lady Duncan that he had prepared one of several volumes of limericks, many of which were later published in the 1st edition of *A Book of Nonsense* (see headnote to [Limericks for the 1846 and 1855 editions of *A Book of Nonsense*]).

The History of the Seven Families of the Lake Pipple-Popple
Written on 13 February 1865.

The MS (*BL*) is inscribed: 'Written & illustrated for Lady Charlotte and the Honbles Hugh and Reginald Wentworth-Fitzwilliam, by Derry Down Derry Edward Lear'. The Fitzwilliams, whom Lear described as 'jolly cheerful children', were staying in Nice, where he was spending the winter. On 1 February Lear visited them, noting in his diary, '... no one was at home: so I drew some birds & made some nonsenses for the children & came away'. He does not specify what these were, but on 10 February he made them an alphabet and three days later wrote 'a most absurd lot of stories for the little Fs'. Pub. *NSSBA*.

When he was preparing *NSSBA*, he borrowed the MS and made a number of alterations to the text. All the variants listed are found in the MS *BL*.

p. 193 l. 6 *Tosh*] Bosh
p. 197 ll. 12–13 *pain in their toes*] headache
p. 197 ll. 31–2 *and guffled, / and bruffled*] not in MS
p. 197 ll. 33–4 *and snapped*] not in MS
p. 198 l. 7 *fourteen*] 3
p. 198 l. 8 *six*] 3
p. 198 l. 10 *himmeltanious*] not in MS
p. 198 l. 13 *sky-blue*] blue
p. 198 ll. 18–22 *chatter-clatter...flatter-quatter*] chatterclatterblatterplatterpatterblattermatterblatter

p. 199 l. 7 *GEESE*] throughout chapter VII, MS has 'Gooses'

p. 199 l. 12 *Geography, and Cookery*] not in MS

p. 200 l. 4 *dreadful*] amazing

p. 200 ll. 10–11 *hopped ... higher and higher*] and jumped like a maniac

p. 200 l. 13 *furiously and terribly*] frightfully

p. 201 l. 2 *Squeaky-peeky-weeky*] Squeakyweeky

p. 201 l. 4 *meaning ... perceive*] not perceiving

p. 201 l. 5 *large*] deep
        superficially] not in MS

p. 201 l. 6 *less than half*] not in MS

p. 201 l. 15 *exclaimed*] called out

p. 201 ll. 16–20 *'Lettuce ... leaves!'*] Lettuce! Lettuce leaves! O let us leave this tree and eat lettuce leaves! Let us, O! let us!

p. 201 l. 22 *extreme*] not in MS

p. 201 l. 22–p. 202 l. 1 *hit ... stalk*] bumped their noses so dreadfully hard against it

p. 202 ll. 1–2 *directly ... transitional*] not in MS

p. 202 ll. 2–3 *worse and worse and worse and worse*] worse and worse

p. 202 l. 3 *till ... Seven*] and killed them all 7 in five minutes time

p. 202 l. 11 *the warning ... had had*] what they had been told

p. 202 l. 14 *commonly to be met with*] common

p. 202 l. 18 *observed*] seen
        entirely] not in MS

p. 202 l. 20 *when they eat*] not in MS

p. 202 l. 21 *or saltpetre*] not in MS

p. 202 l. 24 *though they continued to run*] not in MS

p. 202 l. 25 *afterwards*] not in MS

p. 203 l. 5 *Pipple-Popple*] not in MS

p. 203 l. 7 *15th*] 12th

p. 203 l. 8 *swam after*] pursued

p. 203 ll. 10–11 *spicular, / orbicular*] not in MS

p. 203 ll. 15–16 *great and uncomfortable*] very great

p. 203 ll. 17 *all*] entirely
        very] not in MS

p. 204 l. 16 *circular ... base*] circle

p. 204 l. 17 *all these memorials*] them
        quite] not in MS

p. 204 l. 18 *and a garden-party, and a ball*] not in MS

p. 204 ll. 19–20 *full ... disgust*] with the utmost respect, and pleasure, and satisfaction and sympathy

p. 205 l. 11 *by reading in the newspapers,*] not in MS

p. 205 l. 15 *with air-tight stoppers*] not in MS

p. 205 l. 17 *an affecting and formal*] not in MS

p. 205 ll. 18–19 *numerous ... ridiculous*] select and numerous and responsible

p. 205 l. 23 *each ... bottle*] all of them got into the bottles

        effort] event

p. 205. l. 24 *all died*] were pickled

p. 205 ll. 24–25 *and became ... minutes;*] not in MS

p. 205 ll. 25–26 *(by ... District)*] not in MS

p. 205 l. 27 *Seven*] not in MS

p. 205 l. 29 *principal*] not in MS

p. 205 l. 30 *Tosh*] Bosh

p. 205 l. 30–31 *anti-congenial succedaneum*] congenial substitute

p. 205 l. 31 *marble*] not in MS

p. 205 l. 31–p. 206 l. 1 *with silver-gilt ... contemplation, and*] not in MS

p. 206 l. 4 *Tosh*] Bosh

p. 206 l. 5 *Four hundred and twenty-seventh*] 400th

p. 206 l. 6 *magnificent*] beautiful

The Duck and the Kangaroo

The date of composition is unknown. Pub. *OYF* 6:3 (March 1870), p. 146, where the illustration is not by Lear; *NSSBA*. *Houghton* 1 was published in facsimile by Philip Hofer in 1956.

In his copy of *NSSBA*, Lear has noted: 'Written at Chewton Priory in 1865 or 1866 for the children of Sir Edward Strachey, Bt.' He visited Chewton in June 1865, but there is no mention of the poem in his diary. If the date is accurate, this is Lear's earliest nonsense song. However, he was notoriously vague about dates, and without supporting evidence this cannot be relied upon.

The earliest surviving dated MS is an illustrated fair copy prepared for the family of George Clive, dated 19 October 1868 (*Houghton* 1). There is a further undated, illustrated fair copy in Houghton (*Houghton* 2), and another, probably prepared for the Strachey family, was published in facsimile in *NSS*. In *PM* there is an unillustrated fair copy dated 14 October 1869, made for Mrs Fields, the wife of James Fields, which probably relates to the publication of the poem in *Our Young Folks*. Lear made a fair copy for Daisy Terry on 21 August 1870 (present whereabouts of MS unknown, but there is a photocopy of the MS in *Houghton* 3).

On 18 November 1869, Lear wrote to Fields:

... will you kindly send, as swiftly as possible, or more swiftly than possible if possible – the name & nature & time or times of your magazine. For having been just now at Dr

Lushington's for some days – where billions of that dear old Gentleman's grandchildren have been screaming about the songs I sang, – they all want to know the Magazinious nomenclature, that they may order it 4thwith ... You will I know kindly print my name in full 'Edward Lear' – wh. will, when I get the Magazine, delight my feeble mind, & console me for remaining in this cold foggy place. After all, small as it may be, one does some good by contributing to the laughter of little children, if it is a harmless laughter.

In his diary for 21 May 1870, he noted that he had received a letter from Bush (his London publisher): '... enclosed are the "Young Folks" Pussey [sic] Cat, Kangaroo & Floppy Fly songs. Quaint, that these should be read in America first of all.' On 21 August he wrote to Fields: 'I thought the 3 poems very nicely printed, and capitally illustrated.'

Sources: Philip Hofer, *The Duck and the Kangaroo by Edward Lear. A facsimile of an original manuscript with pen drawings* (Cambridge, Mass., 1956).

3 *fields*] Houghton 3 land
   water] Houghton 1 waters
13 *And we'd*] Houghton 2, NSS We would
   Jelly Bo Lee] Houghton 1, NSS Jellybolee Houghton 2 Jelly golee Houghton 3 Jelly-bo-lee
14 *Over*] Houghton 2, NSS All over
15 *Please take*] Houghton 1 Please let Houghton 3 Please give
18 *This*] Houghton 2, NSS It
   some] OYF, NSS a
19 *Perhaps*] Houghton 3 I think
   might] NSS may
21 *Which ... me*] NSS For – (if I'm permitted to
22 *unpleasantly*] Houghton 2, NSS distressingly Houghton 3 disgustingly
23 *probably*] Houghton 2, NSS certainly
   roo-] Houghton 1, OYF rheu- Houghton 2 rheu= Houghton 3 rheu NSS rheu=
24 *matiz*] Houghton 1, 2, NSS =matiz̄z̄ Houghton 3 =matiz NSSBA Matiz
26 *over*] Houghton 3, NSS of all
27 *I*] Houghton 3 I've
   four] Houghton 1, 2 10 Houghton 3 8
28 *web-feet*] Houghton 1 feet quite
29 *out ... bought*] Houghton 3 myself warm I'll wear
   I've] NSS I have
31 *All to*] Houghton 2, NSS While I
31–2 *true / Love*] Houghton 1, 2, 3 true=/=love NSS true/=Love
35 *to ... well*] Houghton 3 whatever you do
   dear] NSS o my

38 *three*] *Houghton* 1 six *Houghton* 3 five
39 *who*] *Houghton* 1, 2, *NSS* who were
    O *who*,] *OYF*, O who? *NSS* ah! Who?
40 *Kangaroo?*] *OYF*, *NSS* Kangaroo.

'Gozo my child is the isle of Calypso'
Written on 22 April 1866 in a letter to Luard. **MS** *Texas.*

Lear described Luard, whom he had met in Corfu in 1862, as 'a superior youth, & – polyarchacotopochromographical in taste' (letter to Fortescue of 21 January 1862). He was the grandson of the ornithological draughtsman Prideaux Selby (1788–1867), for whom Lear had worked in the early 1830s (see 'Scrawl', note to l. 25).

Lear had spent the winter of 1865–6 in Malta, visiting Gozo for ten days at the end of March. Gozo is the second largest and most fertile of the Maltese islands, the idyllic home of the nymph Calypso. It was here, according to legend, that Calypso entertained Odysseus (Ulysses), the hero of Homer's epic poem *The Odyssey.*

Stratford Place Gazette
Written 7 August 1866. **MS** *Princeton.*

Lear had stayed with George Scrivens and his wife 4–6 August 1866. Mrs Scrivens, who bought a number of Lear's paintings, was the daughter of Sir Thomas Potter (1773–1845), who founded the *Manchester Guardian* and was the first mayor of Manchester. Lear first had rooms in Stratford Place, a cul-de-sac that runs north from Oxford Street, in 1849.

[Three miscellaneous limericks]
The dates of composition are unknown.

There was an old person who said
MS *Houghton.*

There was an old man who felt pert
Pub. *LEL.*

There was an old person who sung
MS *PM.*

The Adventures of Mr Lear & the Polly [& the]
Pusseybite on their way to the Ritertitle Mountains

Written on 23 August 1866 at Upper Hyde Park Gardens, for the children of Emma Parkins (see headnote to 'The Story of the Four Little Children Who Went Round the World'). MS *Houghton*. Pub. *T&Q*.

Writing to Emma Parkins's sister, Gussie, on 18 December 1871, Lear said: 'I cannot recollect the Polly Pusseybite story: is it too large to copy out small, – or too large to be sent to me, as the 4 children MSS was? I should certainly like it to come into the next vol – if I can do another' (Koch). The manuscript must have been sent because in his diary for 7 May 1872, Lear notes: 'After bkft, found out the Pussey Pollybite drawings, made for Emma Parkins children in 1866.' The drawings are on tracing paper, numbered 1, 2, 3, 5, 7 and 8, with a view to publication; the missing sheets are unlocated.

Title *the Polly [& the] Pusseybite*] the Polly Pussey bite

'O Thuthan Thmith! Thweet Thuthan Thmith!'

Written on 24 October 1866 to Mrs Matthew Digby Wyatt from 'Thtratford Plaithe, Okthford Thtreet, W.' MS *Schiller*.

At the end of a previous letter to her, dated '22toothoktobr', Lear had explained: 'P.Eth: I have had a thaddakthident, & have broken off my front teeth, so that I thall never thpeak plain again. Thith cometh of biting crutht.'

5 *Acroth ... thea*: in a letter to Emily Tennyson – wife of Alfred Tennyson – of 15 December 1851, Lear wrote: 'Flights of grey gregarious gaggling grisogonous geese adorn the silver shining surface of the softly sounding sea.' (See also 'When leaving this beautiful, blessed Briánza' note to l. 11.)

14 *thindy*] ~~tumult~~ thindy

The Story of the Four Little
Children Who Went Round the World

Written on 6 November 1867 for the grandchildren of Richard Bethell. No MS appears to have survived, but there is an incomplete set of proofs at *Houghton*. In preparation for *NSSBA*, Lear copied out what he called 'the Slingsby Nonsense MSS' on 15 and 17 September 1869. Pub. *NSSBA*.

Bethell, the first Lord Westbury (1800–1873), whom Lear had met in the early 1830s, had been Lord Chancellor. On 2 November 1867 Lear went to stay with the Bethell family intending to propose to Westbury's daughter, Gussie, a decision from which he pulled back at the last moment. Violet, Slingsby, Guy and Lionel were the children of Westbury's second son, Slingsby. In his diary for 19 September 1868, Lear describes Violet as 'that odious child'. Writing to Gussie after the death of her father in 1873, Lear recalled: 'The Books of Nonsense I wrote from time to time greatly amused him, and when I made that absurd story for Slingsby's children, who went (or didn't go) round the world, it was wonderfully funny to hear the Chancellor read the whole aloud with a solemnity befitting the perusal of grave history.'

The *Dictionary of National Biography* describes Lord Westbury as having 'extraordinary power of sarcastic speech and an unequalled mastery of luminous exposition'. Certainly, he did not always appreciate Lear's turn of mind. Writing to Fortescue on 21 October 1862 after a visit to Westbury's home, Lear said:

The Chancellor – (I was there Saturday and Sunday) was delightful: such an abundance of excellent conversation – with a circle or with me only – one seldom has the luck of getting. He – speaking of 'undique sequaces' – & 'seaquax' – & saying 'let us remember the line & go & look for the translation,' quoth the Landscape painter in a fit of absurdity – 'My Lord I can remember it easily by thinking of wild ducks.' – 'How of wild ducks Lear?' – said the Lord C—. 'Because they are *sea-quacks*' said I. 'Lear,' – said his Lordship, 'I abominate the forcible introduction of ridiculous images calculated to distract the mind from what it is contemplating.' The painter chuckled inwardly – having from beforehand calculated on the exact result of his speech.

The story is a parody of popular books of travel, in particular Captain Cook's *A Voyage Towards the South Pole, and Round the World* (1777), which described the journey, the food they found and the strange people they met. Violet's head-dress (p. 223) is reminiscent of the feathered head-dresses of Tahiti, which Cook brought back and gave to the British Museum, and of the head-dress given to Cortez which was plucked from the South American bird, the Ketzal, whose feathers grew again. Lear also drew on the tradition of fabulous adventures, for example Lucian (c. 115–200), *The True History* and Raspe's *The Travels and Surprising Adventures of Baron Munchausen*.

p. 227 ll. 1–3 *Mainly ... jelly*: writing to his sister Ann on 23 August 1856, Lear explained that while waiting with Giorgio for a boat to take them from Katerina to Salonica on their way to Mount Athos:

... we ate up the last bit of our meat – for the Khan had nothing but coarse bread & a little rhum – & when no boat came on the 25th morning, we began to speculate how Giorgio should cook the large blue jelly fish that the sea threw up. We found 2 small crabs also – & I proposed – as there were blackberries all about, to boil the jelly fish with blackberry sauce, & roast the crabs with rhum & bread crumbs – a triumph of cookery not reserved for us – for at last the boats began to come.

See also headnote to [Nonsense Cookery].

Growling Eclogue

Written on 9 December 1867 in Cannes, for the writer John Addington Symonds (1840–93) and his wife Catherine. Pub. *Atlantic Monthly*, May 1894; *NSS*.

Catherine, whom Lear had known since her childhood, was the daughter of Frederick North, MP, whom he had met in the early 1850s. The sister of John Addington Symonds married Sir Edward Strachey, and was the mother-in-law of the Lady Strachey who edited *LEL*, *LLEL*, *QLN* and *CNB*.

Writing in his diary on 9 December 1867, Lear said: 'I made an Eclogue for the Symonds – funny enough – & wrote it out ... At the V[illa] Josepha – "Johnny" Symonds is better: he & Catherine laughed hugely at my Ekklogg – & say they'll print it.' Although it was not published until after Lear's death, copies were passed round among his friends. Writing to Lear on 4 January 1868, Fortescue said: 'Curious are the coincidence congruities & concatenations of the community of cultivated creatures! This much is caused by the fact that I have this morning received from Ly Strachey, (who is our nicest neighbour here) an "Eclogue" between Edwardus & Johannes, with wh. we are much edified.' On 9 January, Lear wrote to Lady Waldegrave: 'I am glad you and C[hichester] have had that Growling Eclogue I wrote for Lady Strachey ... (The original poem of the Growl, had a line – altered afterwards thus – "*nearly* – run over by the Lady Mary *Peerly*" – stood – "*all but* run over by the Lady Emma *Talbot*" – which was a fact – but I suppressed it as too personal.[)]'

The habit of growling was one that Lear recognized in himself. Writing to Emily Tennyson from Corfu on 15 February 1856, he said: '... though I know I used many phrases of dislike about this place, yet you know my exaggerated mode of writing and talking, and can weigh what I mean: and regarding myself, I have so little real care about mine uncomfortables – (tho' I growl enough about them in my way,) that I could look happily to staying here all my life.'

47–9 *what avails ... Albanian*: Lear's servant, Giorgio Kokali, was an Albanian Christian from Suli. He was living in Corfu when Lear first employed him in 1856. Giorgio picked up rudimentary Italian in Rome, and Lear taught him to speak English. There is no evidence that he spoke Arabic, although Lear himself had a few lessons before his second visit to Egypt at the beginning of 1867.

55 *I needs ... swells*: although dependent upon them for patronage, Lear came increasingly to dislike the aristocratic, idle and often foolish rich who spent their winters on the Riviera, and who condescended to him as a painter. One of the charms of San Remo was that, unlike Nice or Cannes, it was not fashionable and few 'swells' stayed there.

56 *the Estrelles*: the Massif de l'Esterel, a group of isolated, thickly wooded hills above Cannes.

57 *to leave a card*: the convention of leaving a calling card notified friends and acquaintances of a visit.

64 *Jehu*: king of Israel (*c.* 842–815 BC) noted for the ferocity of his chariot driving; in eighteenth- and nineteenth-century England a coach or cab driver was sometimes called a Jehu.

73 *Germans ... strayed*: Lear disliked what he called 'horrid Germen, Gerwomen and Gerchildren' (letter to Fortescue, 12 September 1873).

82 *ics*] NSS Ics. This has been changed in keeping with Lear's usual practice when taking a word over a line-break.

96 *How can ... Palestine?*: Lear was hoping to return to Palestine which he had visited in 1858 and 1867, but this depended on the sale of his paintings.

108 *you're somewhat poorly*: Symonds was wintering in Cannes where he was suffering a period of deep mental despair.

Illustration: the date of drawing is unknown, but it may have been done in 1867 or 1868 for the Symonds's daughter Janet. Pub. *QLN*.

The Owl and the Pussy-cat
Written between 14 and 18 December 1867 for Janet Symonds. Pub. *OYF* 6:2 (February 1870), p. 111, where the illustrations are not by Lear; *NSSBA*.

This was the first of Lear's nonsense songs to be published, and the first for which we have a definite date of composition.

In his diary of 14 December, Lear noted: 'Their little girl is unwell – & all is sad.' Four days later he visited the Symonds, taking with him 'a picture poem for little Janet'. The original MS passed down to Dame Janet Vaughan, John Symonds's granddaughter. In 1937 she sold it at a Red Cross auction to raise money to help the wounded in the Spanish Civil War, and its present whereabouts is unknown. The drawings in this MS were published in *QLN*.

A fair copy in *PM*, formerly in the possession of Lord Strachey, may be the one that Lear sent to Lady Waldegrave on 9 January 1868. In the accompanying letter he said: 'I enclose another bit of fun, for some child or other – (I wrote it for Lady S[trachey]'s niece, little Janet Symonds:) – if Lady S. has a small enough creature not to scorn it, perhaps you will give it to her for its use.' There is a fair copy dated 19 October 1868 made for the family of George Clive (*Houghton*), and an unillustrated fair copy dated 14 October 1869 made for Mrs Fields (*PM*) which probably relates to the publication in *OYF* (see headnote to 'The Duck and the Kangaroo'). At least three other fair copies are known to have existed: for Lord Mount Edgecombe's children made on 24 January 1868; for the children of an Italian neighbour, Giacinta Galletti, on 3 June 1886; and for the sons of his childhood friend, William Nevill.

This is one of the nonsense songs that Lear set to music, and with which he would entertain his child friends. Writing in 1907 (*LEL*, p. xv), Lady Strachey recalled a visit to Lear in San Remo in 1880, when

though much aged and broken by worries and health, still the same sad whimsical personality and undefinable charm of the man attracted as ever, and one day to us was literally shown forth, in his singing of an air to which he had set the 'Owl and the Pussy Cat'. But of that rendering, alas! there is no record, as not knowing music though a musician by ear, he had been unable to transcribe it to paper, and grudged the £5 he said it would cost to employ another to do so.

1 *the Pussy-cat went to sea*: in 'The Story of the Four Little Children Who Went Round the World' the children 'took a small Cat to steer and look after the boat'.

2 *pea-green*: Lear used this adjective frequently. In *The History of the Sixteen Wonderful Old Women* (1820), the companion volume to *Anecdotes and Adventures of Fifteen Gentlemen* (1823), the book that inspired Lear's first limericks, there is a Widow Towl 'Who went to sea with an Owl' in a green boat.

5 *stars*] OYF, PM moon

6 *sang to a small guitar*: in his early years, Lear took his guitar with him on his travels.

9–10 *You are, / You are!*] OYF in each stanza the phrase is not repeated.

13 *charmingly*] OYF wonderful

17 *Bong-tree*] *Houghton* Phloss tree *PM* Palm tree The coach-road along which Lear would have travelled between Liverpool and Knowsley, passes through the village of Knotty Ash, said to have taken its name from a gnarled ash tree which once stood outside the public house beside a group of cottages called 'The Little Bongs'. The tree was known locally as 'the ash tree at Little Bongs', and may have been the inspiration for Lear's Bong tree. On the other hand, he may just have liked the sound of the word.

27 *They dinèd ... quince*: in a note in *NSS*, Edward Strachey wrote: 'Mr Lear was delighted when I showed to him that this couple were reviving the old law of Solon, that the Athenian bride and bridegroom should eat a quince together at their wedding.'

28 *runcible*] *Houghton* muncible *PM* silver This is the first appearance of Lear's most famous neologism. The *OED* (1926) definition of 'runcible' is based on a fanciful idea which has no foundation in fact, and which was probably not meant to be taken seriously. Responding to a reader's query about the

origin of the runcible spoon, Archibald Sparke wrote to *Notes & Queries* 151:24 (11 December 1926): 'A runcible spoon is a kind of fork with three broad prongs or tines, one having a sharp edge, curved like a spoon, used with pickles, etc. Its origin is in jocose allusion to the slaughter at the Battle of Roncevaux, because it has a cutting edge.' In the same edition, H. Askew pointed out that Lear also applied the word to a hat, and asked: 'Does a "runcible" hat mean one of the sort called a trilby? In that case a "runcible" spoon may be one with prongs or teeth.' Lear himself gave it no such meaning; in the alphabet 'The Absolutely Abstemious Ass', the illustration for 'D' shows an ordinary spoon with a deep bowl. He also applied it to a beetle, a bird, a cat, a goose, a raven, a wall, a manner, a state of mind, and, as runcible=scroobious, to a generally praiseworthy way of life. It has no meaning, and dismissing attempts by others to give it one, Lear wrote in his diary for January 1886: 'Letter from ... a school mistress in St Petersburg, wanting to know the meaning of the word "runcible"!!'

29–30 *And hand ... the moon*: this echoes lines that Lear quoted repeatedly in his diary when he was looking back with nostalgia, the source of which has not been identified; for example on 26 August 1861: 'We come no more / To the golden shore / Where we danced in days of old.' One such event is described in a letter to Fanny Coombe on 8 July 1837. He had been staying with friends at Bovisand, near Plymouth, a visit he saw as 'a perfection of all happiness'. Each evening after dinner they would take a long evening walk and then 'we all adjourned to the rocks with guitars ... & there we sate singing to the sea & the moon'.

[Mrs Blue Dickey-bird]
The date of composition is unknown, but probably written in 1867 or 1868, for Janet Symonds. Pub. *QLN*.

'Some people their attention fixes'
The date of composition is unknown. The verse is written on the inside of an envelope addressed to Lear and postmarked 27 August 1868. **MS** *Koch*.

The Broom, the Shovel, the Poker, and the Tongs
Written on, or shortly before, 18 October 1868. Pub. *NSSBA*.

An undated illustrated fair copy (*Houghton* 1), prepared for Mrs Bruce, has an accompanying note: 'My dear Mrs Bruce, Here is the domestic idyll. There will be another of the Goose and the Steam Engine before long.' Henry Bruce, MP

(1815–93), whom Lear had met in Rome, became Home Secretary in 1869 and later Lord Aberdare. The MS was published, in a limited edition and with a foreword by Philip Hofer, in 1977. There is a second, undated illustrated fair copy (*Houghton 2*).

Compare the nursery rhyme 'The sow came in with the saddle', ll. 5–8 (*Halliwell's Nursery Rhymes and Nursery Tales of England* (5th edn, 1853, p. 100)): 'The broom behind the butt / Call'd the dish-clout a nasty slut: / "Oh! oh!" said the gridiron, can't you agree, / I'm the head constable, – come along with me.'

8 *Mrs*] *Houghton* 1, 2 Miss
17 *head is*] *Houghton* 1, 2 noddle
21 *Mrs*] *Houghton* 1, 2 dear Miss
   sighed] *Houghton* 1 said
22 *I'm so*] *Houghton* 1, 2 I am
25 *Ah!*] *Houghton* 1 Oh! *Houghton* 2 O
   when] *Houghton* 1, 2 in
26 *Ah! … complaint!*] *Houghton* 1, 2 Why so deaf to my heartfelt complaint?
27 *Must … so*] *Houghton* 1 Why must you be
30 *You are certainly*] *Houghton* 1, 2 I am sure you are
31 *Mrs*] *Houghton* 1, 2 Miss
   together] *Houghton* 1, 2 looked cross &
32 *you're singing to-day*] *Houghton* 1, 2 you both of you say
35 *homeward*] *Houghton* 1 round
36 *their anger*] *Houghton* 1, 2 the quarrel

'There was an old man who said – "Hum!'"
The date of composition is unknown. **MS** *Houghton*.

On 11 February, 1869 Lear wrote in his diary, 'For 2 days I have suffered greatly from a strained or sprained thumb – somewhat better today.'

Calico Pie
Written in the summer of 1869. There is an unillustrated draft (*Houghton* 1) and an illustrated fair copy (also *Houghton*). Pub. **NSSBA**.

On 24 July 1869 Lear wrote to Lady Strachey regretting that he had little for her youngest son: 'I have been very unpoetical of late, & except one intellectual effusion, "Calico Pie", have made nothing I can send him.'

Compare William Roscoe's popular children's book *The Butterfly's Ball, and the Grasshopper's Feast* (1807) (see headnote to 'The Scroobious Pip').

The refrain echoes Tennyson's lines from 'Break, break, break' (1842): 'But the tender grace of a day that is dead / Will never come back to me'.

4 *wings*] *Houghton* 1 feathers
6 *Till*] *Houghton* 1 ~~Lootilly-loo~~ Till

The Daddy Long-legs and the Fly
Written September–October 1869. Pub. *OYF* 6:4 (April 1870), p. 209; *NSSBA*.

The earliest mention of the song is on 8 September 1869, when Lear was staying with the Lushingtons at Southwold, and noted in his diary: 'Rose at 5.30 – gray –: did little till 8 but a child's song'; in a letter of the same date to Mrs Digby Wyatt he wrote: 'I've written a new child poem here, the Daddylonglegs & the Fly.' On 10 October he went to dinner with Admiral Sir Spencer Robinson, and wrote in his diary: 'There was much fun about my poem of the Daddy Longlegs and Mrs Floppy Fly.' These early MSS have not been traced, but the poem may have undergone changes, for there is an unillustrated draft at *Houghton* which is dated 14 October 1869.

The song was set to music by one of Lear's acquaintances in San Remo, and in his diary for 10 March 1885 he noted: 'Mrs H[assall] played & sang the "Daddy Longlegs & Floppy Fly" set by Miss Josephine Troup – very nicely, – & it seems to me by no means a common place affair.'

2, 4] *Houghton* lines are reversed
12 *battlecock and shuttledore*: see headnote to 'The Absolutely Abstemious Ass' for Lear's 'long nonsense name', and [Lear at the Royal Academy Schools], where his fellow students are playing battledore and shuttlecock. The connection between the game and banishment is echoed in I. Gatty's 'Whiptops and Battledores and Shuttlecocks', *Folklore Journal*, no. 56 (1945), p. 271, where it is suggested that the top in battledore and shuttlecock was 'an inanimate form of "scapegoat" which was flogged with execration out of the village ... while the men were whipping the devil from off the ground, the women were beating him out of the air in the form of a shuttlecock'. The game was so popular in nineteenth-century England that it became a nuisance on the streets.

Battledore was a name given to children's hornbooks, whose broad paddle and handle meant that they were illicitly used by children to play this game.
27 *true I never*] *OYF* true that I don't
41 *awful*] *Houghton, OYF* wondrous
75 *foamy*] *OYF* foaming
76 *sponge-taneous*] *Houghton* ~~spontaneous~~ spongetaneous

82 *reached*] OYF passed
    Gromboolian] *Houghton* Grombolian

[Nonsense Cookery]

Lear gives the date of the *Nonsense Gazette* in which he purports to publish the nonsense cookery and botany (see next item) as August 1870, when it was written for the Terry children (see headnote to 'The Absolutely Abstemious Ass'). It was published in *NSSBA*, and Lear noted in his copy: 'Written mostly 1869 for Bellenden Ker Esq at Cannes.'

There is no mention of the cookery in Lear's diary for 1869, but he certainly met Ker frequently at this time. Ker was the son of the botanist John Bellenden Ker, and was in the south of France because he was ill (he died shortly after this).

In his diary for 19 October 1884, Lear wrote: 'It is funny to see what attention I always pay to dinner/details: but I have a notion that food is a great factor in our fooly life.' He uses food similes frequently in his writings, sometimes putting them into the mouth of his servant Giorgio, as in a description of Petra: '"Oh master," said Giorgio (who is prone to culinary similes), "we have come into a world where everything is made of chocolate, ham, curry powder, and salmon"' ('A Leaf from the Journals of a Landscape Painter', *Macmillan's*, p. 422). See also 'The Story of the Four Little Children Who Went round the World', p. 227 ll. 1–3 and headnote to [The Heraldic Blazons of Foss the Cat].

[Nonsense Botany – 1]

Drawn during the summer of 1870. Pub. *NSSBA*.

On 19 May 1870 Lear wrote from Grasse, in the mountains behind Nice, to Mrs Ker:

As I know how fond you & Mr Ker are of flowers, I have looked out carefully for any new ones all about the Grasse Hills, & have been fortunate enough to find 9 sorts: – they are all very rare, & only grow about here, & in the Jumbly islands, where I first saw them long ago, – & as there happened to be a Professor of Botany there at that time, I got the Generic & Specific names from him. Unfortunately, the flowers all withered directly after I gathered them, so I made drawings of them on the spot, in order to send you a correct illustration of each. (MS *Yale*)

In creating his botanies, Lear may have been influenced by the late fifteenth-century herbal and bestiary *Hortus Sanitatis*, a copy of which is known to have been in the library at Knowsley. As an Associate of the Linnean Society Lear was familiar with modern methods of classification, inscribing both generic and specific names to his natural history drawings.

Bottlephorkia Spoonifolia: see headnote to 'The Absolutely Abstemious Ass'.

The Jumblies
Written on 7 July 1870. Pub. **NSSBA**.

In his diary for that day, Lear says: 'After bkft … completed the Jumblies – wh. I had worked at early this morning.' He does not say whether he was composing the song, or copying it out from earlier workings. *OF* mentions a fair copy made for Mrs Fields in *PM*, dated 14 October 1869, but there is no trace of this; as the poem was not published in *OYF*, it is likely that it was confused with 'The Duck and the Kangaroo', a MS of which was made for Mrs Fields on that day.

The song echoes Sebastian Brant's *The Ship of Fools* (1494), and the traditional nursery rhyme 'Three wise men of Gotham', who went to sea in a bowl. The earliest use of the word 'Jumbly' comes in a letter of 19 May 1870: see headnote to [Nonsense Botany – 1].

In his diary for 31 December 1870, Lear wrote: 'I went to the Sandbachs, but only little Sophy was at hom[e] she sat & heard me read my nonsense songs – & a more delightful little creature I never saw. Of the Jumblies she said – "Do you know, I really don't see how they could have gone to sea in a sieve?"'

Between lines 63 and 64 there is a line missing, giving a thirteen-line stanza. No MS has survived, but since Lear did not amend his copy of *NSSBA* it is possible that he left the line out when he was writing the song, rather than its being a printer's error. In *Edward Lear's Nonsense Songs & Laughable Lyrics* (Stamford, Conn., 1935), ed. Philip Hofer, this line has been inserted and reads: 'And some Barnacle Buns for an early tea'. However, there is no manuscript evidence for this addition, and it is likely that the editor composed the line himself.

'The Absolutely Abstemious Ass'
The alphabet was drawn for the Terry children between 25 and 31 August 1870 (see its title-page). Pub. **MN**.

It is the earliest surviving example of an alphabet in which Lear adopts a different convention (see headnote to 'A was an ant'). The MS was Lear's only known coloured alphabet: it was still extant in the 1950s, but has since disappeared. (There is a black-and-white photocopy at *Houghton*.)

It seems likely that Lear began this alphabet by drawing, on 25 August, a Runcible Beetle and a Scroobious Pig without planning to make them into an alphabet. In a MS of 'The Duck and the Kangaroo' that he made for Daisy Terry on 20 August (*Houghton*), Lear presented 'his best compliments to all the Beetles', which suggests the inspiration for the beetle drawing. When turning the drawings into an alphabet, he changed the beetle into the Bountiful Beetle, and used the pig for the letter S as 'The Scroobious Sucking-pig'. On 30 August 1870, Lear copied the completed alphabet in pen and ink in preparation for publication in *MN* (*Houghton*).

From this time he experimented with different forms of alphabets. There is a draft headed 'Alphabet No. 6', which begins:

> Appaty, Bappaty Appaty A,
> Two nice apples for me today,
> For every Apple a penny to pay.
> Appaty, Bappaty, Appaty A.

Although it promised well, he stopped after the letter P (*Houghton*). In another draft he planned longer verses:

> A those Ants who run about
> Up & down & in & out.
> Corn & oats they bring together
> In the fine & summer weather
> Lest in winter days so cold
> they should —
> When the summer days are done
> And they cannot see the sun
> Then they stay at home & —.

He attempted only one other letter in this alphabet: 'C is spacious London city / Streets & squares & houses pretty' (*Houghton*).

Daisy Terry was a child who was staying at the hotel in Certosa del Pesio where Lear was spending the summer months. He had first met her mother in Rome. Daisy later recalled meeting Lear that summer:

Something seemed to bubble and sparkle in his talk and his eyes twinkled benignly behind the shining glasses. I had heard of uncles; mine were in America and I had never seen them. I whispered to my mother that I should like to have that gentleman opposite for an uncle. She smiled and did not keep my secret. The delighted old gentleman, who was no other than Edward Lear, glowed, bubbled and twinkled more than ever; he seemed bathed in kindly effulgence. The adoption took place there and then; he became my sworn relative and devoted friend. He took me for walks in chestnut forests; we kicked the chestnut burrs before us, 'yonghy bonghy bo', as we called them; he sang to me 'The Owl and the Pussycat' to a funny little crooning tune of his own composition; he drew pictures for me. (Mrs Winthrop Chandler, *Roman Spring* (Boston, 1934))

This is the first record of what was to become the Yonghy-Bonghy-Bò.

The first piece of nonsense Lear did for Daisy Terry is dated 18 August 1870. Below a conventional drawing of a flower he has written his 'long nonsense name': 'Drawn for Daisy Terry, by her affectionate Uncle, Mr Abebiko Krakoponoko, Bizzikato, Katterfelto, Abelgorabolos, Aldeboronty-phosky Phormiostieos, Krohonontonthollogos, Dossy, Flossy, Siny, Tomentilla, Coronella, Polentilla, Poodle Adle Edle Udle Odle Oudle, Battledorra Shuttlecokka Derry Down Derry Dumps Edward Lear' (Houghton). See note to 'There was an old Derry down Derry' in [Limericks for the 1846 and 1855 editions of *A Book of Nonsense*].

A *Absolutely*] *Terry* not in MS
  Barrel] *Terry* tub
B *Bountiful*] *Terry* Runcible
C *Confidential*] *Terry* not in MS
  Red Morocco] *Terry* not in MS
D *Dolomphious*] *Terry* Squashdomphious
  Runcible] *Terry* rosecoloured Runcible
E *and a New … Ear-rings*] *Terry* not in MS
M *Piano-forte*] *Terry* Piano40
P *Parsnip Pie*] *Terry* butter & toast
R *Carpet*] *Terry* Hearth
S *The Scroobious Snake … anybody*] *Terry* The Scroobious Pig, who dressed in blue and wore a bell round his neck, and a hat on his ears to keep them dry In the list of contents prepared by Lear, he calls this 'The Scroobious Suckingpig'.
X *Double-extra … ago*] *Terry* King Xerxes, who drank Extra XX all day long
Y *rather small*] *Terry* somewhat too small for his head
Z *Zigzag*] *Terry* Zigzaggious and
  carried … Jellibolee] *Terry* galloped all round the world with 5 monkeys on his back

'The Uncareful Cow, who walked about'

Written on 8 September 1870 at Certosa del Pesio for Daisy Terry. **MS** *Terry*. Photocopy *Houghton*. Pub. **VN**.

Daisy's sister later recalled: 'Never was there a man who could so live into the feelings of a child. Daisy was a turbulent little creature, always getting into trouble of some kind, and from the first day she learnt to take her disasters to "Uncle Lear", as he taught her to call him, to have them turned into joys by his rhymes and pictures. A frightful bump on her forehead was the origin of the "Uncareful Cow"' (Mrs Hugh Fraser, *A Diplomat's Wife in Many Lands* (Boston, 1910) p. 334).

[Creatures playing chequers]

The date of the drawings is unknown, but probably done in August or September 1870. **MS** *Houghton*.

It is possible that Lear was planning to write a nonsense song about the animals playing chequers.

In the late 1870s and 1880s Lear played with other possibilities for nonsense that were not completed or have not survived. There are various diary entries relating to these: on 31 May 1875 he contemplated making a series of 'caricature spiritual objects', and he illustrated 'a Spiritual snail'; on 22 January 1879 he gave a nonsense song entitled 'The Peacock and the Monkey' to Arnold Congreve, the son of Walter Congreve, his neighbour in San Remo; on 29 January 1881 he 'Conceived a notion of writing stories to each of the "Nonsense" characters'; on 13 July 1882 he wrote, 'Note for poem – the Palm-tree, the pickaxe & the pumpkin'; on 31 August 1884 'I wrote some of a new nonsense poem before bkft, – "Once there lived a little pony, on the road to Abetone"'; and on 27 October 1885 he wrote four lines about characters 'Huntley and Palmer'. In addition there are two undated fragments at *Houghton*: 'The little mouse lived quite close to the oven' and 'Once I had a mucous membrane'.

The Nutcrackers and the Sugar-tongs

Finished and written out on 11 July 1870. Pub. **NSSBA**.

Mr and Mrs Spikky Sparrow

The date of composition is unknown. Written out for publisher on 8 July 1870. Pub. *NSSBA*.

57 *the Monument*: built 1671–7, in the City of London, a column that marks the site where the Great Fire of London broke out in 1666.
62 *Cloxam blue*: sky blue.

The Table and the Chair

The date of composition is unknown. Written out for publisher on 6 July 1870. There is an illustrated draft of nine four-line stanzas (*Houghton* 1) and an unillustrated fair copy (*Houghton* 2). Pub. *NSSBA*.

2–8 'You ... Chair] *Houghton* 1 Let us go & take the air! / And always as we walk / We can have a little talk
21 *everybody*] *Houghton* 1 ~~the people laughed &~~ everybody
22 *hastened*] *Houghton* 1 crowded
26 *the*] *Houghton* 1 a
28 *wandered*] *Houghton* 1 ~~walked about~~ wandered
29 *Till*] *Houghton* 1 So
33 *whispered to*] *Houghton* 1 said unto
36 *Let us dine*] *Houghton* 1 So they dined Let us dine
  Beans and Bacon: Lear's childhood choice of birthday dinner of bacon and small field beans boiled in the bacon broth, a tradition he retained into adult life, recording it as his birthday meal as late as 1871.
37 *So*] *Houghton* 1 With So
39 *Dined, and*] *Houghton* 1 And ~~they~~ each
  their heads] *Houghton* 1 his their head~~s~~
40 *toddled ... beds*] *Houghton* 1, 2 all went off to bed

'A was once an apple-pie'

The date of composition is unknown. MS *Houghton*. Pub. *NSSBA*.

The MS was published in facsimile as *Drawing Book Alphabet* (Houghton, 1954) with an introduction by Philip Hofer. The drawings reproduced here are those prepared for the printer (**Houghton**).

'A was an Area Arch'

Composed between 21 January and 7 February 1871 for the Revd Walter Clay and his children. Pub. *NSSBA*, where (and in all subsequent editions of Lear's nonsense) the illustrations are not by Lear. The drawings reproduced here are those done for the Clays (**Princeton**).

Following his usual habit, when preparing the alphabet for publication, Lear requested the loan of the MS. It appears that Mrs Clay did not return it but copied out the words, so that he did not have his drawings to work from.

[Mr Lear receives a letter from Marianne North]
The drawings, all dated 7 June 1871, accompany a letter written to Marianne North on 8 June. **MS** *Somerville College, Oxford.* Pub. *SL.*

Marianne North (1839–90), traveller and botanist, was the sister of Catherine Symonds (see headnote to 'Growling Eclogue').

Mr and Mrs Discobbolos
The date of composition is unknown, but a fair copy was made on 24 December 1871. Pub. *LL.*

A copy of the sculpture of the Greek discus-thrower, or Discobolos, by the fifth-century Greek artist Myron, was a subject for drawing in the Antique Schools at the Royal Academy when Lear was a student there in 1850.

The Courtship of the Yonghy-Bonghy-Bò
Lear wrote out the song on the morning of 11 December 1871, but it is not known how much of the poem was composed on that day. Pub. *LL.*

In an undated letter to Evelyn Baring, probably written in January or February 1864, Lear has the word 'scratchabibblebongibo', but the earliest mention of 'yonghy bonghy bos' is in the summer of 1870 (see headnote to 'The Absolutely Abstemious Ass'). The turtle on which the Yonghy-Bonghy-Bò escapes is the young *Chelonia Imbricata* for which Lear had made the lithograph for Thomas Bell's *A Monograph of Testudinata* (1836). A later, undated pen-and-ink drawing based on this is subscribed 'ye Turtll' (*Houghton*).

On 21 July 1887, Lear wrote to a friend about some of his paintings: 'O that Lady Jingly Jones could see those! If she were but free I think I would even now propoge to her, for I think we suit admirably.' In his diaries Lear often invokes his nonsense characters, or quotes lines from his nonsense songs, when talking about his own life.

Lear composed his own setting of the song, and Mrs a'Court began to write this down from Lear's playing on 15 March 1872, but the task was not com-

pleted. It was eventually transcribed by Signor Pomé on 1 August 1876 (**MS**
Houghton). In the introduction to *NSS*, Henry Strachey recalled: 'In the
evenings he often sang; the "Yonghy Bonghy bò" was inimitable. His voice had
gone, but the refinement and expression were remarkable.'

The poem echoes lines from mummers' plays, for example, in that of Great
Wolford, Worcestershire, the Fool says: 'In comes I fidler Wit / My head's so
large, me wits so small / I've brought me fidler to please you all. / Toll-de-roll
the tinder box / Father died the other night / And left me all his riches, / A
wooden leg, a feather bed, / And a pair of leather breeches, / A coffee pot with-
out a spout, / A jug without a handle, / A guinea pig without a wig, / And half
a farthing candle' (R. J. E. Tiddy, *The Mummers' Play* (Oxford, 1923), p. 231).

(Angus Davidson has suggested (*AD*, p. 200) that Lear was parodying Ten-
nyson's poem 'Frater Ave atque Vale', but this was not written until June
1880.)

Sources: 'The Yonghy-Bonghy-Bò. Note on the poem by Philip Hofer, on the
music by Randall Thompson', *Houghton Library Bulletin* 15:3 (July 1967),
pp. 229–37.

1 *Coast of Coromandel*: faces the Bay of Bengal in south-east India.

2 *early pumpkins blow*] *Houghton* ~~lofty Bong-trees grow~~

10–11 *Of … Bò*] *Houghton* Throughout the second line of the refrain is not
repeated.

12 *Bong-trees*: see 'The Owl and the Pussy-cat', note to l. 17.

13, 24 *pumpkins*] *Houghton* parsnips

20 *Sits the*] *Houghton* ~~Lovely Charming~~

40 *Gaze … rolling*] *Houghton* In the calm and silent

41 *Fish*] *Houghton* Prawns This line is not bracketed.

50–51 *(Here … I've*] *Houghton* But my Dorking hens look badly, / And besides
– I have

58 *Dorking fowls*: a breed of poultry that has a long, square form and five toes.

63 *Should … send*] *Houghton* ~~If~~ Should my Jones more ~~fowls~~ Dorkings should
send

64 *I … three*] *Houghton* You shall have some eggs

73 *words I needs must*] *Houghton* cruel words I

78 *slippery slopes of*] *Houghton* slopes of musky

81 *Fled*] *Houghton* Rushed

82 *There,*] *Houghton* Far

83 *Lay a large and*] *Houghton* There he found a

86 *Turtle, you shall*] *Houghton* Turtle Turtle

89 *Through*] *Houghton* Plunging through
  silent-roaring] *Houghton* 'roaring' is written above the line.

90 *Did ... swiftly*] *Houghton* Swiftly did ~~that~~ the turtle
91 *Holding*] *Houghton* ~~Sticking~~ Holding
94 *sunset isles of Boshen*] *Houghton* happy isles of Dotion
102–3 *heap ... For*] *Houghton* ~~little~~ heap of stones she mourns / ~~She mourns~~
106–8 *Still ... moans*] *Houghton* She weeps, & warbles airs from Handel. / For
her Dorking fowls she moans, On that little heap of stone, / ~~Parsnips~~ Pumpkins, melody & moans

[Limericks published in *More Nonsense*]

MN is dated 1872, but was available for Christmas 1871. It contained one
hundred limericks, twelve nonsense botanies and the alphabet 'The Absolutely Abstemious Ass'. One hundred and twenty limericks were originally
planned, and the MSS of ninety-seven of these are at *Houghton*.

Lear had been planning a further volume of limericks since 1862, and by July
1863 the material was ready. However, when he approached Routledge about
the possibility, they told him that they were not interested, 'so all these preparations, wh. I have been carrying on for some time – are a failure', he wrote
in his diary on 1 August 1866. The 3rd edition of *A Book of Nonsense* had
made the limerick hugely popular, and as a result it had moved on, so that
Lear's relatively tame verses were no longer so appealing. In the end, as with
all his nonsense books, he brought it out at his own expense, and, like *Nonsense Songs, Stories, Botany, and Alphabets*, which is dated 1871 but was
available in time for Christmas 1870, it was published by R. J. Bush. Writing
to Fortescue, who was then President of the Board of Trade, on 13 September
1871, he said: 'Talking of bosh, I have done another whole book of it: it is to
be called "More Nonsense" & Bush brings it out at Xmas: *it will have a Portrait of me outside.* I should have liked to dedicate it to you, but I thought it
was not dignified enough for a Cabinet M.' (The portrait did not materialize.)

In preparation for *MN*, Lear drafted a sheet of seven limerick verses
(*Houghton 1*). The verses were: Woking, Putney, Brill, Garden, Rhind, Athos
and Dunmore. The first four were put in *MN*, but Lear did not finish the limericks for Rhind (There was an old person of Rhind, / Who rejoiced in an easterly wind) or Dunmore (There was an old man of Dunmore / Who thought all
excitement a bore. / When he tumbled fell off a wall), while that for Athos is
complete: 'There was an old person of Athos / Whose voice was distinguished
by pathos. / He fed upon tripe / and played jigs on a pipe / That excessive old
person of Athos', and has a small, unfinished drawing.

In *More Nonsense*, Old Man etc. was printed in lower-case. This has been
changed here to make them consistent with *A Book of Nonsense*.

There was an Old Man in a Marsh

4 *instructive*] *Houghton* illusive

There was an Old Man at a Station

3 *You have*] *Houghton* For you've
4 *afflicting*] *Houghton* loquacious

There was an Old Person of Woking

2 *mind was perverse and*] *Houghton 1* actions were highly
4 *illusive*] *Houghton 1* abstemious

There was an Old Person of Fife

2 *was*] *Houghton* felt

There was an Old Person of Brill

3 *But ... fish*] *Houghton 1* ~~But~~ When they said, 'its too big', He said, – 'Fiddledefig!'
4 *obsequious*] *Houghton 1* ombrageous

There was a Young Lady in white

In a note for the printer, Lear has written: 'I don't mind how you do the black – as long as you keep the figure quite white with birds gray' (*Houghton*).

There was an Old Person of Putney

2 *Whose food was roast*] *Houghton 1* Who ~~fed upon~~ feasted on
3 *took ... sight*] *Houghton 1* mixed with his tea By the side
4 *romantic*] *Houghton 1* indiginous

There was an Old Lady of France

4 *grieved*] *Houghton* ~~affected~~ grieved

There was an Old Person of Dean

2 *dined on*] *Houghton* ate but

There was an Old Man of Cashmere

3 *slender and*] *Houghton* timid, though

There was an Old Person of Dundalk

1, 4 *Dundalk*] *Houghton* Chalk

There was an Old Person of Shoreham

4 *Which … people of*] *Houghton* And won the respect of all

There was an Old Man of Dunblane

1 *Dunblane*] *Houghton* Dumblayne *MN* Dumblane
4 *Dunblane*] *Houghton*, *MN* Dumblane

There was an Old Person of Cannes

3 *make them feel*] *Houghton* render them

There was an Old Person of Barnes

The idea for this limerick dates from 20 December 1863. Lear had been staying with the Prescott family at Roehampton, near Barnes, and, in a letter to William Prescott, he quotes the first two lines, adding: 'A new idea – & good for my new publication'.

There was an Old Person of Crowle

3 *screamed … screamed*] *Houghton* sang … sang

There was an Old Person of Rye

2 *fly*: a one-horse covered carriage let out for hire.

There was a Young Lady whose nose

3 *exclaimed in a*] *Houghton* grew frantic with

There was an Old Man of Boulak
Written on 19 March 1867 in Cairo. MS *Columbia*.

There was an Old Man of Ibreem
Written on 10 February 1867 in Lear's diary, during a visit to Egypt.

[Extra limericks prepared for *More Nonsense*]
The date of composition is unknown. **MS** *Houghton*. Pub. *OF.*

The drawings and verses were prepared for publication in *MN* but not used.

[Nonsense Botany – 2]
The date of composition is unknown. Pub. **MN**.

'Cold are the crabs that crawl on yonder hill'
The date of composition is unknown. The poem is unfinished. **MS** *Houghton*.
Pub. *T&Q.*

The opening line is a parody of Byron's *Childe Harold's Pilgrimage* (1812–18),
Canto II, xii, 3: 'Cold as the crags upon his native coast'. Line 15 may be an
alternative draft for l. 13. In a final version ll. 15–20 would probably have been
placed before l. 14.

6 *ample*] ~~angry~~ ample
12 *distant*] ~~verdant~~ distant
following 13 ~~Such & so short is life such & so short~~ so sweet
15 *buffaloes*] ~~arabesques~~ buffaloes
17 *pearly ... their*] ~~civil~~ pearly centipedes with pearly adjust their

The Scroobious Pip
Begun in November or December 1871, and continued on 17 January 1872.
The poem is unfinished. **MS** *Houghton*. Pub. *Edward Lear's Nonsense Songs
& Laughable Lyrics*. The final illustration is **Houghton**.

Compare William Roscoe's *The Butterfly's Ball*, ll. 9–16: 'And there came the
Beetle, so blind and so black, / Who carried the Emmet, his friend, on his back.
/ And there came the Gnat, and the Dragon-Fly too, / And all their relations,

Green, Orange, and Blue / And there came the Moth, with her plumage of down, / And the Hornet, with Jacket of Yellow and Brown; / Who with him the Wasp, his companion, did bring, / But they promis'd that ev'ning, to lay by their sting'. The drawings of the Scroobious Pip recall the grotesques in medieval bestiaries and paintings.

Title *Scroobious*: see note to l. 2 of 'There was an Old Person of Philæ' in [Additional limericks for the 1861 edition of *A Book of Nonsense*].
6 *Cow*] ~~horse~~ Cow
7 *Wolf he howled*] ~~lion he roared~~ wolf he howled
20 *rumbling*] ~~raging~~ rumbling
41 *gaily*] ~~quickly~~ gaily
43 *Flippetty ... flip*] Lear wrote the alternative words 'snip' and 'whip' in the margin.
45 *went*] Lear wrote the alternative words 'rushed', 'splashed' and 'squashical' in the margin.
65 *Plifatty*] written over the top of 'Flippaty', cancelling it.
70 *fluttered*] Lear cancelled this word but did not give an alternative.
72 *Gnats*] ~~Spiders~~ Gnats
97 *roared and sang*] snag and roared roared and sang

The Quangle Wangle's Hat

Written on 26 and 27 May 1872 for Arthur Buchanan. Pub. *LL*. There is a fair copy (*Houghton*) made in preparation for publication; and a facsimile of a fair copy that Lear made for Gertrude Lushington on 8 June 1872 (*Edin.*) was published privately in a limited edition of fifty copies in December 1933.

The Quangle Wangle first appeared in 'The History of the Seven Families of the Lake Pipple-Popple' in 1865 as the Clangle-Wangle (or Clangel-Wangel), and reappeared in 1867 in 'The Story of the Four Little Children Who Went Round the World'. In his diary for 30 January 1879, Lear wrote: 'Mr Prentice called – bringing a Mantis, wh. he said he thought had been a model for my Quangle-wangle: – possibly – unintentionally – it may have been.'

The idea of a hat being a convivial gathering place may date back to Lear's travels in Egypt in January 1854, when he wore a broad, flat Leghorn hat and a small boy called after him, 'O thou who wearest a turban resembling a dinner table!' See also 'There was an Old Man of Dee-side / Whose hat was exceedingly wide'.

4 *Beaver Hat*: a hat made of beaver fur, fashionable in the nineteenth century.
5 *For ... two*] *Houghton* His Beaver hat was 12 *Edin.* His Beaver Hat was twelve

15 *plainer than ever*] *Houghton* more than ever *Edin*. plainer and plainer

16 *people*] *Houghton* persons

22 *charmingly airy?*] *Houghton* light & airy? *Edin*. fine and airy!

32 *The Fimble Fowl, with a Corkscrew leg*: this may derive from a popular song of the day called 'The Cork Leg', which Lear used to sing.

34 *build our homes*] *Houghton* build our nests ['& live' below the line] *Edin*. build and live

38 *the Pobble who has no toes*: this is the first mention of the Pobble, who became the subject of his own poem in 1873.

40 *Dong*] *Houghton, Edin*. Bong This is the first mention of the Dong, who became the subject of his own poem in 1876.

43 *Attery Squash, and the Bisky Bat*] *Houghton, Edin*. Ottery=squash, and the Biscuit bat

51 *the Flute*: see 'Letter to Harry Hinde', note to l. 18.

[Receipt for George Scrivens, Esq.]

Drawn for George Scrivens on 2 August 1872.

MS *private collection*. Pub. (text only) *G&F*.

This *The Cedars of Lebanon* was a watercolour; it was also the subject of Lear's largest and most important oil painting (1861), see Introduction.

'Papa once went to Greece'

Written on 19 August 1872 for Gertrude Lushington. Pub. *QLN*.

The Story of the Pobble, who has no toes, and the Princess Bink

Written on, or shortly before, 23 May 1873 for Arthur Buchanan. This MS, which was illustrated with three drawings, was sold at Sotheby's on 20 April 1971. A **fair copy** made on 24 May 1871 for Gertrude Lushington is now in *Edin.*; a facsimile edition of this was published privately in a limited edition of fifty copies in December 1934. A further, handwritten transcript was made by Mrs Bowen from a MS in her possession which is now lost (*Bowen*). Pub. *AD*.

On 5 January 1859, Lear had written to Fortescue: '... it is a mistake to have toes at all: hoofs would have been simpler & less expensive, as precluding boots'.

4 *replied*] *Bowen* replied ~~only said~~

11 *swaddled*] *Bowen* ~~wrapped~~ swaddled

16 *safe – provided*] *Bowen* ~~always~~ safe ~~if~~ provided

25 *gaily*] Bowen ~~quickly~~ gaily
27 *And there*] Bowen ~~Whereon   On which~~ And there
30 *yellow*] Bowen blue
35 *Your beautiful*] Bowen The sight of your
38 *penny*] Bowen ~~groat~~ snap penny
   without] Bowen if he ~~hasn't~~ without
42 *I*] Bowen We
43 *And*] Bowen I'll
44 *That lovely*] Bowen Your wrapper of
45 *And besides that*] Bowen As well as the
46 *trust*] Bowen implore
47–8 *To place ... affection*] Bowen Twill be a striking proof of your deep
affection / To place them in my Father's Museum collection
51 *Which*] Bowen And
52 *She wreathed*] Bowen Wreathed it
57 *Princess – 'O Pobble!*] Bowen Princess Bink
59 *my Pobble! my Pobble!*] Bowen – no!
60 *Never, and never*] Bowen Never – O never
61 *Binky! O*] Bowen Princess!
62–4 *But say ... Said*] Bowen ~~You certainly will not~~ Say would you like at once
to start, / Without taking leave of the ~~King~~ your ancient Father? / Said the
Princess Bink – Jampoodle the King? / Said
67 *winkelty-binkelty-tinkled*] Bowen tinkelty=winklty=binkled
78 *Mice*] Bowen Pease mice
79 *The World in general knows*] Bowen Let the world in general know
80 *Pobbles ... toes*] Bowen A Pobble is happy with never a toe!' / Pobbles are
happier without their toes (*Bowen* gives both lines.)

The Pobble who has no Toes
It is not known when Lear rewrote 'The Pobble and Princess Bink' in this form,
in which it was published in *LL*.

The Akond of Swat
Written on 27 July 1873. Pub. *LL*. Lear enclosed a copy of the poem in a let-
ter to Fortescue on 12 September 1873 (MS *Taunton*).

The poem was prompted by a small news item in *The Times of India* of 18 July
1873: 'It is reported from Swat that the Akhoond's son has quarrelled with his
father, and left the parental presence with a following of 500 sowars, refusing
to listen to the Akhoond's orders to come back.'

On 24 October 1878 Fortescue wrote to Lear: 'I read sometime ago with deep regret the death of the Akhond of Swat – Do you think he knew, before he died, that you had made him more famous than any other Indian potentate?' to which Lear replied wistfully on 28 October: 'The Akhond of Swāt would have left me all his pppproppprty, but he thought I was dead: so didn't. The mistake arose from someone officiously pointing out to him that King Lear died 7 centuries ago, & that the poem referred to one of the Akhond's predecessors.'

When 'The Cummerbund' was published in *The Times of India* in July 1874, Lear made a fair copy of 'The Akond of Swat' to send to them, but then decided against doing so. In a note to the poem in *LL*, he wrote: 'The proper way to read the verses is to make an immense emphasis on the monosyllabic rhymes, which indeed ought to be shouted out by a chorus.' The spelling of 'Akond' follows that in *LL*; in the MS it is spelled 'Ahkond'.

14 *round-hand*: a style of writing in which the letters are round, bold and full.
24 *SHOT*] LL *shot*
26 *prig*: steal.
42 *Like ... SHALOTT*: 'The Lady of Shalott' (1832), a poem by Tennyson.
50 *small beer*: weak, inferior beer.
Illustrations: in a letter to Fortescue of 25 October 1873 (**MS** *Taunton*). Pub. *LLEL*.

'The Attalik Ghaz*ee*'
Written on 30 October 1873 in Lear's diary during his voyage out to India. When writing out his **Indian Journal** (*Houghton*) later, Lear transcribed the first verse into his entry for 29 October, and the whole poem for 30 October, where he noted: 'This poem was knocked on the head by Evelyn Baring who told me that Attálik Gházee was the real pronunciation.' Pub. *IJ*.

Title *Ghazee*: a champion against infidels particularly applied to Muslim fanatics.
10 *Begum* Queen, Princess or lady of high rank in Hindustan.

[Indian limericks]

There was an old man of Narkūnda
Written on 28 April 1874 in his **Indian Journal** (*Houghton*). Lear copied it out on 3 May 1874 in the Dak Bungalow of Fágoo (MS *Texas*). Pub. *IJ*.

1 *Narkūnder*: Narkanda is thirty-nine miles from Simla, the capital of the

Himachal Pradesh state in north-western India. Lear was there to make drawings of the Himalayan mountains, but the weather was bad and the mountains shrouded in cloud and mist. In his diary for 28 April he wrote: '1.20 PM, a big peal of thunder bursts, & the echoes go far & far away, & so it went on growling and with a little rain now & then, till all the distance is covered up with cloud, & one might as well be on Snowdon as at Nārkunda.'

2 *like peals of loud*] *Texas* much louder than

3 *shivered*] *Texas* split
   Colocynth Pills: purgative pills made from the bitter apple *Citrullus Colocynthis*.

4 *trees*] *Texas* mice

There lived a small puppy at Nārkunda

Written on 28 April 1874 in his **Indian Journal** (*Houghton*). Lear copied it out on 3 May 1874 in the Dak Bungalow of Fágoo (MS *Texas*). Pub. *IJ*.

1 *lived ... Nārkunda*] *Texas* was a large Mastiff of Nārkunder

2 *sought for the best*] *Texas* looked for a good

3 *call*] *Texas* say

There was a small child at Narkūnda

Written on 28 April 1874 in his **Indian Journal** (*Houghton*). Pub. *IJ*.

3 *Bonzes*: Buddhist clergy of south-east Asia.

There was an old man of Teōg

Written on 3 May 1874 in the Dak Bungalow of Fágoo. **MS** *Texas*.

1 *Teōg*: Theog is seventeen miles from Simla.

There was an old man of Mahasso

Written on 3 May 1874 in the Dak Bungalow of Fágoo. **MS** *Texas*.

1 *Mahasso*: Mahasu is eight miles from Simla.

There was an old person of Fágoo

Written on 3 May 1874 in the Dak Bungalow of Fágoo. **MS** *Texas*.

1 *Fágoo*: Fagu is twelve miles from Simla.

There was an old man in a Tonga
Written on 5 June 1874 in a letter to Evelyn Baring. **MS** *Brigham Young.*

1 *Tonga*: a small, light two-wheeled Indian carriage or cart.

'Oh! Chichester, my Carlingford!'
Written on 24 April 1874 in a letter to Fortescue. **MS** *Taunton.* Pub. *LLEL.*

Fortescue, whose Christian names were Chichester Samuel Parkinson, had lost his seat in the 1874 election and had just been created the 1st Baron Carlingford.

The Cummerbund
Written on 20 April 1874, during Lear's travels in India. Pub. *The Times of India* (Bombay), 22 June 1874; *LL.*

There is a fair copy, with an **illustration** (Representative Church Body Library, *Dublin*), which is subscribed 'Oct. 8. 1874. Upper Norwood (Surrey)'. The poem was composed before this date, and Lear was not in England then, so this must be a mistake. Although it is unusual for Lear to date a second fair copy with the date of composition rather than when he wrote it out, the MS at Duke dated Poonah, 20 April 1874, was probably made during the summer of 1875. A third fair copy with the same date (Rochester) was probably also made in 1875. There is a fourth fair copy at *Houghton*. A fifth, formerly among the papers belonging to Lord Strachie [*sic*], is written on writing paper stamped *Strawberry Hill, Twickenham, S. W.*, the home of Lady Waldegrave; while staying there on 11 August 1875, Lear noted in his diary: 'Came to bed – utterly outworn at 10.30 & wrote out another copy of The Cummerbund.'

   In *The Times of India* the poem was published in a column entitled 'Whims of the Week', with an introductory paragraph:

A Poetic Interlude. Salaam to the poets! They embellish my prose with agreeable fancies which the world will not willingly let die. One whose harp has been heard in the halls of Poona, and the sound of whose lyre is more loved than the note of the lute in the Palaces of Calcutta, sends me the following, to which I yield the carpet of honour: –

In the *Houghton* MS, Lear gives his own introduction:

The following affecting stanzas founded on fact, have lately been published in England by a Lady whose long residence in India & whose knowledge of its customs & produce, are as widely appreciated in that Country as her Poetical Genius. A glossary of the Indian names occurring in the Poem is added, less as an explanation of their meaning, than as a proof of the Authoress's truthful and talented descriptions united with the adaptation of Hindostanee words with English verse. –

Cummerbund, a sort of Tiger or Leopard of immense size & ferocious nature

Dobie, – a silk cushion

Punkah – a wandering minstrel

Khamsameh, a tree of the poplar kind

Kitmutgar – a sort of convolvulus

It is likely that Lear knew the real meaning of the words. For a similar use of words see 'She sits upon her Bulbul'.

Title *Cummerbund*: a sash or girdle of Anglo-Indian origin, worn round the waist.

1 *Dobie*: Indian washerman. In an undated letter to Lord Northbrook (1826–1904), who, as Viceroy, was his host in India, Lear said: 'Does your Excellency know that in various places in your Empire the dobies fill shirts, drawers, socks, etc. with stones, and then, tying up the necks bang them furiously on rocks at the water's edge until they are supposed to be washed? Surely, no country can prosper where such irregularities prevail' (quoted *P of L*, p. 117).

3 *Punkahs*: large fans made of cloth stretched over a frame, worked by a cord to agitate and cool the air.

4 *Cried*] *Dublin, Houghton, Rochester, Times* Said

5 *Around*] *Rochester* Beside

6 *Kamsamahs*] *Times* Khamsaeh Chief table servants or butlers.

7 *Kitmutgars*: male servants who wait at table.

8 *Tchokis*: police stations, or chairs.

9 *rolled*] *Rochester* flowed *Times* ran

10 *meloobious*] *Dublin* squelodious *Duke* melogious *Houghton, Times* melodious *Rochester* mophibious

11 *Chuprassies*: high-ranking attendants in the households of Indian landowners.

13 *Above … remote*] *Dublin, Duke* And far on lofty trees apart *Times* And while on loftiest branches near

15 *And all … moan'd*] *Duke* has both 'moaned' and 'mourned' *Times* The Mussak warbled all night long

   Mussak: a leather water-bag.

17 *Nullahs*: rivers or streams.

18 *branches … wide*] *Rochester* shadows o'er the tide

19 *Goreewallahs*] *Dublin* Gorrawallahs *Houghton* Gorawallahs *Times* Garrywallahs Grooms or coachmen.

20 *side by side*] *Duke, Times* o'er the tide

21 *Bheesties'*] *Houghton, Rochester, Times* Bheestie's

23 *Jampan*] *Houghton* Palkee Jampan: a type of carriage. (Palkee is a kind of sedan chair used in Indian hill-country.)

26 *Nimmak*] *Dublin* Dooly Nimmak: Salt. (Dooly is a covered chair.)

30 *angry*] *Duke* dreadful *Houghton* hideous *Dublin, Rochester* odious *Times* fatal

31, 36] *Dublin, Houghton, Rochester, Times* have no brackets

33 *They … vain*] *Dublin* In vain they sought

35 *was a dreadful*] *Dublin* is a norfle

37 *wall*] *Houghton* place

39 *underneath*] *Rochester* round about
    words] *Times* lines

40 *yellow, blue,*] *Duke, Rochester* letters pink *Times* letters red

41 *Beware … beware!*] *Times* Ye fair, take care! Take care, ye fair!

42 *sit*] *Rochester* stay

43 *horrid*] *Dublin, Houghton* cursed (Lear also experimented with 'odious' and 'awful' in *Houghton*.) *Rochester* cussed *Times* cursèd

44 *swollow you outright.*] *Dublin* swolly you outright. *Houghton* ~~end your futile flight!~~ *Times* end your futile flight!

Letter to Lady Wyatt
Written on 16 April 1875. **MS** *private collection*. Pub. *SL*.

Using a similar conceit, Lear wrote to Sir John Lubbock on 3 November 1883: I send you in this letter 2 Corpses of the most abominable – or rather, beebominable insects that ever made a florist miserable. The plague of black bees has multiplied here so horribly, and they are so destructive – that there is not a seed of my beautiful Grant-Duff Ipomœas anywhere, as the beestly bees pierce all the flowers and no seed is matured. We are driven mad by these bees, and have bees on the brain; we kill them by scores and the ground is beestrewn with their Bodies. Even the broom we use to sweep them away is called a Beesom. Can you at all enlighten me as to where these creatures build, or if they live more than a single summer? Or is there any fluid or substance which may kill them and save me the trouble of running about after them? I beeseech you to do what you can for me in the way of advice. (*LLEL*)

Poona Observer
Written in May 1875. **MS** *private collection*. Pub. (text only) *G&F*.

On 9 June 1874, Lear wrote to Lady Wyatt: 'I am thinking seriously of becoming a Fakeer: a rice=&=mango diet would be so economical as well as the

Paradise sort of scanty material.'

The New Vestments

The date of composition is unknown. Fair copy made on 9 May 1876. Pub. *LL*.

In some traditional nursery rhymes people dress in garments made of food.

28 *prigged*: stole.

The Pelican Chorus

The date of composition is unknown. Fair copy made on 30 June 1876. MS *Houghton*. There is an undated fragment in *Beinecke*, with the text of the refrain. Pub. *LL*.

Lear's musical setting was transcribed by Signor Pomé on 1 August 1876. **MS** *Houghton*. Pub. *LL*.

Lear had made drawings of pelicans for Gould's *Birds of Europe*, Vol.V, and for plate II of his own *Journals of a Landscape Painter in Albania &c.* (1851). It was, however, the pelicans of the Nile which inspired 'The Pelican Chorus'. Lear wrote in his diary on 9 January 1867: 'O queer community of birds! On a long sand spit are 4 black storks – one legged: apart. – 8 Pelicans – careless foolish. 17 small ducks, cohesive. 23 Herons – watchful variously posed: & 2 or 3 flocks of lovely ivory ibis – (or Paddybirds –) flying all about.' And on 13 January: 'Further on were sand islands – with serene geese & dux – & sentinel plovers – all without Heron guards. But when we arrived – about 4 – or 4.30, nearer the broad river, there were the Herons again. Perhaps the funniest community came thro' the air, just then – 2 immense pelicans – & 20 cranes. These alighted near 2 other Pelicans who put up their heads – (present arms,) & then slept.'

The Two Old Bachelors

The date of composition is unknown. Two fair copies were made on 30 June 1876, one for Gertrude Lushington. Pub. *LL*.

The poem was originally called 'Sage and Onions'. Lear had intended this title for the volume of nonsense songs subsequently entitled *Laughable Lyrics*. The illustration was used on the jacket of the book.

[Nonsense Botany – 3]

The date of composition is unknown. Pub. *LL*.

'ℨ tumbled down, and hurt his Arm'

The date of composition is unknown. Pub. *LL*.

The Dong with a Luminous Nose

The date of composition is unknown. A fair copy, with alterations, for Bush, Lear's printer and publisher, was made during August 1876 (*Houghton*), and another fair copy for Gertrude Lushington (unlocated). Pub. *LL*.

In his diary for 22 August 1876, Lear noted: 'Wrote out the nonsense poem, "The Dong with a luminous nose"'; and on 24 August: 'I quite concluded "The Dong with a luminous nose," & so ends the new Xmas book – spun out to a much greater length than was apprehended.' It is not known if he had begun work on the poem before the 22nd. The other songs for the Christmas book had already been sent to Bush: the Dong seems to have been a last-minute inclusion.

All his life, Lear was haunted by images of past happiness, and the idea of abandonment on a bleak shore recurs frequently. In his diary, especially in his later years, he would echo Thomas Moore's 'I saw from the Beach' (1807), ll. 5–8: 'Ah! such is the fate of our life's early promise, / So passing the spring-tide of joy we have known: / Each wave, that we danced on at morning, ebbs from us, / And leaves us, at eve, on the bleak shore alone!' He returned frequently to the image of dark loneliness lighted by sympathetic companionship. For example, in 1867 he contemplated proposing marriage to Gussie Bethell. On 3 November he discussed the possibility with her sister, Emma Parkins, but, despite her earlier encouragement, she now advised against it. In his diary for that day he wrote: 'Like a sudden spark / Struck vainly in the night / And back returns the dark – / With no more hope of light.' (Tennyson, *Maud* IX, ll. 326–9).

The description of scenery in the first stanza recalls Lear's response to the scenery on Mount Athos which he visited in 1856. Writing to Emily Tennyson on 9 October, he said: 'I never saw any more striking scenes than those forest screens and terrible crags, all lonely lonely lonely … the blue sea dash dash against the hard iron rocks below.'

Compare Thomas Moore, 'A Ballad. The Lake of the Dismal Swamp', in *Epistles, Odes and Other Poems* (1806). The poem is preceded by an introductory note:

'They tell of a young man who lost his mind upon the death of a girl he loved, and who, suddenly disappearing from his friends, was never afterwards heard of. As he had frequently said, in his ravings, that the girl was not dead, but gone to the Dismal Swamp, it is supposed he had wandered into that dreary wilderness, and had died of hunger, or been lost in some of its dreadful morasses.' – Anon. / They made her a grave, too cold and damp / For a soul so warm and true; / And she's gone to the Lake of the Dismal Swamp, / Where, all night long, by a fire-fly lamp, / She paddles her white canoe … / He saw the Lake and a meteor bright / Quick over its surface play'd – / 'Welcome,' he said, 'my dear-one's light!' / And the dim shore echoed, for many a night, / The name of the death-cold maid! / Till he hollow'd a boat of the birchen bark, / Which carried him off from the shore; / Far he follow'd the meteor spark, / The wind was high and the clouds were dark, / And the boat return'd no more. / But oft, from the Indian hunter's camp, / This lover and maid so true / Are seen, at the hour of midnight damp, / To cross the lake by a fire-fly lamp / And paddle their white canoe!

Compare also Tennyson's 'The Lady of Shalott', ll. 96–7 and William Collins's 'Eclogue IV: Agib and Secander; or, the Fugitives' (1742), ll. 1–4.

Title *Dong*: in 1837, when Lear was exploring northern Italy, he visited Dongo, a name that may have resonated in his mind in later years.

2 *Over*] Houghton ~~Around~~ over

12 *A Meteor strange and bright*: marsh gas which burnt above marshy places, otherwise known as Will-o'-the-Wisp or Jack-o'-lantern.

52 *weary*] Houghton earnest

62 *once possessed*] Houghton ~~formerly had~~ once possessed

63 *quite … of*] Houghton ~~certainly left~~ quite gone out

68 *For ever I'll seek*] Houghton ~~I will never stop seeking~~ Forever I'll seek

83 *prevent*] Houghton keep

84 *send*] Houghton throw out

90 *While … vain*] Houghton While ~~he seeks for ever in lake or plain but all~~ While … vain

91 *meet with*] Houghton ~~find~~ meet with

95 *lofty*] Houghton ~~distant~~ lofty

'Finale Marina! If ever you'd seen her!'
Written in his **diary** on 13 September 1877.

1 Finale Marina: a resort on the Italian Riviera.

In medio Tutorissimus ibis
Written on 15 March 1878. **MS** *Houghton*. Pub. *QLN*.

The 'youthful cove' was Arnold Congreve, the son of Lear's neighbour, Walter Congreve, who had been Under Master at Rugby.

33–4 *James … Nastics*: gymnastics.

'O dear! how disgusting is life!'
Written on 3 January 1879 in Lear's **diary**. Pub. *VN*.

See 'Some Incidents in the Life of my Uncle Arly', note to l. 7.

'How pleasant to know Mr Lear!'
Written on, or shortly before, 9 April 1879. MS *BL*. There is a draft at *Houghton*. Pub. *Nonsense Books* (Boston, 1888), *NSS*.

This poem is so well known in the version published in *NSS* that this is taken as the principal source, although in ll. 10, 12 and 24 the *BL* MS is chosen; *NSS* probably came from a MS in the possession of Lady Strachey. Lear said that the poem was a joint composition with Miss Bevan, whose father was Vice Consul in San Remo, and that the opening line was quoted by a friend of Miss Bevan, who passed it on to Lear. In his diary of 9 April he wrote: 'Wrote out my & Miss Bevans verses of "How Pleasant to know Mr. Lear".' It is not known who wrote what, but it is possible that the final composition, apart from the quotation, was Lear's alone. On 14 January, Lear wrote to Mr Bevan: 'I disclose you a Pome, which you may or you may Knott send to the Lady who says "How pleasant to know Mr Lear!" – It may be sung to the air, "How cheerful along the gay mead".'

3 *ill-tempered and queer*: in his years in San Remo, Lear acquired a reputation for irascibility, particularly towards his neighbours. (The word 'queer' did not then have the sexual meaning it has since acquired.)
7 *His visage … hideous*: Lear always spoke of himself as ugly, but this opinion was not endorsed by others. Indeed, when a photographer came to take his picture in 1887, he remarked on the beauty of the old man.
10 *(Leastways … thumbs;)*] *Houghton*, *NSS* line is not in brackets
12 *dumms*] *Houghton*, *NSS* dumbs
15 *He drinks … Marsala*: writing to Fortescue on Christmas Day 1876, Lear said that he had been drinking 'oceans of Marsala & Syphon [soda water],

which mixture it is believed the angels imbibe'.

18 *Old Foss*] BL, *Houghton* Foss. Foss, who joined Lear's household as a kitten in November 1872 and died in September 1887, featured in many of the caricatures that Lear did of himself in those years. See [The Heraldic Blazons of Foss the Cat].

20 *weareth*] BL wears a brown *Houghton* ~~brown~~ wears weareth

24 *O!*] *Houghton, NSS* oh!

27 *pancakes*] BL, *Houghton* jujubes

28 *chocolate shrimps from the*] BL shrimps from the chocolate *Houghton* chocolate froth from the

29 *He reads ... Spanish*: see 'Growling Eclogue', note to ll. 47–9.

31 *pilgrimage*] BL pillgrimage

Mr and Mrs Discobbolos: Second Part

The date of composition is unknown. In his diary for 14 October 1879 Lear noted that he 'Wrote to James Fields – & copied out 2nd part of Mr Discobbolos', but his letter is dated 15 October (*Huntington*). On the 15th he made a fair copy which he sent to the novelist Wilkie Collins (1824–89) (unlocated), and on 18 January 1883 he sent a copy to Sir Edward Strachey (*Taunton*). Pub. *Quarterly Review* 167 (October 1888), *NSS*.

Lear wished to publish the poem in a new edition of his nonsense songs and stories, but he was unable to find a publisher and it was published posthumously.

In his copy of *Laughable Lyrics*, Collins wrote: 'The Second Part of "Mr and Mrs Discobbolos" was written by my old friend Edward Lear at my suggestion. So far as I know, it has not yet been published. / Wilkie Collins / 21 July 1888'. Lear had known Collins since the novelist's childhood. He noted in his diary for 2 November 1879 that he had received 'a letter from Wilkie Collins, – greatly praising the 2nd part of Mr & Mrs Discobbolos'.

This is the blackest of all Lear's nonsense. The despair of Mr Discobbolos, who, in the earlier poem, had climbed to the top of the wall to escape the worry of life, was inspired by the problems Lear was having over the building of a large hotel between his house and the sea. Lear had understood that he would have first refusal should the land ever be sold but, without his being consulted, the olive groves below his house were felled, and by the summer of 1879 building work was well under way. The matter came to obsess him – he called the hotel 'the Enemy' – and he would read the poem aloud to his friends. His studio light was ruined, and he was forced to build another house into which he moved in 1881. Villa Emily remained unsold until 1884, and the financial hardship this caused, together with the sense of betrayal he felt, greatly distressed his last years.

2 *the wall*] *Huntington* a wall
3 *twenty*] *Huntington* Thirty
7 *admired*] *Huntington* belov'd
9 *O*] *Huntington* O!
15 *Up on*] *Huntington* On the top of
16–17 *not … maternal*] *Huntington* never away from our sight have gone, –/ Amply repaying our
21 *O*] *Huntington* O!
23 *lives*] *Huntington* life
24 *Dearest*] *Huntington* ~~Darling~~ Dearest
26 *have even*] *Huntington* even have
31 *darling*] *Huntington* valued
33 *O –*] *Huntington* O
34 *fiddledum*] *Huntington* fiddlestick
35 *runcible*] *Huntington* frightful
39 *And beneath*] *Huntington* Beneath
40 *And*] *Huntington* He
   Dynamite … gench] *Huntington* Dynamite=Gunpowder=Gench
   Gench is a neologism.
42 *sing and*] *Huntington* sing! Let In *NSS* this line is made into two lines.
43 *our*] *NSS* your
   has] *Huntington* is
44 *And*] *Huntington* Then
45 *O!*] *Huntington* O
48 *Discobbolos!*] *Huntington* Discobbolos!!!
51 *and*] *Huntington* and he
53 *sounds*] *Huntington* sound
59 *happened*] *Huntington* come

'O Brother Chicken! Sister Chick!'
Written on 13 June 1880 at The Lodge, Wimbledon Common, the home of Gussie (Bethell) and Adamson Parker (see headnote to 'The Dong with a Luminous Nose'). Pub. *QLN*, 2nd edn (1911).

In his diary for that day, Lear wrote: 'Drew a small sketch from the window, & [ ] a print of a Chicken looking at the Eggshell he had come from.'

12 *Egg-nostics*: 'agnostic' had been coined by T. H. Huxley in 1869, and first appeared in print in 1870.

'Dear Sir, Though many checks prevent'
Written on 29 July 1880 to Sir John Lubbock. **MS** *Beinecke*.

An MP responsible for the Bank Holidays and Early Closing Acts, Lubbock (1834–1913) had commissioned Lear to make a £35 drawing of Sparta and two £13 drawings of Marathon and Athens.

4 *tin*: money.
10 Lear's rather inaccurate Greek seems to mean: 'Besides your letter – also for this letter, which the cheque was in, I thank you.'
14 *Foord and Dickenson*: picture dealers and handlers in Wardour Street, Soho, London, who were Lear's London agents.

Remminissenciz of Orgust 14 Aitnundrednaity
Written on 19 October 1880 in San Remo. **MS** Bibliotheca Bodmeriana. Pub. *English and American Autographs in the Bodmeriana* (Geneva, 1977).

This recalls an incident in August 1880 during Lear's last visit to England. He had been staying at Stratton, the Hampshire home of Lord Northbrook (see note to l. 1 of 'The Cummerbund'). Micheldever was the nearby railway station.

Lear signed the limerick, together with an accompanying drawing of Northbrook's dog, Piggy, from 'Edward Lear, Orther of the Book of Nonsense, weighing Thirteen Stone Four £ and a quorta.'

'I am awfull aged in apierance lately'
Drawn on 30 July 1881 in a letter to Lady Wyatt. **MS** *private collection*.

'There was an old man with a ribbon'
Written on 2 January 1882 in Lear's **diary**, where there is a slight drawing accompanying the verse. Pub. *OF*.

Lear would lend books from his library to other English people living in San Remo, and in his diary for that day he notes: '… took a Gibbon's Rise & Fall up to Mrs Welfords'.

2 *Gibbon*: Edward Gibbon (1737–94), the author of *Decline and Fall of the Roman Empire* (1776–81).

Letter to Mrs Stuart Wortley [The Moon Journey]
Written on 26 February 1882. **MS** *private collection*. Pub. *G&F, VN*.

The MS has no paragraph breaks.

[Chichester Fortescue is appointed Lord Privy Seal]
The date of composition is unknown, but it was sent to Fortescue in a letter of 30 March 1882. Pub. *LLEL*.

In his letter, Lear wrote: 'Sometime back, when I thought you were coming out, I wrote the enclosed for your bemusement.' In April 1881 Fortescue had been appointed Lord Privy Seal, a post he held until 1885. During this time, Lear made frequent play on his title, calling him by the seal's generic name *Phoca*, and arranging suitable watery accommodation for him when he came to stay in San Remo.

The notice was originally written in Italian so that his neighbours might be prepared for his visitor.

[Nonsense Trees]
The date of composition is unknown. **MS** *Houghton*. Pub. *T&Q*.

See Aristophanes' *The Birds*, where there is 'a certain monstrous tree', the Cleonymus, which sheds shields in the autumn (trans. David Barrett (1978), p. 204).

'The Octopods and Reptiles'
Written on 13 September 1882 in Lear's *diary*. Pub. *OF*.

Lear spent the summer months in a hotel in Monte Generoso in the Italian Alps. He had a great dislike of any kind of crowds, and loathed the convention of table d'hôte, where all the guests sat down together for meals. To Anthony Mundella he wrote on 30 August of 'the disgusting noise and riot of Octopod Hotel life', and in his diary he referred several times to the Octopods: on 15 September, 'Bkft and talk with various Octopods', and on 19 September, 'The horrid noise made by Octopod children is acutely horrid.' (Mundella (1825–97), Liberal MP for Sheffield and Vice President of the Council of the Committee on Education.) In a letter to Edgar Drummond of 19 September, he wrote: '110 people boxed up here ... Of this mob I see but little, having had the good luck this year to have old friends in the Hotel: Adml Sir Spenser & Lady Robinson, – the Mundellas, – and for the last fortnight Alfred and Mrs A. Drummond. We three dine & sup together, free from the noise of the mixed multitude whom we call the Octopods & Bobblichoffs.' See also 'Mr and Mrs Discobbolos: Second Part', l. 36.

[The Heraldic Blazons of Foss the Cat]
Drawn for Henry Strachey in January 1883. Pub. *NSS*.

In his introduction to *NSS*, Henry Strachey recalled:

When staying at Cannes at Christmas 1882, I was invited by Mr Lear to go over to San Remo to spend a few days with him ... on the last evening after dinner he wrote a letter for me to take back to my father, sending him the then unpublished conclusion of Mr and Mrs Discobbolos; and when this was done he took from a place in his bureau a number of carefully cut-out backs of old envelopes, and on these he drew, to send to my sister, then eight years old, the delightful series ... of heraldic pictures of his cat. After he had done seven he said it was a great shame to caricature Foss, and laid aside the pen.

They were published as 'The Heraldic Blazons of Foss the Cat', a title that was almost certainly added by the editor. Henry Strachey was the brother-in-law of Lady Strachey. On Foss, see 'How pleasant to know Mr Lear!', note to l. 18.

In the Preface to *LLEL*, Hubert Congreve gives a menu that Lear drew up shortly after the arrival of Foss:

Potage	Potage au Petit Puss.
(Pour Poisson)	Queues de chat, à l'Aigùille.
1st Entrée	Orielles de Chat, frites à la Kilkenny.
	Pattes du Chat – aux chataignes.
2nd Entrée	Cotelettes de petit chat (sauce doigts de pied de Martyr –
	Tomata Sauce.)
Roti	Gros Chat Noir.
Pour Legume	De Terre – sans pommes. Petite pierres cuites à l'eau chaude.
Gibier	Croquet aux balles.

Canards de Malta.

Sauce au poivre.

Sauce au sel.

Patisserie   Pâté de vers de soie sucre.

Breadcrumbs à l'Oliver Cromwell (all of a crumble).

Boudin de Milles Mouches.

Compôt Mouches Noires.

'Mrs Jaypher found a wafer'

Written 30 January to December 1883. The earliest mention of the poem is on 30 January 1883 when Lear wrote in his diary: 'Wrote out "Mrs Jaypher" verses.' The following day he was visited by a friend who 'laughed to shivers on reading "Mrs Jaypher"'. By March he was writing to E. Carus Selwyn: 'Mrs Jaypher is altogether shunted: I have sad & serious letters to write.' He sent the second stanza in a letter to Amelia Edwards on 14 July 1883, explaining: 'I have been writing a pome called "Mrs Jaypher's advice" lately: but I can rarely write nonsense now, and it hangs fire' (**MS** *Somerville College, Oxford*). On 31 December he sent another version of this stanza to Lord Aberdare (*Aberdare*), adding: 'This is part of a poem I lately wrote called Mrs Jayphers Wisdom: I wish it were bupplished' (**MS** *Florida*). The first stanza was published in *QLN*, where the text was taken from a MS formerly in the possession of Lord Northbrook. This text has been assembled from the two sources.

Lady Strachey notes that 'Lear adds the stage direction that the verse is to be read sententiously and with grave importance.' Lines 11–14 were also published in *QLN*, where they are described as 'A verse of another version'.

13 *a pound*] *Aberdare* ~~some curried~~ a slice

From a letter to the Hon. Mrs Augusta Parker

Written and drawn on 19 February 1883 in a letter to the Hon. Mrs Augusta Parker, formerly Gussie Bethell. **MS** *private collection*. Pub. *SL*.

p. 449 l. 6 *inganno*: deception.

[The Later History of the Owl and the Pussy-cat]

Written on 12 January 1884 in a letter for the sister of James Cameron Grant. **MS** *Koch*.

Title *Pussy-cat*: in the letter, Lear has 'Pussycat' and 'Pussy cat'. Since there is no apparent reason for these variations, they have here been given uniformly as 'Pussy-cat', following the original poem.

p. 450 l. 20 *sauce*] ~~source~~ sauce

p. 450 l. 33 *Tears idle Tears*: a song in Tennyson's poem 'The Princess' (1847), which Lear set to music and performed for his friends. He published the setting in 1853, and the sheet music for it was painted by Holman Hunt in his *The Awakening Conscience* (1853–4). Lear would quote the words in his diary and in letters when he was overborne with sadness and loneliness.

p. 450 l. 34 *My Pætus*: the Emperor Claudius ordered Pætus to commit suicide, but as he was too cowardly his wife plunged the sword into her own heart, saying 'See Pætus, it is not painful.'

A year later, in about April 1885, when Lear was ill in bed, he made drafts for a poem describing the later history of the Owl and the Pussy-cat on the end-papers of Addison's *Essays from the Spectator* which he was reading. **MS** *Sir David Attenborough*. Pub. *AD*. There are many alterations and deletions, and in places it is impossible to read. The provisional text reads:

> Our mother was the Pussy-Cat, our father was the Owl,
> And so we're partly little beasts and partly little fowl,
> The brothers of our family have feathers and they hoot,
> While all the sisters dress in fur and have long tails to boot.
> > We all believe that little mice,
> > For food are singularly nice.
>
> Our mother died long years ago. She was a lovely cat
> Her tail was 5 feet long, and grey with stripes, but what of that?
> In Sila forest on the East of far Calabria's shore
> She tumbled from a lofty tree – none ever saw her more.
> Our owly father long was ill from sorrow and surprise,
> But with the feathers of his tail he wiped his weeping eyes.
> And in the hollow of a tree in Sila's inmost maze
> We made a happy home and there we pass our obvious days.
>
> From Reggian Cosenza many owls about us flit
> And bring us worldly news for which we do not care a bit.
> We watch the sun each morning rise, beyond Tarento's straight;
> We go out ——————————— before it gets too late,
> And when the evening shades begin to lengthen from the trees
> ——————————————— as sure as bees is bees.
> We wander up and down the shore

Or tumble over head and heels, but never, never more,
Can see the far Gromboolian plains
Or weep as we could once have wept o'er many a vanished scene:
This is the way our father moans – he is so very green.

Our father still preserves his voice, and when he sees a star
He often sings ————————————— to that original guitar.
The pot in which our parents took the honey in their boat,
But all the money has been spent, beside the £5 note.
The owls who come and bring us news are often ——————
Because we take no interest in poltix of the day

The draft then becomes unintelligible, the final jottings referring to some of the themes that angered Lear in his later years – Gladstone and the Eastern Question, mendacious priests and General Gordon's death at Khartoum.

'When "grand old men" persist in folly'

Written on 9 February 1884 in a letter to Fortescue. MS *Taunton*. Pub. *LLEL*.

1–4 *When 'grand … teaze?*: W. E. Gladstone (1809–98), four times Prime Minister, was known as the 'Grand Old Man'. Lear, who had met Gladstone briefly in Corfu in 1858, was a fierce critic of his foreign policy, in particular the way in which he dealt with the Eastern Question. Writing to Fortescue on 1 January 1885, Lear said: 'I think that in future times that personage will be far less renounced anent the "inevitable constitutional change" than he will be for Majuba, the advance of the Russians to India, & the giving Russia a Port on the Adriatic – Duleigno: not to speak of other matters such as his Midlothian babooneries, insults to Austria &c &c. – Pah! But I have no doubt he cuts down trees beautifully, & is hugely eloquent.' Gladstone enjoyed chopping down trees on his estate at Hawarden, in north Wales. Although he counted many among his friends, Lear generally had a low opinion of what he called 'Polly-titians'.
7–8 *Is first … Sanremo*: Lear persistently tried to persuade his friends to come to stay with him in Italy.

'He lived at Dingle Bank – he did'

Written on 19 March 1884 for Revd E. Carus Selwyn. MS *Selwyn*. Pub. *QLN*.

Selwyn lived at Dingle Bank, on the Mersey, where he ran a small private school for boys. The idea of the school obviously caught Lear's imagination, for, writing to Selwyn on 14 February 1883, he said: 'As to the increase of 5 or 6 in your upper School & the decline of the Lower ditto, I advise you to mix them all up together & feed them with honey & mustard. Mrs Jaypher said "it's safer".' However, in a letter of 11 March he recanted: 'I repented having in my last spoken of your Upper school in a runcible & ossplivvious manner, but I didn't mean any disrespect, though I believe I recommended them all to be boiled in mustard.' Two years later, on 24 May 1885, he asked Selwyn: 'Have you any frogs & snails in your Dingly Bank garden? If not, purchase a large number immediately, & place them in a row in a glass case, which will be highly ornamental & abomalous.'

'And this is certain; if so be'

Written on 30 April 1885 in a letter to Fortescue. **MS** *Taunton*. Pub. *LLEL*.

Lear had been very proud of his garden at Villa Emily, with its English flowers, as well as plants grown from seeds he had gathered elsewhere on his travels. He had to begin again when he moved into his new house, and he wrote frequently about its progress in letters to friends. On 12 March 1882, he told Emily Tennyson:

My new garden is *beginning* to be interesting, but it has suffered hideously from 2 gt rainstorms which carried away all the gravel, & busted a new wall, as still remains unbemended. But I suppose everything will come right some day, as the Caterpillar said when he saw all his legs fall off as he turned into a Chrysalis ... The unfinished state of the Garden – till lately without gates, – led to vexatiums – German bands & mucilaginous Mendicants entering spontaneously and irruptively. One day there was a big Bishop (Sydney) walking on the Terrace, and a little Bishop (Sierra Leone) in the Gallery, Lord Aberdare's children on the middle walk, the Milkman and a Norgan Grinder on the cross path, & worse than all, Mrs Weld and her daughter Agnes unbespectedly in the midst.

On 28 September 1884 he wrote to tell Fortescue of its latest glories: 'Them is flowers highly ablopumpshious in themselves, & squagglibeetious to others, on which I shan't diffuse, as you can't see them'; and on 20 October 1884 Fortescue wrote back: 'I like to hear of your garden and I hope please God to see it! My recollection of it is that of an apparent rubbish heap with the great Italian wall at the bottom half built.'

The illustration follows the verse in the letter.

Eggstrax from The Maloja Gazette
Written on 30 August 1885 for Mary Mundella. Pub. *Call Back Yesterday*, ed. Lady Charnwood (1937).

Accompanying the Eggstrax was a covering letter:

When now I have at length from Barzano parted, and to the city of Milan reluctiously returned am, I send you to Maloja this billet.

For I have heard with scratchifaction that your so excellent and venerable papa has a Polybingular monument on the very top of the Superior Engadine Mountain to be directed ordered, – representing of a Colosshial Marble Polar Bear, with 83 small marble sepulchral stones in a circle placed, so as to remain for an internal Bemorial Commensuration of the lately occurred dreadful & frightfully pullulent History-Fact, that so large a number of deservingly aspiring British scholars suddenly by Polar Bears devoured were, – leaving nothing but a posthumous howling and disconsolate tears for the consideration and contempt of past and future posterity, ever to be bitterly and with feelings of prostrate acerbity and benign gripes justly lamented.

At my advantageous age, and upper all circumstances, it is but too probable that we shall not ourselves again encounter, unless in your Italian progress-journey by Sanremo you purpose to travel. And therefore I this obvious and pneumatic communication conclude by wishing that you may all return with safety and increased appetites to your shadowy and chocolate abiding Fireplace in All-of-a Crumble [Cromwell] Road.

Pray regard this as the moblivious and suffused wish of,

Dear Miss Mundella,

Yours pistilentially, Edward Lear

'When leaving this beautiful blessed Briánza'
Written on 8 September 1885 for the Mundella family. Lear sent a **fair copy** to Hallam Tennyson the same day, with the caricature of himself with Foss (*Lincoln*). There is a MS draft at *Houghton*. Pub. Lady Charnwood, *An Autograph Collection* (1930).

On 31 August 1882, Lear wrote to Fortescue that 'Mundella is ultra Tennysonian, & always carries his works with him in one vollim.'

1 *Briánza*: a village in the Italian Alps where Lear was passing the summer months, and where he met the Mundella family.
3 *mancanza*: mistake.
7 *that*] *Houghton* though
10 *stamping*] *Houghton* ramming

11 *A Tennyson ... puffing*: Lear was a friend of Tennyson, and admired his poetry. In 1850, prompted by Lear's gift to the poet and his new wife, Emily, of a copy of *Journals of a Landscape Painter in Albania &c.*, Tennyson composed a poem 'To E.L. on his Travels in Greece'. At about this time, Lear conceived the idea of making a series of drawings in which his landscapes and lines from Tennyson's poems were set side-by-side. This project occupied the last years of his life, and he came to see it as his *Liber Studiorum*; it was still uncompleted at his death.

In a letter to Fortescue on 12 September 1873, Lear set out the subjects of five of the Tennyson illustrations:

1. And the crag that fronts the Even / All along the shadowing shore (Eleänor).
2. To watch the crisping ripples on the beach, / And tender curving lines of creamy spray (The Lotos-Eaters).
3. Tomorhrit, Athos, all things fair, / With such a pencil, such a pen, / You shadow forth to distant men, / I read and felt that I was there (To E.L. on his Travels in Greece).
4. Illyrian woodlands, echoing falls / Of water, sheets of summer glass, / The long divine Peneïan pass, / The vast Akrokeraunian walls (ibid).
5. Or night dews on still waters between walls / Of shadowy granite, in a gleaming pass (The Lotos-Eaters).

He then parodied the lines, telling Fortescue that these were 'some parodies I have been obliged to make, whereby to recall the Tennyson lines of my illustrations: – beginning with those mysterious & beautiful verses,

1. Like the Wag who jumps at evening / All along the sanded floor.
2. To watch the tipsy cripples on the beach, / With topsy turvy signs of screamy play. –
3. Tom-Moory Pathos; – all things bare, – / With such a turkey! Such a hen! / And scrambling forms of distant men, / O! – aint you glad you were not there! –
4. Delirious Bulldogs; – echoing, calls / My daughter, – green as summer grass; – / The long supine Plebian ass, / The nasty crockery boring, falls; –
5. Spoonmeat at Bill Porter's in the Hall, / With green pomegranates, & no end of Bass.

I hear you say – 'you dreadful old ass!' but then my dear child, if your friend is the Author of the book of nonsense, what can you expect?

16 *the 'Lord]* Charnwood only

Some Incidents in the Life of my Uncle Arly

Written May 1873–March 1886. The earliest drafts of this poem date from May 1873. Ill in bed and reading *The Letters of Horace Walpole, Earl of Orford*, Lear made several drafts on the endpapers of Vols. VIII (1858) and IX (1859) (*Beinecke*). In January 1886, again ill and confined to bed, he returned to the poem. On 22 February he wrote in his diary: 'Kept always in bed – &

read – (also writing "my aged Uncle Arly" –).' Writing to John Ruskin on 1 March, he said: ' "E'en in our ashes live" – & lying as I do here, I have just now finished an absurd "History of my aged Uncle Arly" begun long ago. And I esteem it a thing to be thankful for that I remain as great a fool as ever I was.' On the same day he wrote to the wife of his doctor: 'I have just written (the last Nonsense poem I shall ever write,) a history of my "Aged Uncle Arley" – stuff begun years ago for Lady E[mma] Baring', the daughter of Lord Northbrook. On 5 March he copied out the poem in its final form, and over the next few days he made twelve fair copies which he sent to various friends (including Ruskin). Pub. *NSS*.

Lear wrote on 7 March 1886 to Wilkie Collins: '"E'en in our ashes live" &c &c – so, – though I have been in bed since 14 weeks, I have nonetheless written an absurdity which I fancy you may like – whereby I send it.' Collins responded enthusiastically, and, on 19 May 1886, Lear wrote to Selwyn: 'After I sent your letter to the preconcerted predacious Poast – I remembered your wish to know about "Uncle Arly" – of which Wilkie Collins writes to me that he thinks it the best of all "my poetry!" – There is another pome about the same ingividgual begun – but shunted – / Accidental, on his hat, – / Once my Uncle Arly sat: / Which he squeezed it wholly flat. / (Incomplete MSS – found in the brain of Mr Edward Lear on dissection of the same – in a post mortification examination.)' He is known to have made at least two further copies. Lear's own copy is at *Houghton*, one of unknown provenance is at *Texas*, that for Selwyn is still in the family, and that for Wyatt was in the family until it was sold at Sotheby's on 16 December 1980.

Lear seems to have returned to the theme late in 1886 or 1887. On the end-papers of a copy of *At Home in Fiji* by C. F. Gordon Cumming (1885) (*Sir David Attenborough*), which he bought in July 1886, Lear had written: 'Quacks vobiscum Uncle Arly / Sitting on your heap of barley / Quacks vobiscum – every Duck / Quacks vobiscum – two by two / Quacks vobiscum – as they flew / Through the morning sky so blue / Quacks vobiscum – what a lark!'

With a few alterations, noted below, the text is based on the *NSS* version; there are several variants in the surviving MSS and no text has priority over others.

Title *Some Incidents*] NSS Incidents *Texas* Certain Incidents *Byrom* suggests (p. 219) that the poem 'is much more revealing, once we spot Lear hiding "unclearly" in "UncLE ARly".'
3 *All*] NSS Thro' *Texas* ~~Through~~ All *Wyatt* Through
4 *Close … thicket*] Houghton, Texas line is bracketed.
7 *shoes … too tight*: looking out over his garden from his sick-bed, Lear wrote in his diary on 14 June 1886: 'The big magnolia flowers – also the nightingales

& robins are a satisfaction – "but his boots were far too tight" – i.e. my chest oppression & cough are a sad set off.' The idea of the oppression of ill-fitting shoes is first found in Lear's diary for 3 January 1879: see 'O dear! how disgusting is life!'

9 *goods away*] *Selwyn* worldly goods

10 *Timskoop*: in various MSS Lear played with the possibilities of Timskip, Timskop, Teegos, Clobbsbobb, Flúmpious, Frumphy, Jumpshm and Phobbly. *NSS* has Tiniskoop, probably a misreading.

13 *Orb*] *Texas* Sun

14 *How … are*: l. 2 of the children's rhyme 'Twinkle twinkle little star'. Lewis Carroll also drew on this song which he parodied as 'Twinkle, twinkle, little bat!'

after 14] *Beinecke* Soon he saw that patent matches / Caused the light

15–16 *Like … exertions*] *Beinecke* lines in inverted order. In 1831, at the age of eighteen, Lear had written: 'I had rather be at the bottom of the River Thames than be one week in debt, – be it never so small. For me – who at the age of 14 and a half was turned out into the world, *literally without a farthing* – and with nought to look to for a living but his own exertions you may easily suppose this is a necessary prejudice' (*PM*).

18 *Whiles … spelling*: in the late 1820s and the 1830s Lear earned money by giving drawing lessons, first in London and later in Italy.

19 *merely*] *Houghton, Texas* simply

21 *Propter's Nicodemus Pills*: it is not known if this was a patent medicine of the time, but the reference seems to be to the commercialization of Lear's work. He may mean the 'uncommon queer shop sketches' (*NSS*, p. xiv) and other hack drawings such as designs for fans which he did to make money before becoming an ornithological draughtsman. It could also refer to his later attempts to sell his work. Writing to Lord Derby on 27 June 1884, Lear said: '… the annual notice of my gallery I should like to make known to all who have had my works … this annual notice is as much an Advertisement=universal as Eno's Fruit salt or Epps's Cocoa, or any other.' Lear may also have been playing with the idea that his books for children resembled the products of John Newbery, from 1744 an influential children's publisher, whose other occupation was as a purveyor of patent medicines.

22–4 *Later… disclose*] *Beinecke* Over among the dewy grasses / Trampled on by sheep & asses / He found a square of white saw a square of paper white This stanza probably refers to Lear's going to live at Knowsley, the home of the earls of Derby, and to his introduction there to the limerick.

24 *square and white*] *Houghton* white and square

26–8 *But … Nose*] *Beinecke* Then one morning in a thicket / He perceived a railway ticket / Stooping [ ] the ground to pick it / Forth there leaped a lively cricket

26 *in*] NSS on

27–8 *Off ... Nose*] *Beinecke* From the ground there skipped a cricket / And ~~it perched upon~~ lighted on his nose

28 *Settled on*] *Houghton* Leap'd upon *Texas* Jump'd upon

29–30 *Never ... ever*] *Beinecke* Never more by night or day / Has the cricket gone away

33 *cheerious measure*] *Beinecke* cheerful fervour *Houghton, Texas* cheery measure

36 *So ... winters*: forty-three years passed between 1827, when it is believed that the Lear family finally moved out of Bowman's Lodge and Lear began to earn his own living, and 1870, when he found his first permanent home in San Remo.

38 *All those ... o'er*] *Beinecke* Up & down those hills he went / Waddled to his last abode

40 *Borly-Melling*] NSS Borley-Melling. There is a town called Melling five or six miles from Knowsley.

42 *And he ... no more.*] NSS (But his shoes were far too tight.) It is not known why this line was used in NSS; it is not in any known MS, and it does not rhyme with l. 38, but it was possibly mistakenly repeated from ll. 7, 35 and 49. *Illustration: Beinecke.*

'He only said, "I'm very weary'
Written on 10 December 1886 in a letter to Fortescue. **MS** *Taunton*. Pub. *LLEL*.

This is a play on the refrain of Tennyson's poem 'Mariana' (1830): 'She only said, "My life is dreary, / He cometh not," she said; / She said, "I am aweary, aweary, / I would that I were dead!"' Lear parodied these lines frequently in his diary, e.g. 2 January 1882: 'He only said – "My life is dreary! There seems no hope" – he said, He said – "I'm aweary, aweary, ————!" '

'I must stop now'
Written on 30 May 1887 in a letter to Hallam Tennyson. **MS** *Lincoln*.

'I think human nature is pretty much the same all along'
Written on 10 July 1887 in a letter to Selwyn. **MS** *Selwyn*.

Appendix

Illustration: from a **letter** to Hallam Tennyson of 16 June 1884 (*private collection*). Pub. *VN*.

All similes are from Lear's **letters,** except for one from his **diary.**

Index of Titles

Index of First Lines
(Poems, Nonsense Songs and Alphabets)

Subject Index